Martha Graham in Love and War

Martha Graham in Love and War

The Life in the Work

MARK FRANKO

OXFORD
UNIVERSITY PRESS

Oxford University Press, Inc., publishes works that further
Oxford University's objective of excellence
in research, scholarship, and education.

Oxford   New York
Auckland   Cape Town   Dar es Salaam   Hong Kong   Karachi
Kuala Lumpur   Madrid   Melbourne   Mexico City   Nairobi
New Delhi   Shanghai   Taipei   Toronto

With offices in
Argentina   Austria   Brazil   Chile   Czech Republic   France   Greece
Guatemala   Hungary   Italy   Japan   Poland   Portugal   Singapore
South Korea   Switzerland   Thailand   Turkey   Ukraine   Vietnam

Published by Oxford University Press, Inc.
198 Madison Avenue, New York, New York 10016

www.oup.com

Oxford is a registered trademark of Oxford University Press

Library of Congress Cataloging-in-Publication Data
Franko, Mark.
Martha Graham in love and war : the life in the work / Mark Franko.
p.   cm.
Includes bibliographical references and index.
ISBN 978-0-19-977766-2 (alk. paper)
1. Graham, Martha. 2. Dancers—United States—Biography. 3. Choreographers—United States—Biography.
4. Modern dance—United States—Psychological aspects. 5. Hawkins, Erick—Influence.
6. World War, 1939–1945—United States. I. Title.
GV1785.G7F73   2012
792.802'8092—dc23[B]   2011034099

This book has been supported by a research fellowship from the National
Endowment for the Humanities, designated a "We the People" project, and a
University of California President's Faculty Research Fellowship in the Humanities.

Source information for the image on page ii:
Martha Graham and Erick Hawkins, Bennington College, 1938. © Barbara Morgan/Barbara Morgan Archives.
Courtesy of the Haggerty Museum of Art, Marquette University, Milwaukee, WI.

1 3 5 7 9 8 6 4 2

Printed in the United States of America
on acid-free paper

CONTENTS

Martha Graham in Love and War

Introduction

Martha Graham has been celebrated as a paragon of feminine spirituality.[1] But, she has also been admitted into the pantheon of modern male geniuses. Howard Gardner ranks her with Freud, Einstein, Picasso, Stravinsky, Eliot, and Gandhi as one of the most creative minds of the twentieth century.[2] Biographies have provided indispensable information on the artist's life from Don McDonagh's *Martha Graham* (1973) to Agnes de Mille's *Martha* (1991).[3] Yet, biographers tend to be so in awe of Graham's accomplishment that they have not always given her work the quality or quantity of analysis that has been devoted to Freud, Einstein, Picasso, Stravinsky, Eliot, or Gandhi.[4] Graham died some 20 years ago, providing us with the distance to reevaluate her work from the perspective of politics and world events, literary modernism, and major trends in anthropology, psychoanalysis, and criticism.[5] This is a historically contextualized and biographically informed analysis of her work between 1938 and 1953, arguably her most productive period.

From her retirement from the stage in 1969 until her death in 1991 Martha Graham already experienced what one might call an afterlife.[6] As Selby Schwartz pointed out in her recent discussion of Graham impersonator Richard Move, the end of Graham's career as a dancer in 1969 was a first death.[7] In the years between her recovery from a grave illness in 1971 and her biological death in 1991 Graham's image reentered circulation to an unparalleled degree. One has only to think of the 1976 advertisement for Blackglama ("What Becomes a Legend Most?"), the much publicized friendship with Madonna who was to play Graham in the film version of her life, the Apple "Think Different" advertisement spots that also featured Einstein, and the Presidential Medal of Freedom bestowed by President Gerald Ford in 1976 through the good auspices of First Lady Betty Ford (Elizabeth Anne Bloomer), who had studied with Graham at Bennington in the 1930s. The magnitude of this exposure combined with Graham's declining creative powers in those 30 or so years engendered a Graham-fatigue that has little to do with her actual contribution to dance and culture.[8]

During this time, many of her early works were revived, but she was rarely engaged in their restaging, and was ambivalent about younger dancers performing roles she had made for herself.[9] In fact, she had little interest in her own choreography once it was no longer vitally connected to her. Although Graham continued to be productive after her recovery, creating 30 new ballets at the rate of between one to three a year from 1973 through 1991, her "afterlife" engendered a distorted and disjointed replay of what had already transpired in the 1940s.

This is why I consider it essential to examine how Graham's image was constructed in the 1940s, the period of her personal and political coming of age. Without such an examination, her legacy remains muddled. I take on Amy Koritz's challenge to discuss Graham in terms of popular culture for the aim of Graham's image, which was widely disseminated in that decade, was to reach the broadest public possible.[10] "Graham was . . . engaged in an inherently mixed endeavor," writes Koritz, "—producing both a commodity offered for consumption by her audiences and a 'pure' aesthetic object."[11] This statement makes sense when one thinks of the commodity not as the live dance, but as the image. While I do not believe her live performances were intended to be "pure aesthetic objects," I also do not believe that they can or should be reduced to mere images or commodities. But, Graham did lend her person to commodification in the media. The subject of this book is the enablement and constraint of Graham's creative freedom that resulted from the construction of her image by the media in which she actively collaborated.

Graham's relation to the image and images was complex: her dance had been related to the fixity of an image as in dance critic Edwin Denby's perspicacious remark about her early solos: "I have the impression that [she] would like to keep a dance constantly at the tension of a picture. She seems to be, especially in her solo dances, clinging to visual definition."[12] But, Graham's dancing also opened out onto a fluid space of the *imaginary*, which was experienced by many who saw her in the 1930s and 1940s as astounding and deeply moving. One somewhat naïve example of this sort of reaction is worth quoting because it suggests that Koritz's "mixed endeavor" was not something that Graham herself concocted, but that the audience itself actually felt despite the choreographer's esotericism.

> The evening's surprise lay elsewhere. It was to be found in the very telling reaction of hundreds of people in the audience. Their enthusiasm, their unrestrained ovation signified a vital development taking place today. Such dynamic response to purely spiritual values is good. On this scale, it is practically unknown. Whatever the explanation, here is a living example of great art moving countless people to a quickened

experience. When the great art happens to be something so esoteric, so recondite as the contemporary dance the occasion is notable.[13]

This passage from a 1944 Cincinnati newspaper review of one of Graham's performances captures in a very precritical way a counterintuitive experience in which abstraction as "the spiritual in art" touches the general public, a phenomenon having no previous explanation in American culture.

Graham built her reputation on the gradual development of an unusual relationship to the audience, a relationship that was also nurtured by the projection of her image in the media, which extended its reach throughout the decade. The celebrity image of Graham the press and ultimately radio cultivated throughout the 1940s attained mythological proportions by decade's end, and was augmented by Graham's myth-based work of the immediate postwar period. Commoditized aspects of Graham's public image, however, ran counter to some of her most deeply held convictions about her identity as an artist and a woman, and thus caused internal conflict and resistance. I study her work in function of this conflict and resistance, which also involves situating her dances in the immediate context and milieu of their creation, and gearing the analysis to how the dances may have appeared and been received when first performed. This is not a study of dances that withstand the test of time, the sort of analysis designed to claim for Graham the status of artistic immortality. Instead, I write as if these dances had disappeared and must be rediscovered even though my knowledge of them in many cases relies on later performances.[14] They actually have disappeared in their original form.

This is not a biography. My recourse to biographical findings in this book serves to explain the aesthetics of Graham's productions. I am interested in Graham's life only insofar as it can illuminate her work. But, I hope this will not be confused with the hackneyed idea that life is directly expressed in art. This would lead us straight to a mythical proposition. As Eric Gould reminds us: "There can be no myth without an *ontological gap between event and* meaning. A myth intends to be an adequate symbolic representation by closing that gap, by aiming to be a tautology."[15] This has been, in a nutshell, the critical weakness of biographies of Graham that testify to how large her image loomed in her life and afterlives. Going back to the life can rehumanize Graham if we give critical attention to how her myth was constructed and the effect it had on her work. I situate the life *in* the work as the life *of* the work. This life, like most lives, is both personal and political.

The historical context of Graham's choreographic flowering was the global crisis of Fascism, the conflict of World War II, and the postwar years that ushered in the Cold War. A sociological split in the decade between the war years (1941–45), which were marked by economic austerity and fear, and the postwar years (1946–53), which were characterized by unbridled consumerism compounded with psychological anxiety, is mirrored in Graham's engagement with anti-Fascism before and during the war, and her involvement with psychoanalysis after the war.[16] Fascism and psychoanalysis provide the two pivotal sociological axes upon which Graham's most productive period turned. Graham's public position on anti-Fascism was in some sense unexpected because she had remained aloof from left-wing politics of the early 1930s. With what is called the Popular Front, however, the focus of the left shifted from worker's rights to a reassertion of democratic values in the face of the violent authoritarianism and expansionism that were to bring about World War II. Graham's adoption of a recognizable political position with *American Document* (1938) led to a major success that relaunched her career with a renewed vigor and momentum at this extremely uncertain time. This book is in part the narrative of Graham's ascension to stardom from 1938 until 1948 and how this new status was reflected in her work through the construction of her image on and off stage.

The turn to psychology was necessary for Graham to formulate her particular approach to myth in dance whereas her turn to psychoanalysis was motivated by conflicts in her personal life related to her lover and husband-to-be, Erick Hawkins. But the question of myth in relation to the personal also had a political dimension. Nazi ideology had an unmistakable mythic dimension that accounted for some of that regime's attraction, and which was thought to contain some explanation for the willing submission of Germans to authoritarian rule. Sociologists and psychoanalysts with connections to the Frankfurt School were called upon by the CIA to study the psychological underside of nihilistic social behavior in Hitler's Germany. In the postwar world a theory of the abiding forces of Fascism in the West was considered urgent. After World War II, psychoanalytically inflected cultural commentary—sometimes called modern man literature—served to replace prewar anti-Fascism with what was thought to be a more nuanced understanding of human destructiveness. Perhaps because the psychoanalytic movement had evoked Greek myth earlier in the century, postwar visual artists and modern dancers explored human destructiveness and apocalyptic historic events in a mythic mode. As poet Ben Belitt, who was close to Graham, noted: "[T]ragedy in 1946 was forced upon both of us; we were both versions of some innocent identity who had thought the world was reasonable."[17]

Graham's work is the privileged terrain upon which to study the influence of psychoanalysis and psychoanalytic theory on modernism. Psychoanalytic theory and psychotherapy influenced not only Graham's personal life, but also her postwar choreographic output. Graham is a prime example of *psychoanalytic modernism*—a tendency in twentieth-century art that serves to focus the interpretation of her work in a way that generalizations about spirituality and genius do not. While the practice of modern dance was based first and foremost on direct and visceral communication with an audience, psychoanalytic theory introduced many mediating factors that rendered the directness of that communication mysterious but attractive in giving rise to sublimated areas of meaning. Audiences were convoked in the dual role of analysts and analysands, and this is in part why Graham became known, as *Life Magazine* put it, as the "intellectual priestess" of dance. The *priestess* suggests myth and belief whereas the adjective *intellectual* suggests the power of analysis. Myth, then, provided not only a psychoanalytically inflected subject matter at a time when Jungian psychology was popular in the United States, but also a way to choreograph through a process of self-analysis in which personal ritual became encrypted within the mythic framework. Finally, myth also provided a means to navigate between issues of feminine identity and male-identified power.

I focus primarily on four works: *American Document* (1938), *Appalachian Spring* (1944), *Night Journey* (1948), and *Voyage* (1953). My thesis is that Graham's choreography evolves across the decade from anti-Fascism—becoming veiled as patriotism during World War II—to the archetypal use of myth in the immediate postwar period (1946–48), and is then briefly but unsuccessfully exchanged for a psychodramatic approach to choreography in the early 1950s (1953–55). The two broad themes of anti-Fascism and psychoanalysis break down into three distinct choreographic phases: the dramaturgical, the mythographic, and the psychodramatic.

The dramaturgical phase at the most basic level is marked by the development of large-scale works lasting approximately one half hour and involving both sexes on stage as "characters." It is also characterized by the use of texts in a variety of ways: the spoken word on stage, program notes to help orient the audience, libretti and scenarios used in the process of setting the work, and notes used in the conceptualization of work. The spoken word was introduced in *American Document*, used again in *Letter to the World* (1941), and seriously considered, although ultimately not used, in *Deaths and Entrances*, *Appalachian Spring*, and *Cave of the Heart*. But, the dramaturgical phase was more importantly one in which Graham developed a way to evoke both the visible and the invisible on stage. This cultivation of the possibility that in seeing her work we were exposed to both the seen and the unseen promoted a sensibility for the secret, or, what I call *encryption*, which can be understood as the insinuation of absent characters and actions beneath or within what is visible.[18] Although this was a subtext to be sensed rather than literally seen, it led to the engenderment of what I call the unconscious of the dance work inasmuch as an audience could intuit elements they did not see before them. This promoted in turn the sensation of absolute space on the stage, the idea of an above ground and an underworld both participating in the action. One compelling reason for Graham to resort to encryption was the need to convey hidden messages of a political and personal nature. These involved both a critical view of American history in war-time and a resistance to marriage within a paean to the American family, both of which occurred in *Appalachian Spring*.

The mythographic phase, on the other hand, involved choreographic adaptations of known narratives taken from Greek mythology—Medea, Theseus, Oedipus, and Jocasta—but narratives in which the unseen and the numinous were still known to play a role. The changing use of program notes by the late 1940s is revealing of how Graham wished her audience to perceive these narratives archetypally as a way to identify with a universal pattern the character's action suggested. *Cave of the Heart* and *Night Journey* (as well as *Clytemnestra* in 1958) were among Graham's most narrative works. Still, a personal ritual that remained invisible to the public was also played out on stage lending a peculiar intensity to what was seen, but also deflecting the viewer's attention from meanings personal to Graham by focusing attention on the universalizing narrative and its mythical symbolism, which induced the viewer to project their own life experience into the choreography. The mythographic phase, in other terms, transformed the vertically oriented encryption into a horizontal myth-ritual relation between stage and audience: what was ritually enacted on stage was read as myth by the audience. The operations of absolute space were still in effect, but the audience became the analyst of its own complexes, the investigator of its own unconscious tendencies. This was, of course, promoted by the strong belief at the time that psychology had a basis in myth. The unconscious of the work was its ritual, performed before, yet invisible to, the audience. The personal reading of the myth by the audience became in its turn a ritual, or functioned as ritual for the viewer. The place of the underworld had shifted to what is called in theater language, "the house," that is, the space occupied by the audience. To see the work was to expose oneself to self-analysis. In the mythographic, which reached its peak with *Night Journey*, Graham truly made her audience into collaborators.

The third phase, which I call psychodramatic, was a failed experiment conducted in an attempt to relinquish both encryption and the ritual-myth structure in order to confront life in a more disabused and contemporary sense. Here there could no longer be hidden drives with symbolic meaning and psychological complexes with universal extension, but instead sexual needs and emotional devastation in a less than perfect world. In the psychodramatic phase absolute space gave way to abstract space in which all the forces at play between people were out in the open and visible on the surface. *Voyage* typifies this approach.

Appalachian Spring and *Night Journey* are canonical works about which much has been written; *American Document* and *Voyage* are thought to be minor works that have no established place in the Graham canon. The lesser-known works, however, respond to the beginning and the end of Graham's intimate and professional relationship with Hawkins. Erick Hawkins first appeared with the Martha Graham Dance Company in 1938, when her art was taking on new dramaturgical complexity and political commitment. As a relationship between a young man and a mature woman as well as between a fledgling and an established artist, the Graham-Hawkins story was a tormented one. Graham's productions in the 1940s were bound up with her relationship to Hawkins in several important respects. She featured Hawkins in ways that decisively determined the shape and sense of her most important work. The intricate workings of myth she arrived at were determined by the need to both publicly perform and conceal from public awareness personal rituals concerning their relationship. Although the structures Graham devised were rigorously designed to protect her privacy, there are also indications that life and art were becoming difficult to tell apart. Moreover, Hawkins's multiple contributions to Graham's production values were salient, and they require analysis and acknowledgment in themselves, along with a fuller account than has yet been provided of Hawkins's own work in the 1940s, which frequently existed in critical counterpoint to Graham's, but which she nevertheless produced. The conflict between them was most evident in the contrasts between their individual outputs that passed unnoticed in the criticism of the day. The prominent response of critics in the 1940s was to pan Hawkins rather than to take him seriously as a choreographer. As a dancer Hawkins was competitive with his contemporary Merce Cunningham while they both appeared with Graham. Once Hawkins became an independent choreographer with his own company he continued to compete with Cunningham for recognition as a leading avant-garde choreographer. But, no one else beside musician Louis Horst, whom Hawkins displaced in her affection, shared an intimacy with Graham that crossed the lines of the personal and the artistic. Horst was senior to Graham, but with Hawkins Graham reversed this relation to herself, becoming the mentor of the younger artist. Thus, in Graham's two most serious relationships with men there was a significant but quite different age discrepancy.

Graham's reading was vast, but her literary influences can be traced back to the Anglo-American modernist poets launched with Imagism circa 1916 and, from there, to the authors who most crucially influenced them: James Frazer, Jane Harrison, and Jessie Weston. Graham's frame of reference was not only that of Anglo-American literary modernism, but extended to this movement's most inspirational source texts as well. From the perspective of these influences, Graham appears to be the contemporary of T.S. Eliot, Ezra Pound, William Carlos Williams, and James Joyce. Born in 1894, she was actually only six years younger than Eliot (born 1888) and 12 years younger than Joyce (born 1882). Although Graham's choreographic work was not fully launched until the early 1930s—her first solo concert took place in 1926—she did not fully sort through these influences in choreographic terms until the 1940s.[19] She is thus, at one level, a belated Anglo-American modernist whose work recovers the roots of that brand of modernism as its own "tradition."

The literary aspect of Graham's creative process in the 1940s was accentuated by her own writing, some of which is to be found in *The Notebooks of Martha Graham*. "The *Notebooks*," writes Susan Jones, "provide one of the century's most striking examples of a choreographer's engagement with literary texts during the choreographic process, illustrating a discrete relationship between poetic and choreographic arts."[20] Graham also produced libretti and scenarios for many of her productions, which is surprising since it recalls a nineteenth-century ballet tradition. The libretto for *American Document* was the only such text that found its way into print, and it was called a libretto because of the use of the spoken word. But, Graham also wrote scenarios in order to facilitate collaborations with composers. They contained character sketches, sequences of action without steps, and poetic reflection on the effects and meanings she aimed for. Overall, Graham's words were more than vehicles for thinking about a dance: they constituted in themselves a discourse on dance making. Toward the end of the decade the scenarios begin increasingly to resemble her notes and notebooks. The three libretti for *Clytemnestra* (1958) are exceptions because they are almost exclusively spoken text. However, the scenario for her solo *Judith* (1950) exposes a contradictory dynamic between the scenario as "an emotional springboard into idea" and the plethora of quotations and scholarly footnotes of which the script is comprised, fragments of literary exegesis in which all traces of story disappear.[21] In the case of *Judith*, Graham assured composer William Schuman "it is the way I have been thinking and feeling at this time and it is the nearest I can come to being concrete."[22] Despite its basis in literary texts, Graham was never able to reconstruct this solo once she had stopped performing it. Citations become a method with which to conduct choreographic movement, a kind of *ductus*, or way of moving through an imagined composition made up of word-images.[23] Further, Graham's notes and scenarios began to take on an increasingly matrixial or generative character toward the end of the decade, one that brought language closer to movement rather than using language to provide the representational framework within which movement was to be set. With *Judith* the highly subjective character of choreography became the leitmotif of Graham's verbal mappings, creating an apparent gap between research, writing, and movement. In other terms, these were not blueprints for performances in any obvious sense. This state of affairs augmented the already existing tension between her theoretical recourse to literature and what Kandinsky called the artist's "guiding principle of inner need."[24] At the same time, it speaks to the necessity to interpret her work as much through her writing as through the phenomenal appearance of that work. The question is how to interpret the writing.

Graham's preparation for choreography was thus mediated not only by the texts she read, but also by the texts she wrote. The scenarios provide insight into her process extending over a considerable time period—sometimes two years— prior to an actual premiere. *Night Journey*, for instance, premiered in New York in 1948 but began as a text written for composer William Schuman in 1946. "I work slowly on an idea," she wrote to Schuman, "although I can sometimes work quickly on a dance."[25] In her writing one recognizes many works in progress or to come in the literary and philosophical context from which they initially emerged. This permits us to study the genesis of her work as well as the phenomenal end product, what I shall call the geno- and the pheno-choreography, respectively. Graham's scenarios are complemented in turn by letters, choreographic notes, and the *Notebooks*, which, taken together, bring one into her labyrinthine reflections on subjectivity and creativity. Her writing also permits one to reconstitute to some degree her reading. Wherever possible I trace her extensive readings in literature, psychology, anthropology, and what has become known as "modern man literature" but should probably be called "modern woman literature" as exemplified by the work of Jung's female disciples Maud Bodkin, Esther M. Harding, and Frances G. Wickes.

Another major influence on Graham was psychology and psychoanalysis. I distinguish between her readings in psychological literature and her actual experience of psychoanalysis. She and Hawkins consulted with Erich Fromm, Geza Roheim, and Frances Gillespy Wickes during the 1940s and early 1950s. Graham and Hawkins read Jung, but also Rank and Fromm. The influence on Graham of psychoanalytic theory ranged from the politically radical Jewish émigré psychoanalytic community in New York of which Rank and Fromm were a part, to the more Anglo-patrician and generally more politically conservative Jungian community. Although Jung is usually assumed to be the strongest influence on Graham's work, my research shows that Erich Fromm and Otto Rank were equally, if not more, influential. Although Graham knew Fromm personally, the influence of Rank, whom she never met (he died in New York in 1939) was fundamental. For Graham inserted woman into psychoanalytic theory in a very un-Freudian, but quite Rankean, way. As the analyst Abram Kardiner remarked: "It was Otto Rank who made this contribution, pointing out that the mother as a figure other than as a sexual object was totally neglected in the literature."[26] Graham is often called the "mother" of contemporary dance, but it is time to understand how the figure of the mother was itself instrumental to her choreographic imagination, and what the vicissitudes of mother are in her work. "There is an inescapable correlation," writes Adrienne Rich, "between the idea of motherhood and the idea of power."[27] Graham's image was not in itself maternal, but she manipulated mythic concepts of the Great Mother that may still hold the key to her much disputed "feminism."

I have benefited in researching this book from the work of two predecessors who shared my interest in Graham. Don McDonagh interviewed Hawkins extensively in the 1970s as well as many others for his biography of Graham. I am grateful to him for giving me permission to listen to his recorded interviews. Some aspects of the testimony he elicited take on new meaning in the light of the archives of Graham and Hawkins housed at the Library of Congress. Dance critic David Sears was fascinated in the 1980s by Graham's work, and recorded important oral histories with Hawkins, Bertram Ross, and Joseph Campbell, among others. Without the groundwork Sears laid, much of the information essential to this book would simply not exist.[28] Because he was unable to gain direct access to Graham, Sears turned to Hawkins. On the track of the classical literary references in Graham's work, he studied Greek at Hunter College in 1988 to better understand her myth works. He began to perceive the complex relation of Graham's work to literature. "We need someone to decode . . . the notebooks," he wrote. "But it's all in there. Erick—I came upon Erick, again, as an innocent—trying to see what he could give me in terms of Graham. And I discovered great pain. He didn't want to deal with that."[29] Still, it is to Sears's credit that he did get Hawkins to say much about the 1940s. In exploring Graham through Hawkins, Sears also did important research on Hawkins's own choreography.[30] The untimely death of David Sears in 1992 prevented him from carrying his research further, but what he left us contains many intriguing leads as well as much irreplaceable historical evidence.

The insightful and unorthodox thoughts of Bertram Ross, Graham's most important dance partner and collaborator after Hawkins, have been recorded in many of his interviews up until his death in 2006. Without his perspicacious reflections we would know substantially less about Graham than we do. I am grateful for the interviews accorded me by Yuriko, Ethel Winter, Stuart Hodes, Robert Cohan, Helen McGehee, and Mary Hinkson. I thank Stuart Hodes for allowing me to read relevant sections of his manuscript *Part Real/Part Dream* before it was published. For facilitating these interviews I wish to thank Henrietta Bannerman, Marnie Thomas, William Schneider, Pam Risenhoover, and Victoria Geduld. For research questions I am much indebted to the resourcefulness and generosity of Elizabeth Aldrich at the Library of Congress, Charles Perrier at the Dance Collection, and Mary Marshall Clark at the Oral History Office of Columbia University. I appreciate the support of Janet Eilber, director of the Martha Graham Center for Contemporary Dance Katherine Duke, director of the Erick Hawkins Dance Foundation, and David Prensky (brother of Bertram Ross). For valuable critical responses and inspiration I thank Gay Morris, Janet Wolff, Susan Jones, Ramsay Burt, Fiona Macintosh, Arnold Rampersad, Martha Schoolman, Katherine Duke, Vincent Pecora, Christie McClure, Don McDonagh, Leslie Getz, Adam Blatner, Juliet Neidish, Christine Dakin, James Rubin, Linda Langton,

Donna Haraway, Carrie Noland, Janice Ross and Paul Sanasardo; and special thanks to Alessio Franko for his clerical work. I am grateful for the support of Norman Hirschy at Oxford University Press, who believed in this project from the beginning. I was able to bring it to completion thanks to a Senior Research Fellowship from the National Endowment for the Humanities, designated a "We the People" project, and a UC President's Faculty Research Fellowship in the Humanities. Jay Barksdale welcomed me in the Allen Room at the Stephen A. Schwarzman Building of the New York Public Library, which was a wonderful environment in which to pursue research, replete with receptions graced by incomparable deviled eggs. Earlier phases of my research were supported by a Special Research Grant awarded by the Committee on Research from the University of California, Santa Cruz, and by a grant from the Arts Research Institute, University of California, Santa Cruz.

1

Myth, Nationalism and Embodiment in *American Document*

"This is a time of action, not re-action"
—Martha Graham (1937)

Despite Martha Graham's distaste for the sectarian politics of the early 1930s, her refusal of the Nazi Culture Ministry's invitation to dance at the 1936 Berlin Olympic Games was politically motivated.[1] Graham's anti-Fascist politics starts with her letter to Rudolf von Laban:

> I would find it impossible to dance in Germany at the present time. So many artists whom I respect and admire have been persecuted, have been deprived of their right to work, and for such unsatisfactory and ridiculous reasons, that I should consider it impossible to identify myself, by accepting this invitation, with the regime that has made such things possible. In addition, some of my concert group would not be either welcome in Germany or willing to go.[2]

Graham became active in labor-related causes following the Soviet declaration of the Popular Front against Fascism in 1935. On December 15, 1935, she danced for the International Labor Defense at Carnegie Hall, and on December 31, 1935, she danced at the International Celebration under the auspices of the Worker's Training School at the Venice Theatre.[3] Whereas at the onset of the Great Depression class struggle had promoted a cult of the artist as worker, the Popular Front chimed with Graham's sense of artistic freedom. The anti-Fascist turn in left politics engendered a cultural climate receptive to the aesthetic innovations of modernism. "Praise for greater conceptual complexity in the Soviet Union," notes Cecile Whiting of anti-Fascist modern art, "went hand in hand with acceptance of a certain degree of diversification of style and artistic individualism, which had been anathema in the early thirties."[4] Where even abstraction was considered of value to the anti-Fascist cause, Graham felt it safe to align herself politically.

The anti-Fascist position in American art dates officially from the 1936 American Artists' Congress. Graham collaborators Barbara Morgan and Isamu Noguchi were signers of the original call for the Congress; Morgan's name also appears in 1939 on the Executive Board list of the New York branch.[5] Graham addressed the second national convention of the Congress in 1937.[6] [Figure 1.1] At the public session at Carnegie Hall, Erika Mann read a message from Thomas Mann, and Pablo Picasso spoke to the assembly by telephone. Graham also addressed the symposium "Nazi War Over Europe" held by the American Committee for Anti-Nazi Literature, of which she was a member, on February 14, 1937.

The political agenda of the American Artists' Congress consisted not only of its opposition to Fascism abroad; it also opposed curtailment of civil liberties at home. The 1941 call, "In Defense of Culture," states:

> Today the Fascist threat has come full circle. In a traditionally free and liberty loving America, Fascism comes in the name of anti-Fascism. All the enemies of progress suddenly become defenders of democracy. Our liberties are destroyed to defend liberty and the policies to which our people are committed by their government, in the name of peace, border ever closer on overt war.[7]

As the call indicates, anti-Fascism was not limited to the celebration of democracy; it was equally, and perhaps more importantly, a critical response to the erosion of democratic values resulting from opposition to Fascism itself. "Fascism comes in the name of anti-Fascism." As Eric Hobsbawm has pointed out: "[A]ntifascist nationalism was patently engaged in a social as well as a national conflict."[8] The mood was that of Sinclair Lewis's *It Can't Happen Here* (1936), a Federal Theatre Project production that sounded the alarm over Fascism on the home front. The play was adapted from Lewis's novel of the same name, published in 1935. The novel depicts the process of emerging homegrown Fascism in the United States when Berzelius Windrip displaces Franklin Delano Roosevelt for the Democratic nomination and wins the 1937 presidential election. It is not surprising that Graham engaged with the social critique announced by the American Artists Call and the insights of Sinclair Lewis.[9] The greatest danger lay in taking democratic traditions for granted and casting a blind eye on the threats engulfing it from all sides.

Of her new work, *American Document* (1938), she said in an interview with the *Daily Worker*: "This dance is supposed to bring back to its full meaning what has largely become meaningless in America through familiarity."[10] The danger

AMERICAN ARTISTS CONGRESS

2nd Annual National Convention
PUBLIC SESSION:
Friday, December 17, 1937 at 8:30 p. m.
CARNEGIE HALL

FOR PEACE - FOR DEMOCRACY - FOR CULTURAL PROGRESS

RALPH M. PEARSON, Chairman

PABLO PICASSO
The Defense of Culture in Spain
By Direct Wire to the Congress

FIORELLO H. La GUARDIA
New York as a Cultural Center

MAX WEBER
Reasons for an Artists' Congress

GEORGE BIDDLE
The Artist Must Organize: A Realistic Approach

ERIKA MANN
A Message from Thomas Mann

Rep. JOHN M. COFFEE
The Federal Arts Bill

MARTHA GRAHAM
The Dance, an Allied Art

PHILIP EVERGOOD
President, Artists' Union of New York

YASUO KUNIYOSHI   CHEN I-VAN

Tickets: $2.20, 1.65, 1.10, .83, .55; over 800 .35
Tax Included

On Sale at Carnegie Hall Box Office and at the
AMERICAN ARTISTS' CONGRESS, Inc., 100 West 13th St., New York, N. Y.
Tel.: GRamercy 5-9647
ORDER FORM

Figure 1.1 A flyer for the American Artists Congress 2nd Annual National Convention Public Session, December 17, 1937 (Gerald Monroe research material on WPA, American Artists' Congress, and Artists' Union, ca. 1930–1971). Courtesy of the Archives of American Art, Smithsonian Institution

was that democracy could drift insensibly toward Fascism. But, there was also another alarm that Graham seems to have taken seriously. Lewis Mumford warned of the dangers of inaction in *Men Must Act*. It was necessary to fight Fascism on the battlefield.[11] In his article "Call to Arms" (1938) it was clear that the term *action* invoked militant nationalism.[12] *American Document* suggests that Graham shared the interventionist position of liberal-traditionalists such as Archibald MacLeish, Carl Sandburg, John Dos Passos, and Mumford himself.[13]

A report on the talk Graham delivered in 1937—"Nazi Destruction of the Arts"—shows that she learned of Laban's fall from favor with the Culture Ministry after the Olympic Games, but that she thought Mary Wigman "received no support from the Reich."[14] Discussion in the New York dance press about Wigman's possible collaboration with the Nazi regime found its way into print between 1935 and 1937, yet remained inconclusive.[15] Graham asserted in 1939 that dance itself in Germany had been "proscribed; bound down."[16] But she also conceded: "What conditions exist today, at this time, I do not know, because very little comes out." What took place in the world of German modern dance between 1933 and 1945 was not to come out for at least another sixty years.[17] It is not a matter of what Graham knew and when, but of understanding how Fascism politicized Graham and how she expressed that politicization choreographically.

The Problem with Myth

Graham's enormous productivity during the 1940s peaked in the second half of the decade with her myth works. But, her use of myth in the postwar era—also typical of abstract expressionist painters—was preceded by a prewar anti-Fascist period in which myth, which had been appropriated as a Fascist mode of representation, was a definite liability to a progressive American artist.[18] The Third Reich appealed to a classicizing past to create an aesthetically persuasive if ultimately kitsch image of national glory and strength. Hitler himself had said in a speech on September 1, 1933: ". . . [E]ach politically historical epoch searches in its art for the link with a period of equally heroic past. Greeks and Romans suddenly stand close to Teutons."[19] The opening of Leni Riefenstahl's *Olympia*, a documentary film on the 1936 Berlin Olympic Games and a recognized piece of Nazi propaganda, showed classical statuary coming to life as a prelude to the games themselves. Riefenstahl, formerly a modern dancer, appeared nude in these scenes. The athletic feats bodies performed for Riefenstahl's cameras acquired a new range of political implications enhanced not only by genuflecting to classical aesthetic norms but through innovative montage and camera angles thanks to which dynamic movement acquired the irresistible quality of the embodied energy necessary to political will.[20] Given the Nazi celebration of male athletic prowess with bellicose aspirations, Graham knew she would have to include men in her choreography. Before the appearance of Hawkins on the scene she unsuccessfully approached José Limón.[21]

Had Graham accepted the invitation to appear at the Berlin Olympic Games in 1936 she might have found herself in 1938 on the screen in Riefenstahl's *Olympia* just as she was premiering *American Document*. Graham knew that an anti-Fascist political statement in American dance demanded a rational conception of the historical past to counteract the appeal of Nazi myth, or what Walter Benjamin called its "aesthetic politics."[22] In creating a dance that would not only defend democracy but also demonstrate its superiority to authoritarian regimes, origin narratives could be tricky to avoid. Both Fascism and democracy were yoked to national identity and hence to myths of the national past. This chapter is about how Graham conceived her pro-democratic statement in 1938 as aesthetically anti-Fascist while drawing upon American history as a backdrop.

Graham's alignment with anti-Fascism was already evident in *Chronicle* (1936), which bears some relationship to David Smith's *Medals for Dishonor* in its antiwar stance.[23] But, with her boycott of the 1936 Berlin Olympic Games followed in 1937 by two solos supporting the fight for democracy against Fascism in Spain—*Immediate Tragedy* and *Deep Song*—her choreography itself became identified with the Popular Front. *American Document* in 1938, however, was the watershed work in which Graham mobilized an ethical concept of history as a springboard for national purpose. It was a large-scale work that introduced a new focus on dramaturgy. Fragments of film remain, but the piece has never been reconstructed if one discounts two loose adaptations, one in 1989 and the other as recently as 2010. Although largely forgotten for almost fifty years, renewed scholarly interest in racial representation and casting on the modern dance stage brought it back into focus among dance scholars as a significant work in cultural terms.

Both Susan Manning and Julia Foulkes interpret Graham's borrowing of formal choreographic features of minstrelsy as well as the performance of Native Americans and emancipated slaves by Caucasian dancers as a reflection of policies of racial discrimination in the United States.[24] I interpret Graham's use of the conventions of minstrelsy as intentionally ironic and inherently critical of this aspect of American history. To do this, I rely on the ethos of anti-Fascism, which was politically allied with the Popular Front as of 1937. With respect to casting, Graham did not "cast" dancers for specific works, but took dancers into her company and trained them to perform her evolving repertory. According to Francis Fergusson there were no African American students at Bennington College in 1938.[25] By 1944 the Japanese American dancer Yuriko was performing one of the Followers in *Appalachian Spring*; African American dancers Mary Hinkson and Matt Turney joined the Martha Graham Dance Company in 1950.

The absence of students of color at Bennington in 1938 was not necessarily Graham's fault, but I have been unable to find documentation of admission policy. On the other hand, Graham's brilliant seamstress and costume maker Ursula Reed, who was African American, appears in the film *A Dancer's World* in 1957 as a maid attending to Graham in her dressing room. The question is whether political ideals, personal attitudes, representational codes, and social practices (including those of choreography) are always perfectly in sync. Graham herself, according to Bertram Ross, wished to appear Japanese in the film, for which her makeup man "taped up her eyelids—flipped them over inside-out and lifted the corners." "Martha," commented Ross, "was terribly taken with Japanese culture."[26] Graham's understanding of the American film audience in the 1950s may have led her to play with markers of exoticism and colonialism in the process of "becoming" Jocasta before the dressing room mirror, which in Hollywood film had to be the process of playing the Other without becoming Other. Her Orientalist identity was a way station between the antibourgeois choice to "be" Jocasta and the upper-class society matron sufficiently imaginative to make this choice palatable. *A Dancer's World* both builds on the exposure she had gained from *Life Magazine* in the late 1940s and responds to *Life*'s epithet of Graham as "the grim practitioner." In the film she says the dancer's world is "not grim." Despite the avant-garde nature of the dance, Graham clearly considered this film to have mass exposure potential.

Although Graham's public position was antiracist, there is scattered anecdotal evidence that she sometimes saw ethnic differences as barriers. In his unpublished memoir Bertram Ross writes of comments Graham made in the late 1940s and early 1950s that indicate she believed dancers of color might be limited in their understanding of certain roles by their ethnic background. On the other hand, Yuriko remembers that Graham told her "in art . . . there is no racial feeling. If one is good, one is accepted . . ."[27] The complexity of Graham's figure, as in all else, is present here. There is some evidence of a social anti-Semitism habitual in the white Anglo-Saxon moneyed elite Graham liked to frequent, among people such as, for example, Merle Armitage, the opera impresario, who published a book on her work and also was instrumental in hosting her in Santa Fe, which became her habitual retreat. Armitage deeply admired Graham's performance qualities, but his grasp of Graham's interest to others betrays a certain narrow mindedness:

> In every city, as you well know, you've got all these strange, weird, unreal kind of people who live in an imaginary world of their own. They won't accept the filth and the traffic and the cacophony that the city has become. Martha became high priestess to a great many alienated people. She also attracted homosexuals. The audiences were the strangest audiences you

could imagine because she also had a following of wealthy society women. So, I don't think the Graham audiences exist any other place. It's a slice right from the top to the basement of life: just strange![28]

In a letter of January 16, 1944, Graham wrote to David Zellmer, one of her dancers who was a pilot in the Pacific theater of World War II, that Pearl Lang would never be a true artist because her Jewish heritage was too important to her.[29] Graham herself was Presbyterian. Zellmer seems to have commented on this indirectly later. As Zellmer's employer, Graham received notice of his discharge from the army. On June 5, 1945, she responded to his "initialed postscript at the bottom" of the printed discharge notice, which read: "'Plie inspected & OK.' The initials I cannot make out. They look like JEW. Does all this mean anything to you? I thought it was highly entertaining."[30] Was this Zellmer's reply to Graham's assessment of Lang? When Graham later became interested in Old Testament sources and biblical heroines, beginning with *Judith* in 1950, she consulted with Lang, who spoke Yiddish and read Hebrew.[31] Lang believed Graham did not identify with any one cultural or religious tradition given her ecumenical interest in world culture.[32] Clearly, *American Document* did not cater to the white Anglo-Saxon Protestant milieu that Graham identified with socially. The priestess had no difficulty being a black sheep.

Given the audience range, the socially critical edge of *American Document* emerged at its premiere precisely because the work was not structured as a piece of left-wing propaganda. The materials Graham worked with were not homogeneous. In addition to the patterns of minstrelsy, as Ellen Graff points out, Graham also "incorporated many elements that had proved popular in the revolutionary dance movement, including moral fervor, archetypal historical pageantry, and spoken text."[33] This disparity of elements points to the discontinuities typical of literary utopia, to which I shall return later in this chapter. At this point, suffice it to say Graham conjoined a nationalist pro-democracy agenda with Popular Front politics. What I find missing from the recent critical treatment of *American Document* is a serious consideration of the anti-Fascist context in which it was made and which by 1936 was beginning to undermine the revolutionary agenda of the left-wing dance movement of the early 1930s. The challenge Graham took on with *American Document* was to fashion a counterweight to the Nazi myth of national unity and destiny without resorting to fabulous origin narratives which had become tainted by Nazi ideology. This had neither to do with class struggle nor revolution, but it did contain elements of a broader social agenda associated with the Popular Front.

Graham decided upon a national-utopian vision for *American Document* in which she could view the American past critically rather than embrace it unconditionally. The "no-place" of utopia allowed Graham to celebrate democratic values while still pointing to national ideals as an unfulfilled project. The most compelling reason for Graham to reject myth was its most salient narrative: "a nation is the political expression of the race," or, in other terms, the Nazi agenda of national identity through blood and soil (*Blut und Boden*).[34] Graham sought an alternative vision of national identity and resolve based on document and utopia. We shall see in what follows how deeply the sensibility for utopia is woven into *American Document*. The archival document held a key to the future precisely because it was not an earlier version *of* the future. While myth depends on an archaic past conveyed in archetypal narrative, utopia looks to an uncertain future, which is imagined both from an idealistic ethical perspective and through a viewpoint that permits criticism of the present.

Graham chose not to represent a utopian future as much as to enact it in ritual form. Despite the historical panorama staged in *American Document*, the Inter-locutor (actor Housley Stephens, Jr.) who spoke all the words, started by estab-lishing an awareness of the present place and time, which serves not only as a bridge between past and present but also between individual and collective, par-ticular and general:

> Ladies and Gentlemen, good evening
>> This is a theatre.
>> The place is here in the United States of America.
>> The time is now—tonight.[35]

As the Interlocutor's greeting suggests, historical representation works on the stage through real time ("good evening," "now," "tonight") so that place ("here") can be multiple ("a theatre" or "the United States of America"). The libretto defines documents as "our legends—our poignantly near history—our folk tales."[36] André Jolles makes a distinction between legend and myth: legend situ-ates words and gestures in a certain field of significance whereas myth fashions a creation story out of them.[37] Even were we to take legend as a synonym for myth, "*Left-wing myth,*" as Roland Barthes has remarked "*is inessential.*"[38] If the radical right exploited myth to create an aura of national-political essentialism, Graham's competitive stance toward Fascism was to deploy similar tactics to opposed ends. In this regard, her choice of the term *legend* over *myth* is strategic. *American Document* did not propose an essential and timeless narrative of origins arising from a classicizing past—as in Riefenstahl's *Olympia*—but instead a call to memory arising from a historical past that could be documented in *texts* such as the Declaration of Independence of 1776, the Gettysburg Address of 1863, and so forth. The past only existed in the present as texts. The document that associates national identity with archived words rather than with blood and soil is an alternative to Fascist demagoguery and, by extension, a rejection of the mysticism characteristic of Nazi ideology. *American Document* nevertheless competed with Fascism on a terrain of imagery that promoted the mythical importance of the national state and its borders, and the folk aspects of its traditions. Ballets on American folklore—the Settler, the Pioneer, the Indian—were in fashion, but they did not constitute strong alternatives to Fascist strategy because they lumped democratic values and folk legends so as to avoid, as did the Fascists, any hint of cosmopolitanism. In *American Document* Graham privileged texts over mythical folk heroes, focusing on texts that were not uniform in meaning. For example, it was clear in the counterpoint between her love duet with Hawkins and the puritan text accompanying it that not all the documents in *American Document* were praiseworthy. This suggested free intellectual activity and a nondogmatic approach to history.

Such a vision was barely narrative in nature as it relied more heavily on quotation, fragments, episodes, eroticized bodies and repressed desires, agitprop-type statements like newspaper headlines, and a fair amount of New Deal imagery. History functioned as a series of exempla related to statements that could be assembled in a montage-like suite of episodes containing the gravitas of a return to neglected traditions of thought but also disillusionment with the present. The cast enacts not so much moments from American history as the statements that make up its archive. As William Carlos Williams said of writing *In the American Grain* (1925), "The plan was to try to get inside the heads of some of the American founders or 'heroes,' if you will, by examining their original records."[39] Influenced by Williams, Graham thought of the historical record itself as a nontendentious response to the Fascist voice whose screaming tones were a feature of daily life in this period, not only through the radio and the newsreel, but through loudspeakers in Fascist countries.

"Listening to the vicious and terrifying words sent over the air from the Axis countries," Graham conceived *American Document* as a national "wake-up call" that, like those broadcasts, also used words.[40] A brief introduction to the *Theatre Arts Monthly* publication of the libretto, probably written by Francis Fergusson, states that Graham had conceived *American Document* as a response to the demagoguery of Nazi speechifying: "our own country—our democracy—has words, too, with power to hearten men and move them to action."[41] Fascist orality, as Alice Yaeger Kaplan has called it, was a political phenomenon of the 1930s that depended on the radio.[42] Graham's use of words in *American Document* was a response to the use of communications technologies in the battle to win minds. A "new culture of the senses," as Inge Baxmann named it, wedded a pulsating kinesthetic imaginary of the body and the voice to the broadcasting potentials of radio, film, and photography.[43] This culture of the senses bore witness to the power of live and mediatized embodiment as the weapon of choice in ideological struggle. New communication technologies not only took up the body and the voice as the proper starting points for such effects, *these technologies emulated and simulated embodiment as such.* If radio produced a voice that invaded the privacy of the home, film and photography projected dynamic impressions of corporeality into public space, magnifying bodies manifold on the screens of movie theaters and in the glossy pages of magazines and newspapers. To understand how Graham's choreography expressed anti-Fascist politics we need first to understand that the ideological contest between Fascism and democracy was not only conducted across a common symbolism, but *in embodied terms.* In fact, the term "symbol" as it is frequently associated with ideologically inflected images is most likely a misnomer. I will conclude this chapter with a discussion of Barbara Morgan's influential photographs of *American Document*, which also projected a utopian rather than a mythic vision of the future, and increased the reach of Graham's live performance into the mainstream media.

Myth, Embodiment, and the Image

The collaboration between embodiment and the image in film and photography lent corporeality a mythic and hence persuasive power. As Georges Sorel, the theorist of revolutionary syndicalism, wrote: "A myth cannot be refuted since it is, at bottom, identical with the convictions of a group, being the expression of these convictions in the language of movement."[44] Although Sorel did not write about theatrical dancing, he did pinpoint the most crucial component of dance—the "language of movement"—as a factor in social life, and as essential to the fundamentally irrational mythical effect. Sorel further related this mythical awareness of "the language of movement" to the unique sensation of commitment:

> It is very evident that we enjoy this liberty pre-eminently when we are making an effort to create a new individuality in ourselves, thus endeavouring to break the bonds of habit which enclose us . . . It seems to me that this psychology of the deeper life must be represented in the following way . . . To say that we are acting, implies that we are creating an imaginary world placed ahead of the present world and composed of movements which depend entirely on us.[45]

Sorel likened myth to something whose image lies before us in and as the future. In a certain sense, the "expression of convictions in the language of movement" is always an incipient phenomenon. In *Olympia*, as Erin Manning analyzes it, "we feel the incipient force of movement moving."[46] Sorel's moment of decision is impregnated with emotion: "[W]hen the masses are deeply moved," notes

Sorel, "it then becomes possible to trace the outlines of the kind of representation which constitutes the social myth."[47] Thus, he also specifies, "The myths are
not descriptions of things but expressions of a determination to act."[48] Emotion,
will, and incipience were transmitted to audiences through the example of
dynamic movement.

Philippe Lacoue-Labarthe and Jean-Luc Nancy have discussed the Nazi myth
as a past that must be (re)lived. "The characteristic of Nazism (and in many
respects that of Italian fascism) is to have proposed its own movement, and its
own State, as the effective realization of a myth, or as a living myth."[49] This gives
us a second and important ingredient of embodiment, according to which
bodies are not only required to convey an unshakable conviction in movement
as incipient action at the visceral level, but must also, in so doing, relive a mythical past that prescribes such action. It is in this connection that Graham's con-
strual of the historical text of national origins as a document rather than as a
myth both competes with Fascist symbolism on its own terms and opens a gap
between itself and Fascist representational strategies.

Utopia for Sorel, on the other hand, is an *intellectual* project.[50] He distinguishes between myth and utopia in the same manner as he distinguishes
between emotion and intellect. As Willy Gianinazzi puts it in his discussion of
Sorel: "utopia is an ideological process that derails and bogs down the action of
the masses."[51] One would most readily associate myth, as David Gross points
out, with what he calls "the action-image."[52] Myth animates images but risks, in
the process, confusing life with the image; utopia tempers this alchemy with
critical thinking. Graham attempted to move men to action without resorting to
myth, and her use of utopia was designed to make people think, but not to bog
them down. The action to which she referred as early as 1937 with the phrase
"This is a time of action, not re-action," was war. In 1938 Mumford Lewis wrote:
"Fascism has already declared war . . . The time for action is now."[53] In a few
years, it was abundantly clear that the American public understood *American
Document* as a patriotic pro-war statement. The particular flavor of *American
Document* at the beginning was a call for intervention compounded by a critical
utopian hope for the future.

American Document and Civil Rights

American Document evoked a historical canvas representing a struggle over the
meaning of America and an ongoing story of rights and injustices. There were
scenes that evoked the betrayal of indigenous peoples and the history of slavery.
In the Second Episode—"Occupation"—dated 1811, the Interlocutor spoke
words attributed to Red Jacket of the Senecas: "You have got our country."[54] To

these words, Graham danced a solo with "a black and white striped blanket on her dress" entitled "Lament for the Land."[55] [Figure 1.2] In the Fourth Episode—"Emancipation"—dated 1863, the Interlocutor spoke of the states that had slavery, and of the abolition of slavery under Abraham Lincoln. The all-Caucasian female chorus danced the emancipation of the slaves. As composer Ray Green remembered: ". . . [T]he idea of Emancipation being a very active piece, which it turned out to be, and the dance was also that. I used the suggestion of a Spiritual, only in kind of a tone-cluster pattern, very fast moving, and she liked that very much."[56] "What is an American?" and "What is America?" asked the Interlocutor.[57] The dramatis personae were reminiscent of Langston Hughes's 1935 poem "Let America Be America Again."

> I am the poor white, fooled and pushed apart,
> I am the Negro bearing slavery's scars.
> I am the red man driven from the land,
> I am the immigrant clutching the hope I seek—
> And finding only the same old stupid plan
> Of dog eat dog, of mighty crush the weak.[58]

Figure 1.2 Martha Graham in "Lament for the Land" solo from her *American Document* (1938). Photo: Barbara Morgan Courtesy of the Haggerty Museum of Art, Marquette University, Milwaukee, WI

"The Interlocutor calls to mind," noted Graham, "things we are ashamed of . . . Sacco-Vanzetti, share-croppers, the Scottsboro boys . . ."[59] Hawkins remembers: "One of the things she talked about originally—then later she cut this out—was the Scottsboro boys."[60] Specific references to current events of the 1930s were not presented because according to Hawkins she concluded they might clash with the legendary aspect of the historical documents and injustices evoked. As William Carlos Williams remarked in his Introduction to *In the American Grain*, which had served as a model for Graham, "I wanted nothing to get between me and what they themselves had recorded."[61]

The focus of my analysis will be to show that Graham skillfully opposed a Fascist mythical conception of history as a national past to be relived with an approach to the use of fragmentary texts having documentary historical significance. Historical documents used as spoken texts to accompany dance allowed Graham to sidestep the mysticism inherent in Fascist ideology while still stirring popular convictions about national identity with which her audience could and did identify. In a radio interview of June 23, 1937, on WQXR Graham stated that ". . . [the modern dance] must of necessity reveal certain national characteristics because without these characteristics the dance would have no validity, no roots, no direct relation to life."[62] *American Document* located democracy in the American national space, but its import was in the measuring of words against deeds. In this sense, the idea of dance itself as fundamentally different from words, and exemplary of deeds that escape language, served the utopian project.

Hawkins, Erdman, and Campbell

During the process of creating *American Document* in 1938 Graham acquired two new dancers—Jean Erdman and Erick Hawkins—both of whom became under her influence quite invested in the use of the spoken word in dance.[63] In the midst of summer rehearsals for *American Document* in 1938 Jean Erdman, who had just married Joseph Campbell, came to study with Graham at Bennington College, and joined the Company.[64] Through Erdman, Graham met Campbell, the mythologist and soon to be popularizer of Jungian ideas.[65] Campbell can be credited with establishing the compelling positioning of the dream between the psyche and myth.[66] "In his talks with her up at Bennington," remembers Erdman, "he must have gotten going on his favorite subject, mythology. She started reading the Greek myths and she got very excited about doing them."[67] For Campbell true artistic inspiration was irrational and hence the body was the most appropriate vehicle for such inspiration. In terms of dance, Campbell tied myth and the unconscious to embodiment: "Myth comes from the realm of the Muse, the realm of inspiration, inspiration that comes from below the level of consciousness."[68] The consequence of these ideas was that the dancing body was also placed below the level of consciousness.

In March of 1938 the Nazi annexation of Austria took place. In June Sigmund Freud expatriated from Vienna to London, where he would die in 1939. Kristallnacht (The Night of Broken Glass) followed in November of 1938. In that ominous year, Graham met the politically conservative Campbell, whose enthusiasm for myth, along with his devotion to Jung, would come into vogue in the United States only after 1945, to continue well into the 1950s. Although Graham would only choreograph her overtly mythical works once the war had ended, she began to read Jung avidly according to Campbell in the summer of 1938 between the creation of her two anti-Fascist solos and the premiere of *American Document*.[69] Campbell's refusal to take an anti-Fascist position in a talk he gave at Sarah Lawrence College in 1940, "Permanent Human Values," received a stern rebuke in 1941 from Thomas Mann, whose advocacy Campbell had hoped to enlist. Mann's position on Hitler had changed since he expatriated—like Brecht and Adorno—to Santa Monica.[70] Graham's postwar engagement with Greek myth took root in the prewar anti-Fascist moment even as Jung was establishing an institutional presence in the United States. The Analytic Psychology Club of New York (now the C.G. Jung Center), with which Graham's analyst Frances Wickes was affiliated, was founded in 1936.[71] In the fall of 1937, Jung himself came to the United States to lecture at Yale University. Otto Rank, then also living in New York City, wrote on October 15th to his disciple Jessie Taft: "Jung is coming next week to this country, seemingly an apostle of Nazism. In today's issue of *Saturday Review of Literature* he has an article on 'Wotan' justifying fascist ideology."[72] In Jung's article he identified Wotan as the archetype responsible for the "awakening" of National Socialism; but he dramatically underplayed the importance of anti-Semitism: "The coincidence of anti-Semitism with the reawakening of Wotan is a psychological subtlety that may perhaps be worth mentioning."[73] The conservative politics of Club members is reflected in its Bulletin as of 1937. In the second Bulletin an editorial casts doubt over the validity of the American Artists Congress to which Graham belonged.[74]

Nevertheless, Campbell, a conservative, if not to say politically retrogressive element in Graham's midst, inspired her interest in myth and the "mythopoetic mental condition."[75] Graham consulted with Campbell through 1943 while she was working on *Deaths and Entrances*, which he considered to be her first mythologically inspired work. Yet, in the contest between democracy and Fascism—utopia and myth—Graham opted in 1938 for utopia. Myth, however, was in the wings, and destined to become a major preoccupation of her postwar work as well as hallmark of her creative life from the 1950s until her death.

The role of Erick Hawkins—the first male dancer for whom Graham choreo-graphed and the first with whom she performed—also contributed to her new dramaturgical phase.[76] Hawkins introduced a male presence into the formerly uniquely female enclave of Graham's company, counteracting the sexual homo-geneity audiences and the Company itself had come to expect. [Figure 1.3]. The possibilities for narrative were enlarged by the presence of both sexes on stage. As McDonagh put it, Graham "let Hawkins serve as the instrument through which she would enter the theatrical mainstream."[77] But the use of words them-selves on stage should not be underestimated. Hawkins, too, was to be influ-enced throughout the 1940s by Graham's use of the spoken word. "By Martha doing that," he explained to David Sears, "I had very definitely a precedent and a pattern of thinking about words and dance. I could very easily see just from *Doc-ument* that there were times when you had to use words."[78] Hawkins observed that words were particularly necessary to choreography with an ethical dimen-sion, as would be the case with his *John Brown* (1945). But, he was also to use poetic texts in his *Stephen Acrobat* and *The Strangler*.

Figure 1.3 Erick Hawkins in Graham's *American Document* (1938). Photo: Barbara Morgan Copyright Barbara Morgan/Barbara Morgan Archives Courtesy of the Haggerty Museum of Art, Marquette University, Milwaukee, WI

Hawkins had studied modern dance briefly with Harald Kreutzberg in Salzburg in 1933 after which he returned to the United States to enroll in Georges Balanchine's School of American Ballet.[79] He became a member of Lincoln Kirstein's Ballet Caravan and debuted in the premiere of Balanchine's *Serenade* in White Plains, New York, on June 9, 1934. Hawkins's debut as a modern dancer, however, was in the first performance of Graham's *American Document* at Bennington on August 6, 1938. From the beginning of his dance training, Hawkins wanted not only to be a dancer but also a choreographer, and he soon came to feel that Balanchine's vision of himself as dancer would not lead him to discover a personal choreographic language.

Kirstein was an impresario who aimed to create an American brand of ballet. He wrote extensively on dance and although not a choreographer or dancer himself, was a major force in the development of dance as an American art form. Kirstein was also an outspoken opponent of modern dance and a virulent detractor of Graham's innovations in that field. Kirstein encouraged Hawkins, along with Lew Christensen and Eugene Loring, to set choreography on his fledgling Ballet Caravan.[80] In 1936 Hawkins created *Show Piece*, a ballet designed to display the strongest qualities of each member of Kirstein's Company.[81] Graham apparently first met Hawkins at a performance of *Show Piece* in Bennington. Hawkins next turned to a ballet on the Minotaur, the idea for which originated with his translation of Catullus's *Marriage of Peleus and Thetis*. He had majored in Greek civilization at Harvard University, graduating in 1932 with a bachelor of arts degree. Catullus wrote of sacrifices of young men and women to the Minotaur.[82] Thinking of this depiction of the sacrifice of innocents alongside Picasso's use of the image of the Minotaur—he may have been referencing *Composition avec Minotaure* of 1936 although Picasso produced many other variations of this image[83]—Hawkins worked with designer Philip Stapp on the concept of a barbed wire maze, and a costume sketch for the Minotaur was created: "a kind of a white mask on with big black eyes, and one red glove."[84] Kirstein commissioned a score from Charles Naginski and gave Hawkins the piano reduction and three weeks to set the choreography.

Hawkins, however, did not feel he could do justice to the idea in such a short rehearsal period.[85] Ultimately, *The Minotaur* never went into rehearsal for another reason: Hawkins realized classical ballet was the wrong idiom for it. Seeking a unique theatrical and choreographic formality, which he associated with a play by Sophocles or Uday Shankar's mime, he decided to study modern dance. The idea of a work on the Minotaur thus became the impetus for Hawkins to seek out Graham, whom he had first seen at the New England Conservatory in 1931 when she performed a solo on *Electra* in collaboration with actress Blanche Yurka. With Kirstein's blessing and a small travel loan Hawkins went to study with Graham in the summer of 1938 at Bennington, where she

had taken up summer residency.[86] He continued to perform with Ballet Caravan through 1939 although by then his own compositions were no longer part
of the company's repertoire.[87] But Hawkins's choreographic notes throughout
this period suggest that he hoped Kirstein was still interested in the Minotaur
project. It so happened that Kirstein did not forget about it, as John Taras choreographed a ballet called *The Minotaur* for Ballet Society in 1947.[88] It was in
that same year that Graham herself would do her own version of a Minotaur
ballet: *Errand into the Maze.*

Although with hindsight Hawkins dismissed *The Minotaur* as just another
unrealized youthful idea, his choreographic notebooks show the extensive preliminary planning he did for the ballet in 1938, which continued once he was
already working with Graham in 1939.[89] In 1938 Hawkins's notebooks indicate
that the connection of the Minotaur to Fascism became definitive: he reimag-
ined the piece in modern dress with the Minotaur as a dictator and Theseus in
workman's overalls; he renamed the ballet *Death by Minotaur.* The break with
Kirstein was not immediate. Graham billed Hawkins as a guest artist from Ballet
Caravan until 1939. There was, however, an intrigue surrounding Hawkins and
Kirstein, which their letters expose but do not elucidate in detail. Hawkins was
holding onto his position in Ballet Caravan and Kirstein appears to have been
pushing him out. At the same time, Graham was grooming Hawkins to be her
stage partner. She even admonished him in the early 1940s that hitchhiking was
inappropriate to his new star status.[90] Graham was infatuated with Hawkins
and, as he reciprocated, she became deeply and sensuously in love with him.[91]
"The reason people grow old," she wrote him at the start of their relationship, "is
that they do not worship Sex as the great immortality—and because they do not
know it is to be practiced deeply with concentration and simple delight."[92]
Hawkins's letters to Graham and his diaries reveal a driving ambition to succeed
as a modern artist, but also a nagging self-doubt. He appears, in fact, to have
been obsessed by the desire to create great art, and was particularly hungry for
recognition. "I want to be an artist like Martha, Lawrence [sic] Olivier, Picasso,
Stravinsky, Hindemith, Joyce, Klee, Miro, a Noh actor, Bartok, . . ." he noted
down in his diary in 1946.[93] Graham was blinded to his ambition, which
although not necessarily a negative quality, would eventually unsettle her own
self-security. Hawkins gave as much as he wanted to take, but Graham saw her
artistic identity as autonomous, and frequently took as a theme the destiny of
being alone. As Otto Rank pointed out in his book *Art and Artist* (1932), the
immortality of the artistic personality was an ideological given of the artist in
modern society. In conversation with Don McDonagh in 1971 Hawkins said
Graham had "the idea that she could live through her fame, or experience life as
a sort of immortality." "I feel the saddest thing about Martha," added Hawkins,
"is that she thought she could take it with her, and she can't."[94] In 1938, however,

Graham was not yet the major figure of twentieth-century choreography she was to become. That year was a turning point for Graham: a moment of artistic, emotional, and political expansion.

Nerves, Bones, and Blood

Just as Graham scrupulously differentiated utopia from myth, so she also made crucial theoretical distinctions between nerves, bones, and blood. She wrote in the Dance Libretto: "[Dance] communicates its participation to the nerves, the skin, the structure of the spectator."[95] This dissection of the body into receptive zones of nerves, skin, and skeletal structure omits the category of blood, an image Graham would evoke later for *Appalachian Spring*.[96] In a letter to Bertrand Russell of November 8, 1915, D.H. Lawrence distinguished between what he called "blood consciousness" and "mental consciousness."[97] Lawrence took the notion of blood consciousness from his reading of Frazer's *The Golden Bough* and *Totemism and Exogamy*. He relates blood consciousness to sexuality in a manner parallel to the relation of mental consciousness to the visual. "There is the blood-consciousness, with its sexual connection, holding the same relation as the eye, in seeing, holds to the mental consciousness."[98] Lawrence also relates mental consciousness to the nerves. Hence mind, eye, and nerves participate in intellectual activity. Blood consciousness, however, does not. If anything, blood consciousness is a variant of the myth because it epitomizes the identity whose roots evade intellectual scrutiny. We touch here upon aspects of embodiment in modernism that were already in circulation just before and during World War I. Approximately ten years later Graham would grow interested in what Lawrence called "the half of life, belonging to the darkness."[99]

Another important aspect of myth harks back to the past. Here we might invoke that other anatomical receptor of the effects of movement—the bone structure—Graham elaborated on the skeleton in one of the libretti for *Appalachian Spring*, when she wrote: "This is a legend of American living. It is like the bone structure, the inner frame that holds together a people."[100] The skeleton is the armature of living matter but also a sort of *futur antérieur*—what *will have been*—that interrupts the flow from present to future with a past that is always about to be—an anticipation of the end of life. The skeleton not only gives form to the living, it is what remains of the body after life is complete. Hence, the "legend of American living" flirts with the past as well as with the future through action in the present. Becoming movement, the about-to-be of action, and the legacy of the past that bodies may draw upon, are facets of a common imagery over which the ideological battle between democracy and Fascism was being fought.

The Workings of Utopia

Since hers was a conception of utopia with a political program, it is important to put some flesh and bones on the workings of utopia itself. One important characteristic of narrative utopia has been identified in literary criticism with "generic discontinuity."[101] At least four substyles in *American Document* fostered discontinuity in a formerly homogeneous style: (1) elements of agitprop, notably in the use of language throughout and in the "Afterpiece"; (2) the influence of the historical pageant, of which a good example is the 1936 WPA production *America Sings*[102]; (3) Graham's nativist modernism of the early 1930s, evidenced in her solo "Lament for the Land," which drew upon the movement vocabulary developed in earlier dances inspired by Native American culture such as *Primitive Mysteries* (1931); (4) Erick Hawkins's athletic and classically trained body that breached both the aesthetic and the gendered homogeneity of Graham's work until then. Graham now replaced her austere experiments of the 1930s with a new iconoclasm. While most of the women of Graham's company were already well-trained in her style, many having also contributed significantly to the development of her technique, Hawkins was something of an interloper by virtue of both his gender and his classical training.[103] "There is sometimes a slight disparity," noted one critic, "in his interpretation of the style so particular to Graham's art."[104]

Given these heterogeneous elements, *American Document* did not supply a stable representation of national identity, but its *figuration*. Figuration can arise out of discontinuity between text and dance. More than one dance critic stressed the antiphonal relationship of dance and text throughout *American Document*. It also arose from the more subtle discontinuity between modern and balletic styles of dancing. Also contributing to figuration were intentional discontinuities between past and present, ritual and myth, *sensus communis* and invocation. Taken together, this is evidence of a strategy to deal with democracy figuratively. As the libretto and Graham's comments to the press made clear, democracy was not a given, but a possibility—indeed, an almost forgotten possibility. "Freedom has been hunted around the globe"[105] is a line from the libretto that has a certain ambiguity, for it can indicate persecution, but also a quest that is related to the question: "what is an American?" It is answered with the words "Emancipation" (referring to abolition) and "Democracy," by naming the attributes of America as if it were a proper name:

> America! Name me the word that is courage.
> America! Name me the word that is justice.
> America! Name me the word that is power.
> America! Name me the word that is freedom.

> America! Name me the word that is faith.
> Here is that word—
> Democracy![106]

America is called upon to "name the words" that encapsulate its own essence. The territorial identity is displaced by a conceptual identity inherent in a political system. The country is exhorted to name a word that equates it with the five abstract nouns: courage, justice, power, freedom, and faith. The script promotes a blurring of word and name ("Name me the word that is . . ."), and promotes a willful confusion between history, document, legend, folk tale, and performance. National identity may speak through those present, but the performance—unlike the athletes born of classical statuary in *Olympia*—does not pass for a creation myth. Democracy must come into being—be created—in the present, as if the performance were the very ritual of its creation.

Langston Hughes expressed a similar sentiment in his poem "Freedom's Plow" (1943), a later version of "Let America Be America Again" published in 1935.[107] Hughes asked, "Who is America?" while Graham asked, "What is an American?" Like Graham, Hughes viewed democracy as a possibility rather than a given:

> Democracy will not come
> Today, this year,
> Nor ever
> Through compromise and fear.[108]

In his earlier poem upon which this one was based, Hughes's position on history and the future was clearly utopian and hence figural: "O, let America be America again—/The land that never has been yet—."[109] Because of the figural quality of the performance, what transpired on stage had the qualities of quotation, antithesis, irony, and temporal play.

The meaning of America as a democracy—democracy as America's "name"— contrasted with the floor patterns, roles, and steps of minstrelsy, indicate that America is a presence that must be named precisely because it lacks stable existence: it exists in words that have an uncertain relation to movements. In this way, movements themselves—or action—ensure its meaning, but also risk betraying it. Graham's final solo is called "Invocation" and the naming of America that the Interlocutor evokes is equally an invocation. His final words express hope for "a just and lasting peace among ourselves and all nations."[110] But, that hope is far from conclusive. The nation exists outside of itself as a potential that must be named, and in this way the entire piece is framed by a utopian quality of figuration. Democracy is not only under threat from foreign Fascisms; it is actually the object of an ongoing *internal* struggle. Hughes cited two enemies. The first was the Nazi army, but the second was "the enemy who would divide and conquer us from within." Hughes referred to "Hitlerism at home."[111] Graham evoked the power of the archival word not to glorify the national past, but to reinvigorate efforts toward racial equality in the present.

Graham took a formal framework for *American Document* from the minstrel show walk around, which may have been an attempt on her part to discover an indigenous pageant structure that would contrast with the classicizing German Olympic Games. Susan Manning has referred to the "complicated politics" of *American Document* with respect to the work's evocation of minstrelsy in what the Dance Libretto calls a "definite dance pattern."[112] Minstrelsy (recognized by one critic at the time as "despised") could, however, be considered within the utopian framework to furnish a foil against which democracy is sought.[113] *American Document* does not wear its politics on its sleeve. Rather than rendering Graham's politics ambiguous, however, the choreographic reference to the patterns of minstrelsy provided a formal counterpoint to the Emancipation Episode to follow, just as the "Lament for the Land" solo was meant to be compared with the later "Lament for the Living" of the Fifth Episode—"Hold Your Hold!"— dated 1942, the moment at which *American Document* rejoins contemporary reality. In this way, the relation of spatial histories—the patterns of minstrelsy, the land confiscated—to the temporality of the nation as an unfinished project is stressed to the detriment of the nation as a mythic totality that characterized Fascist representations of national identity and national will.

As dance critic of the *New Masses* Owen Burke noted of Emancipation Episode: "It brings the knowledge that the struggle for Negro liberation was (as is today the struggle for Negro rights) part and parcel of the constantly urgent struggle for democracy." Burke was also the only critic to connect the Indian Episode not just with the problems of dispossession brought on by the Great Depression, but also with the threat of Fascism abroad. "'Indian Episode,'" he writes, "takes on current significance, brings to mind migratory workers, the increasing ranks of the jobless—land becomes a symbol of security and the composition connects with the streams of refugees leaving their fascist-invaded lands and home. The Indian Episode loses it nostalgia."[114] This nostalgia refers to the Indian as a symbol of the vanishing American.[115]

The Third Episode—"The Puritan"—referring to the arrival of the first Pilgrims to American shores in 1620 interspersed a 1741 sermon by Jonathan Edwards with a love duet for Graham and Hawkins. [Figure 1.4] The text of the sermon ("Sinners in the hands of an angry God!") alternated with lyrical and erotic excerpts from the Old Testament "Song of Songs" ("Let him kiss me with the kisses of his mouth"). A program note for a performance at the Civic Theatre in Chicago on March 10, 1940, mentions additional text by Cotton Mather.[116] These texts "are woven into and around the dance to suggest the conflict that took place in Puritan hearts when faced with the choice of a simple life or an angry life of denial."[117] Arnold Kaye wrote: "The protagonists are two lovers and they are alternately drawn to each other by passion and parted by the taboos and inhibitions of their society."[118] The personal nature of the duet might appear to set it apart from the civic dimensions of *American Document*.[119] But it may have forged what Jeffrey Schnapp, in a different context, called "individualistic patterns of desire and identification."[120] These very patterns anchor the desire for community in embodied and sexualized identifications. Democracy becomes the Beloved. The audience coalesces its desire for community later in the work around Hawkins as One Man, a portrayal of the Common Man.

Figure 1.4 The first duet for Martha Graham and Erick Hawkins in Graham's *American Document* (1938). Courtesy of the Music Division, Library of Congress

The Impact of *American Document*

When *American Document* premiered in New York City on October 9, 1938, it engendered a new sense of community between the general public and the dance world. Graham's work had up until then been appreciated by a small, elite audience. The spoken word and the pageant framework made *American Document* accessible and appealing to a general audience. *American Document* also virtually closed ranks within the dance world itself.[121] Despite previous gripes Lincoln Kirstein extolled "the quality of Graham's idiosyncratic gesture formulating just what she meant to say."[122] The left-wing press set aside persistent political misgivings about Graham's oeuvre: *New Masses*—the most prominent left-wing cultural publication of the 1930s—sponsored the New York premiere at Carnegie Hall. Graham's success with *American Document* demonstrated her ability to make artistic impulse, political savvy, and public image cohere. The mainstream media took notice of her growing celebrity status.

The potential for publicity and career building in the wake of *American Document*'s success was nothing short of unparalleled. "Martha Graham," one critic wrote, "has not only succeeded in interpreting America but her vital art has enabled America to interpret modern dance."[123] The first national tour of an American dance company in 1939 confirmed *American Document* as the first American modern dance to address national identity, and Graham as the first American modern dancer to reach a national, if something short of a mass, audience. Graham's new political and sexual orientation made her work more legible to the general public. "I want the audience," she said in a rare interview with *The Daily Worker*, "to feel no obscurity or doubt at any time about what is happening on stage."[124] To like *American Document* became almost a patriotic duty. The *Hollywood Citizen News* asserted: "If there is any American who can witness Martha Graham's new dance composition 'American Document' without emerging from the experience a finer, prouder citizen, that person is impervious to reason, numb to emotion, insensible to art."[125] Graham's clearly stated political engagement meshed flawlessly with the public visibility afforded by the work's success, which also confirmed that modern dance could be an accessible idiom. Its success propelled Graham to national prominence.[126] Graham's anti-Fascist stance was indistinguishable from her artistic success, and the nascent celebrity image was to be useful in the coming American war effort on the home front.

Graham's newfound iconicity went hand in hand with a more pronounced heterosexual identity. "She developed aggressive qualities in his [Hawkins's] dancing so that her own natural aggressive qualities would not be too much, and she also toned hers down so it was the manly man and the womanly woman, you know, sort of thing."[127] If the "womanly woman" was uncharacteristic for Graham, her stage persona in *American Document* reflected a changed identity with political as well as personal ramifications. One left-wing critic saw Graham's performance in *American Document* as a personal transformation into political consciousness through lyric self-awareness:

> Her face was an expressionless mask when she began dancing—white, hollow cheeks, straight eyelashes, and hair, steady eyes, crimson mouth. Her face now flushed through its powder, her hair, lashed free, tumbled roughly and her expression softened with her flush.[128]

This critic renders Graham's transformation from impassive modernist abstraction to sexualized emotional vibrancy in critical language that reverses the left-wing critique of her work throughout the 1930s as cold, emotionless, and formal.[129]

Action Photography

If Riefenstahl claimed the moving image, Graham claimed the still image. Beginning in 1935 and continuing through 1941 Barbara Morgan undertook the photo-documentation of Graham's dances in a "small, non-commercial theater" using "complex lighting constructions."[130] Morgan's photographs of Graham reached a broad public by 1941 with the publication of *Martha Graham: Sixteen Dances in Photographs*. This portfolio was advertised in the Book of the Month Club's "Say, Is this the U.S.A." section, and featured in *The New York Times* Sunday Magazine (September 28, 1941). The dissemination of the photographic documentation of *American Document* augmented its impact. Morgan's work showed that modern dance could compete with Fascist orality and innovative cinematographic editing as a transmitter of visceral effects in the image. "This is the first decade of action photography," she wrote, "in which it has been possible technically to photograph unrestrained dance action."[131] Morgan set herself the task of capturing peak moments thanks to which the dance inscribes itself in memory. "It is the role of photography to seize such moments; to fuse reality, art, and time."[132] Dance photography could extend the reach of movement's call to action without undercutting its visceral qualities. "The still photograph," writes Morgan, "[is needed to] clarify the significant instants [of the dance]."[133] But, it does more than that: the photograph also sustains the movement of dance toward the future. It preserves the positive effects of action, as it were, in a permanent future. Morgan's action photography has a utopian approach to movement that appropriates the energy Sorel attributed to myth.

The notion of action in the photograph relies on the future of movement in the image. "Nothing," notes Morgan, "seems emptier to me than merely 'stopping' action. . . . So-called 'stopping' or achieving un-blurred form and detail in focus should be done with such a fine logic of movement that it seemingly continues even though arrested by the camera shutter."[134] Morgan names the optimal moment of photographic capture "the moment of greatest tension before the peak, . . . or the peak explosion of that tension."[135] To capture the continued flow of dance in the still image, explains Morgan, the photographer must anticipate movement. The photograph is only true to dance when it shows us where movement will go, and this can only happen if the photographer anticipates the moment she captures by clicking the shutter before movement actually happens. "If the photograph is shot in the tension peaks before the release, the picture should nevertheless imply continuity."[136] Morgan understands action as continuity in the image between a past, a present, and a future. But, action is equally a discontinuity or, rather, the occasion for the spectator to do the work of missing emplotment.

This counterpoint between movement and image—between dance and photography—indicates that we are dealing here with a phenomenon of figuration. As the photograph documents its historical and performative moment, it also suggests, to paraphrase Benedict Anderson, a style of imagining that engages both the past and the future.[137] Imagined community, which Anderson has identified with national identity, is also, as Phillip E. Wegner points out, *imaginary* community.[138] It is this gap in the representation between the imagined and the imaginary that also characterizes the performance of Graham's anti-Fascist politics. *American Document* enacted an affirmation of democracy as a utopian invocation of national community. It is this *utopian* aspect of the performance that issues from the gap between image and motion, or the gap between the image and the motion that follows it, a gap that haunts dance photography. The photograph is utopian because in it the body moves toward the future but does not reveal it. We do not *see* where movement will go. Graham and Morgan point to a place in which the body discovers its own political self-definition as futurity. Dance photography renders action as the search for continuity toward the future, and captures it through anticipation in the past of a present that had not yet occurred. Action photography is both functionally and visually anticipatory.

This Is One Man

The final episode of *American Document* takes the Great Depression as its theme, the very historical conjuncture within which the dance was created. The text for "three women" (Sophie Maslow, Jane Dudley, and Frieda Flier) invites identification: "We," intones the Interlocutor's voice, "are three women/We are three million women."

We are the mothers of the hungry dead.
We are the mothers of the hungry living.
We are the mothers of those to be born.
Listen to what we say.
Ours is a lament for the living.[139]

The sense of the women as individuals who merge nevertheless into a mass of human suffering squares with the New Deal photographic aesthetic in which sharecroppers, tenant farmers, and their families were photographed by government agencies for documentary purposes. The tragedy of the women, as in Erskine Caldwell's and Margaret Bourke-White's *You Have Seen Their Faces*, is inextricably bound to the fate of their children.[140] "By restrained yet fluid motion, the tragedy of the unemployed was starkly evoked," wrote a critic of the *Memphis Commercial Appeal in 1939*.[141]

The text for the three mothers contains reprieves just as the women's choreography, captured in Morgan's time-lapse photograph, seems to have consisted in diverse rotational movements.[142] The look of the three performers suggests the "emotional" orientation of left-wing modern dance.[143] Erick Hawkins's entrance

Figure 1.5 "We Are Three Women." Sophie Maslow, Jane Dudley, and Frieda Flier in Graham's *American Document* (1938). Photo: Barbara Morgan. Copyright Barbara Morgan/ Barbara Morgan Archives

directly upon their exit was captured in another famous Morgan image. [Figure 1.6] The scene is described as follows: "They [the three women] walk off in silence. Erick enters from opposite side, seeming to be about to follow them off. Instead he turns in center stage. The Interlocutor speaks . . . This is one man. This is one million men."[144] The text of these two scenes was so closely associated with the dance that it appears under the plates in Morgan's book. The transition between the three women and the one man is also marked by the change from "we are" to "this is." The transition, in other terms, contains a shift from the identification *with* to the objectification *of* national identity. Such objectification takes the form of a male body walking.

The Interlocutor's final words in *American Document* exhort America to "name the word" that has five ontological predicates: courage, justice, power,

Figure 1.6 "This is One Man." Erick Hawkins in Graham's *American Document* (1938).
Photo: Barbara Morgan Copyright Barbara Morgan/Barbara Morgan Archives

freedom, and faith. The word is "Democracy!" At this point Hawkins becomes a walking allegory of democracy: "This man has a faith/It is you/ . . . This man has a fear/it is you/This man has a need/It is himself/And you."[145] Democracy is pictured as a state of relative faith, fear, and need between the members of its political community. Thus, I would argue that the figuration of democracy is a more important and decisive preoccupation of *American Document* than that of national identity per se. Hawkins's energy appears barely contained within the frame, yet the breadth of his stride also suggests a rootedness. He creates a space ahead of himself that he is at the point of attaining.

Graham exploits Hawkins's presence here with reference to contemporary iconography of the common man/worker. His enterprising energy suggests the democratic ethos. "This is one man," announces the Interlocutor, "This is one million men . . . This man has a power. It is himself, and you." Ellen Graff notes that "Hawkins' solo portraying the struggles of the work force [was] probably the most explicit representation of working class America in Graham's dances."[146] Although Hawkins's appearance does bring the iconography of the worker to mind, I would suggest he should be read as a figure of participatory democracy. The issue of representation—both aesthetic and political—emerges in the photograph with a certain complexity. "One Man" walking across the stage is proposed as the aesthetic representation of a great plurality of men ("one million men"). His standing (or walking) for others is a function of universal democratic representation. As Charles Beard and Mary Beard wrote in *America at Midpassage*: "It took the great economic depression, the domestic conflict, the rise of Hitler, and the consolidation of fascist forces abroad, to arouse what appeared to be a fierce affection for democracy and to produce a tumult of praise for the idea and its institutional embodiments."[147] Hawkins was embodying an institution. Not only could the history of injustices be the object of a reassessment of America's past, but the system of democracy itself could be salvaged. Charles and Mary Beard described Graham as "engrossed in the American scene and with leftist sympathies," and saw in *American Document* Graham's "feeling for time, place, perils, and prospects of survival."[148]

One Man's "power" is forceful only inasmuch as it is a (political) representation: "This man has a power. It is himself, and you." His power resides in his equality with others; he shares his power with others and he draws it from them. Hawkins, then, is an individual inasmuch as he represents, or is (a) representative. The worker, in other terms, enters Graham's universe under the aegis of representation. Hawkins not only represents the worker in Graham's oeuvre; he also stands for the work of (democratic) representation. Kirstein observed that Hawkins "stood and walked like a workman's best idea of himself as a dancer," suggesting that the worker becomes a dancer in order to stress his equality with other workers.[149] Yet, representation also has a political dimension here. In this dance celebrating democracy, Hawkins stands apart from the millions (or walks alone) precisely because he *represents* them, as the representative would stand for the electorate.

F.R. Ankersmit argues in *Aesthetic Politics* that one of democracy's most positive if least understood traits is to sunder thought and action, and thus to instance the "brokenness" of political reality.[150] Democracy, in other terms, works on analogy with the "crisis in representation" of the aesthetic sphere. Just as no absolute match is possible in modern art between the artwork and what it represents—this relationship being recognized as in "crisis"—so political representatives retain a vexing autonomy from those whom *they* represent. This autonomy of the political agent (action) from the democratic constituency (thought or intention) for Ankersmit is a positive if still troublesome trait of democracy.

In the "Afterpiece," Hawkins collapses the representative and the represented into one body. But this collapse does not create a totality as much as a divided state. He allegorizes democracy as the broken state of political reality. And it is precisely for this reason that democracy in *American Document* is something that needs to be sought for, something that is not yet thoroughly established. The dance photograph itself testifies to this brokenness. It is brokenness between mobility and stillness, between performance and its visual reproduction; and, in the dance, between ritual presentation and historical representation, conventional patterns and undefined national space. If the document is a figure of America's past evoked by the choreography, and a mechanism whereby the urgency of democratic processes can be critically conveyed to a national public, it is also a vector of movement rendered by Morgan's action photography. But, the very figure of the document is subject to a discontinuity: the discrepancy between image and flow. Brokenness itself constitutes the figure of community proper to *American Document*, and points toward that community's possible future political practices. Under the rubric "Disturbing Sequel" a critic of the *Los Angeles Times* reported: "There is an air of righteousness about 'American Document' that is strangely upset by the 'After Piece' with its implication of responsibility un-shouldered today. It is a challenge, a disturbing aftermath that sends one home with facts to think upon."[151]

The symptom of this political brokenness—the divided body of democratic political reality—is also gendered male. Hawkins is showcased in *American Document* despite his evident classical training. Although this disparity may have contributed to the ends of utopic discontinuity, his centrality to the work's core meanings also usurped some of Graham's gravitas. Inasmuch as Graham chose to embody American identity, she now had to do so as an American woman; that is, according to the conventions of American scene art with its iconography of the comradely ideal and companionate marriage. Yet, as Kirstein points out, it was Graham herself who danced the key idea of Democracy in the work, an idea that Hawkins had merely introduced in his brief solo. "In the end, in a plain bright red dress, with her dancing balance of suavity and abruptness, her somber levity and steady stops, *she seemed an incarnate question of everything we fear and hope for in our daily lives.*"[152] These are the very terms of Hawkins's solo—"a man who has a faith and a fear." Here there is neither a man nor a woman, but, in Kirstein's terms, an incarnate question, as danced by Graham. This moment in which the feminine body performs the main theme of the work occurs only at the end, but it does so through a daring form of abstraction that was apparently quite effective. Graham herself embodies the allegory of precariousness and the question of social survival that hovered over the entire work, making it, at its beginnings at least, less a work of propaganda than a thoughtful and urgent meditation on the fate of democracy. Nevertheless, the heterosexual couple is stressed in the final image: "[W]hen the reader says, at the end of the Document,' 'that government of the people, by the people, and for the people shall not perish from the earth,' while the Man and Woman, Erick Hawkins and Martha Graham, pass slowly from the stage together.'"[153]

Afterpiece

American Document was purged by 1942 of its popular front critical barbs. The Dance Libretto was published that year.[154] Susan Manning points out the political changes incorporated after the Pearl Harbor attack and the entrance of the United States into World War II.[155] Dance critic Edwin Denby, never a great fan of the work, called the 1944 version of *American Document* a "smug glorification" of national identity.[156] But, positive popular response to the work continued undiminished. *The American Dancer* reported that Graham's company performed in "convention halls, sport palaces on the scale of Madison Square Garden" where "the response was so thunderous that the performers were often frightened at the sound, the cheers being as mighty as for a new world's record in some sport."[157] Although *American Document* brought Graham to national attention in 1938 through 1939, the work disappeared from Graham's repertory after 1944. The anti-Fascist political community *American Document* had mobilized in the late 1930s gave way by the mid-1940s to patriotic nationalism.

The fact remains that Graham's national breakthrough had a political basis.[158] And, this basis was initially not that of nationalism, but instead a critique of nationalism under the banner of anti-Fascism. The meaning of *American Document* changed as the nation approached war and Graham was forced to the political center. Conjoined with her increasingly iconic status, her politically mercurial quality doubtless facilitated her later role as cultural diplomat in the State Department tours of the Cold War between 1954 and 1974.[159] One wonders, however, what she would have thought had she known of the US government protection of ex-Nazis immediately after World War II, which has only recently been revealed, but has yet to be fully explained.

In 1944, the year of the last performance of *American Document*, Graham unveiled a new work—*Appalachian Spring*—destined to become an abiding popular success, and also to be her last Americana ballet. In *Appalachian Spring*, as we shall see in the next chapter, Graham did not entirely abandon the socially critical dimension of her anti-Fascism. Although she did not live under Fascism, Graham learned how to camouflage her views, a lesson with direct implications for her interest in addressing the unconscious of the audience and concealing the most personal meanings of her work, which would become her major concern of the postwar era.

2

Politics Under Erasure

Regionalism as Cryptology

"The monstrous body or, rather, monstrous bodies alone can serve as
the subject of any conceivable history of the body"
—Hayden White[1]

Appalachian Spring (1944) is considered one of Graham's most lyrical and
accessible works as well as an enduring masterpiece of American modern
dance. It has rarely if ever been compared with *American Document* from an
aesthetic or political perspective. As a picture of rural American life, *Appalachian Spring* has invited more frequent comparison with Graham's other piece
of Americana, *Frontier* (1935), although this last had also faded from memory
until it reentered the repertory of the Martha Graham Dance Company in
1975.[2] Some considered *Frontier* a sketch for Graham's role of the Bride in
Appalachian Spring.[3] One reason might be that the Graham character in both
works cradles an imaginary infant. Musicologist and Copland specialist Vivian
Perlis reminds us, however, how topical the ballet was in 1944: "*Appalachian
Spring* confirmed traditional American values that were being challenged by
Nazism."[4] It was, indeed, a patriotic affirmation of national identity in terms of
folk legend. "This is a legend of American living," wrote Graham. "It is like the
bone structure, the inner frame that holds together a people."[5] The question I
ask is, did *Appalachian Spring* retain the socially critical dimension of Graham's
prewar anti-Fascist stance?

Despite its timelessness as a modern dance classic, *Appalachian Spring* does
bear the imprint of the popular front interest in American folk materials. It is
performed in something like period costume, which links modern dance to a
national past.[6] Both choreography and music aim at an evocation of national
identity through historical markers of a vague regionalism. The score makes references to Shaker music, and the choreography to folk dance even as both remain
resolutely modernist through engagement with dissonance, angularity, tension,

and counterpoint. Particularly significant is the hymn "'Tis the Gift to be Simple" orchestrated by Copland. As was well known since Doris Humphrey's *Shakers* (1931), the Shakers were a dancing and singing religious sect located on the East Coast and in the Midwest. They reached their greatest numbers in the pre–Civil War period. "Shaker ritualism was a true folk art," writes Edward D. Andrews. "Though the tunes, songs, marches, ring dances and other forms of devotional 'exercises' were composed by individuals, they were intended for communal use. Their character and form were peculiarly social."[7] And, he adds: "[I]t may yet be claimed that the Shakers represent the oldest, most successful, and most consistently pure communism in the new world."[8] With this reference to the Shakers, a historical primitive Christian sect of the new world, Graham nodded to the left.

As in much federally subsidized art of the prewar period, Graham glorified the American heartland that was geographically located between the East and West Coasts of the United States. "During the war," writes William Graebner, "the regional Americanism of the 1930s was easily transmuted into the theme of rural patriotism."[9] In 1940 leading regionalist artist Grant Wood asserted: "In our present unsettled times, when democracy is threatened on all sides, the preservation of our folklore is more important than is generally realized."[10] Howard Mumford Jones wrote in "Patriotism—But How?" that "America needed to promote patriotism through its national mythology."[11] Effective patriotism seemed to require a depiction of the country rather than the city, and the roots of the folk in customs of particular regions. The fact that *Appalachian Spring* is set in the Appalachian Mountains distances it from the high-modernist, urban milieu of New York City where Graham lived and worked. But, there were also dissenting views about the connotations of folk culture. Grant Wood, for instance, had written an essay entitled "Revolt against the City," which set him apart from other Regionalists as a crypto-Fascist. Impugning the political as well as the artistic value of regionalism, artist Stuart Davis, whose work, like that of Graham and David Smith, was engaged with both abstraction and anti-Fascist politics, linked regionalism with Fascism. Davis "condemned the regionalists for being anti-modern, regressive, and even fascist in style and subject matter."[12] In 1946 art historian H. W. Janson published a similar critique of Benton and Wood, which announced the decline of regionalism and the ascendancy of abstraction in postwar American art.[13]

Despite Graham's gesture toward regionalism, abstraction predominated in her work. While the characters of *Appalachian Spring* were recognizable types whose costumes placed them in a generalized regionalist context, the plot contained lacunae, discontinuous moments, and absences of clearly interpretable meaning that highlighted gesture for its own sake. In preparing *Appalachian Spring* Graham wrote that she wanted to avoid any resemblance to "a mural in a middle western railway station or post office"—images that evoke regionalist public art of the WPA era. Isamu Noguchi's set destabilized the implied region-alism of the costumes so that spatial abstraction would counterbalance the ele-ments of plot. Noguchi's choices were in line with Graham's intent to destabilize time with respect to narrative action.

Graham herself thought about how the set could serve to blur temporal and historical fixity. She envisioned the stage set as suggesting "the inside and the outside of a house, something still in the building, something unfinished."[14] And, she added, it should be "like the bones of a dwelling."[15] [Figure 2.1] The outlines of this house suggest a metaphor for the entire piece being about "the bone struc-ture of a people's living."[16] Bones suggest basic structural outlines, but also ruined remains. The sense that the piece will convey the outlines of a structure whether it be the body ("the American body frame"), "a people's living," unornamented design (the "bone-like simplicity" of the Shaker rocking chair that is called for) or that which lasts after life is expended ("things that last like bones"), space pre-dominates over time, because the latter is not stabilized from a narrative or his-torical viewpoint.[17] Graham stresses that time is a fluid concept because subjectivity is also not fixed in time: "Some things happen to our mothers and

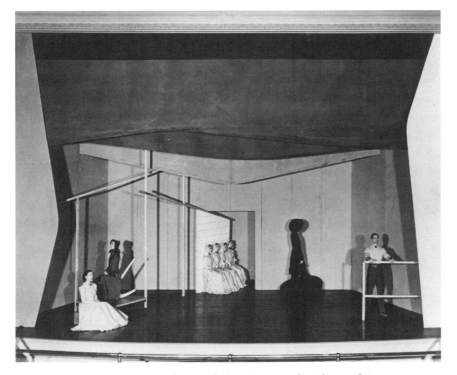

Figure 2.1 Isamu Noguchi's set for *Appalachian Spring* at the Library of Congress (1944). Courtesy of the Music Division, Library of Congress

some things happen to us, but they all happen to us."[18] These shifting temporalities are contained within the stability of a place, although place, too, can endure the ravages of time. "It should all by theatrical clarity add up to a sense of place."[19] Space that retains remnants of the past could be called PLACE (capitalized by Graham as though it were a character in its own right), which accedes to its own uncanny temporality: "Certain things are alive and present for us although far in the actual past as far as time is concerned."[20] For Graham, place was haunted space. This rendering transparent of the space in terms of that which is unfinished or that which is, to the contrary, in a state of decay, corresponds to the simultaneous superimposition of different historical moments. Its contradiction—pristine wilderness and a "bone orchard"—replaced historical consciousness. With *Appalachian Spring*, the body becomes archetypal in that it cannot be governed by a single narrative logic. "All this," she wrote to Copland, "is rather more like a poem than a dramatic happening, although many of the happenings will be very dramatic in themselves."[21]

The Coolidge Commission

The Elizabeth Sprague Coolidge Foundation commissioned Aaron Copland to write the score for *Appalachian Spring* through the auspices of the Library of Congress. The "Ballet for Martha," as Copland named it, received its premiere on October 30, 1944, in the auditorium of the Library of Congress in the nation's capital. The commission and the resultant performance were part of a much larger initiative. In 1924 the Coolidge Foundation endowed the Library of Congress with an auditorium, and in 1925 the Congress approved the creation of a Library of Congress Trust Fund Board to administer the Coolidge Foundation gifts, which were meant to promote the development of modern chamber music.[22] The venue evoked for *The Dance Observer* the recently dismantled WPA arts projects. The Coolidge commissions were seen as a model of government arts sponsorship, "a working model of a national department of fine arts."[23]

In 1942 when she began work on the scenario for Copland, Graham had been unable to present an annual New York season and the Bennington summer program had closed down. The war was taking its toll. Although she had accepted loans to support her work, Graham had never solicited a contribution. Hawkins realized that financial contributions were crucial for their survival. He first wrote to Mrs. Max Schott, a Graham acquaintance from Santa Barbara, to request $2,000. To their surprise, a check for this amount arrived in the mail. In a diary entry of August 8, 1943, Hawkins notes: "In July 1943 I sat up in bed and crystallized my desire to raise $20,000 for Martha. We raised $26,000."[24] He convinced Katharine Cornell, her agent Gertrude Macy, and Bethsabee de Rothschild, who was studying at the Graham studio, to hold a Sunday afternoon gathering of potential patrons at Cornell's apartment. Out of this came the "Plans for the Formation of a Limited Partnership for Financing Martha Graham and Dance Company." Limited Partnership referred to changes in the 1943 tax law providing a way to finance "most theatrical enterprises" wherein the choreographer is designated "the general partner." There is a tax write-off in the case of financial loss for a "bad business debt." The implementation of contributions on this basis permitted the Company to finance two consecutive Sunday night performances in December 1943 in a Broadway theater with a small chamber orchestra and rehearsal pay for the dancers.[25] As de Mille put it in an interview with Gertrude Macy recorded in preparation for her biography of Graham: "Erick was responsible for getting Martha off the rehearsal studio floor."[26] De Mille did not include this comment in her biography of Graham, however, which is resolutely anti-Hawkins from the perspective of the couple's ultimate separation.

Graham received the Coolidge Commission for a new score by Aaron Copland thanks to the initiative of Hawkins, who took it upon himself to write to Mrs. Coolidge on May 21, 1942: "I feel that it is extremely important, now that she [Graham] is at the height of her career, that she should be able to use the music of the finest composers of the time for her dance."[27] Up until *American Document*, Graham had only been able to afford piano accompaniment in performance, whereas *Appalachian Spring* was performed with a nine-instrument ensemble made up of four strings, four winds, and one piano (Copland wanted two pianos, which shocked Hawkins). After all parties agreed to the commission, but before it was implemented, Hawkins wrote again to Elizabeth Sprague Coolidge on October 7, 1942, to propose that she support his staging of a new ballet to Copland's *A Lincoln Portrait* at the Library of Congress with a symphony orchestra. The terms in which he conceived the idea were derivative of Graham's way of conceptualizing Americana, except for his use of the term *myth*: "I wouldn't be Lincoln, but the myth of the American man that he is the prototype of."[28] Hawkins's timing was ill chosen, and the response was elusive and politely negative. For Hawkins to move in on funding and collaborators with a competitive project must have been unnerving for Graham. Hawkins was in search of a dramatic vehicle for himself that would match Graham's signal achievements, which is entirely understandable as he was a major proponent of her conception of dance theater, but unique in that he was a man. In 1948 he approached Copland a second time with the idea for a ballet based on Herman Melville's *Moby Dick*. In a letter of April 28, 1948, he wrote: "I feel that I have lived long enough to be ready to tackle a tragic role [Ahab]." He added: "I am setting a permanent nucleus for a small ensemble to tour with; flute, oboe, clarinet, bassoon, piano and percussion."[29] Copland responded on May 19, 1948, that he thought Melville "cannot be successfully translated into any other medium" and certainly not without "the aid of a full symphony orchestra."[30] The tragic role that Hawkins would eventually tackle successfully in the Graham mode, however, was that of John Brown in the ballet of that name, which he mounted in 1945. This work has important connections to *Appalachian Spring* to which I return later in this chapter.

Political Continuities

Because Copland was in Hollywood and Graham in New York during the preparation of the score in 1943 she sent him two scenarios from which to compose. The first, "House of Victory," was sent in a letter dated May 16, 1943; the second, to which she gave the title "NAME?," in all capital letters with a question mark, was sent in a letter dated July 10, 1943. The scenarios provide a way to track the initial development of the work. Copland requested certain changes in the first scenario, but his compositional sequencing depended upon the second scenario, and musicologists have studied the scenarios closely for this reason.[31] Jacqueline Shea-Murphy was the first dance scholar to do a close reading of the scenarios.[32] My analysis complements hers in many respects, but makes a few different points. Shea-Murphy's emphasis is on the Indian Girl who is evoked in one of Graham's scenarios for *Appalachian Spring*, but never actually portrayed on stage by one dancer. Shea-Murphy sees this presence in the mode of an absence in Graham's thinking on the work as evidence of Graham supporting "other troublesome government policies and rhetoric, such as those asserting the trope of the 'Vanishing American' and of a paternalistic 'Great Father' looking after his children."[33] In this chapter I stress two other figures who never made it onto the stage—the Escaped Slave and the Abolitionist—in order to make a connection between the anti-Fascism of *American Document* and the absence of all three figures in *Appalachian Spring* five years later.

It is impossible to understand how these absences become ghostly presences without taking active account of the music in the ballet and its relation to the characters Graham projected in her scenarios. Certain characters not visible on stage because they were cut are nonetheless present in the relation of sound to the movement we do see. Copland composed music for them, which remained part of the integral score. I want to argue that no character is actually fully present as each one we see is a composite of the erased others. While I rely on the foundational work on *Appalachian Spring* by musicologists Vivian Perlis and Howard Pollock, it should be noted that they do not in general address the political dimension of the work's compositional history. More recently, musicologist Elizabeth B. Crist has placed *Appalachian Spring* in the context of the Popular Front, but she has relied chiefly on musicological rather than choreographic evidence and hence she finds the relationship of the scenarios to the finished version seamless. How we perceive the preliminary scenarios in the final version is not explained.

We can address the political dimension of the work through the three politically sensitive characters Graham wrote into the scenarios: the Fugitive (an escaped slave), the Indian Girl, and the Citizen, also called the John Brown figure. The Fugitive and the Indian Girl are suggestive of the "Emancipation" and "Lament for the Land" Episodes of *American Document*. John Brown was the subtext of the final section of *American Document*—Hold your Hold—as indicated in Langston Hughes's poem "Freedom's Plow" (1943). In the part of his poem that describes John Brown, Hughes explained the meaning of "hold your hold" as the labor of plowing the earth. Keeping the hand on the plow is not enough. One must hold on to one's grasp, as the plow itself takes on a movement of its own.

The slaves made up a song:

> Keep Your Hand On The Plow! Hold On!
> That song meant just what it said: Hold On!
> Freedom will come!
> Keep Your Hand On the Plow! Hold On!
> Out of war it came, bloody and terrible!
> But it came![34]

The war to come was, of course, the Civil War, which was a metaphor for the civil rights struggle. John Brown was still pertinent to the Popular Front of the 1940s. Holding your hold was about holding on to the ability to struggle. Hence, the significance of Graham's evocation of the Civil War period in *Appalachian Spring* was not only as a metaphor for World War II, but also as metaphor for the ongoing struggle against racial oppression and for civil rights in the United States. Although Graham and Fergusson may have been influenced by Hughes's 1935 poem "Let America Be America Again" when they wrote the libretto for *American Document*, it is possible that *American Document* influenced Hughes when he wrote "Freedom's Plow."

Although Graham considered setting *Appalachian Spring* in the Civil War period, she ultimately kept historical references ambiguous so that different temporalities could be manifested in movement.[35] "The different parts and different characters," wrote Graham in the second scenario "NAME?" "span a long time length and do not fit into any period of history. In that sense there is no historical development."[36] *Appalachian Spring* engages with *historicities*, rather than with *history* properly speaking. Or, one could say that it is intentionally episodic. This very quality could be identified as having political import since, following the reflections of Hayden White on the relation between time and narrative, it is worth noting that unclarity of temporality points to ideological uncertainty in the truth claims of narrative.[37]

The scenarios for *Appalachian Spring* included a larger array of characters and situations than Graham ultimately put on stage: a Mother, a Daughter, a Younger Sister, Two Children, and Neighbors (perhaps more neutral versions of the Followers). The final version, which was not scripted, limited the dramatis personae to the Pioneer Woman, the Revivalist, the Husbandman, the Bride, and the Followers. At the premiere, the characters portrayed were all Anglo-Saxon as were the dancers portraying them (except for Yuriko, who played one of the Followers).[38] *Appalachian Spring* was originally received as a piece of transparent story telling. One critic called it: "A pleasant, good-humored ballet with no hidden meaning at all . . . comprehensible even to the bored businessman."[39] The original program notes promoted the impression of pastoral clarity and simplicity: "Spring was celebrated by a man and a woman building a house with joy and love and prayer; by a revivalist and his followers in their shouts of exaltation; by a pioneering woman with her dreams of the Promised Land."[40] [Figure 2.2]

The preliminary scenarios, however, present a different picture. In the first, Graham sketched out the Fugitive. "House of Victory," contained an Uncle Tom's Cabin scene. This scene, not unlike the first act of Bill T. Jones's *The Promised Land*, was to review events from the Harriet Beecher Stowe novel:

Figure 2.2 Erick Hawkins in the first production of *Appalachian Spring* (1944). In the background, left to right: the four Followers, Martha Graham, May O'Donnell. Courtesy of the Music Division, Library of Congress

In the midst of this tranquility there appears on the opposite side of the stage a small stage set framed in a kind of luminous frame. By its size, its appointments, its decoration, it gives the feeling of an old fashioned theatre set, a showboat stage. A play takes place within the frame. It is essentially condensed and highly dramatic but is in no sense satire or burlesque. There is no comedy but a sense of the tragic. The action centers about the crucial scenes in "Uncle Tom's Cabin." Rather than playing it exactly as written it should have the effect of the pictures that take place in one's mind upon hearing that name. It will be played simply but with a theatricality. These were the crucial scenes that turned the attention of the world to slavery and precipitated the crisis. It is like putting a grave truth in the mouth of a child. It has the innocence and power.[41]

Although Copland's letters to Graham do not survive, we gather from Graham's letters to him that the composer disagreed with the Uncle Tom's Cabin scene, and discouraged Graham from using it.[42] The second scenario, "NAME?," took Copland's objections into account: "I have as you will see taken out the Uncle Tom's Cabin episode altogether. I think you were right that it was dragged in by the hair of the head and I did not seem to be able to fix it so I started on a different aspect."[43] She nevertheless retained the Fugitive and his scene of escape—Fear in the Night: "This is a man who is hunted, persecuted, who almost becomes a clown in his unconscious agony for freedom. He is really the slave figure of the CIVIL WAR but should have a broader meaning as well."[44] The Fugitive, however, was cut from the final version. The different aspect she referred to in "NAME?" was the Indian Girl whom Graham intended to be a dream-like figure not fully present on stage, but present to the imagination of the other characters. In the final version Graham also cut the Indian Girl.

But, there is a third suppressed character that has not received sufficient attention from either musicologists or dance scholars. Having deleted the Uncle Tom's Cabin scene in "NAME?" Graham specified that the Citizen—her first designation of the Husbandman—should suggest the abolitionist John Brown: "He is shy, fanatical, with the overtones of the Puritan ancestor about him."[45] Graham gives a character reading of the Citizen: "It is the name of the man that became the Abolitionist, the John Brown. He is the type of simple man who would fight to the death for civil rights for mankind." The Citizen was to have his own solo in "The Day of Wrath"—"angry, violent, possessed"[46]—coming directly after the Fugitive's solo, and clearly as a reaction to it. The Citizen's dance "is fanatical, at times mad."[47] Graham was evoking the pre-Civil War period through the Harpers Ferry incident that precipitated the Civil War. As W.E.B. Du Bois wrote in his 1909 biography of John Brown: "John Brown began the war that ended American slavery, and made this a free republic. Until this blow was struck [the Harpers Ferry raid], the prospect for freedom was dim, shadowy, and uncertain."[48] As Du Bois makes clear, the raid on Harpers Ferry presaged the Civil War.

Once Graham had excised the Uncle Tom's Cabin play within a play and the Fugitive's scene of escape, she identified the Citizen decisively with John Brown. The problem of slavery was transferred from a black man who was tangential to the plot to a white man integrated into the plot, but who could be like the Abolitionist, "a man descended from the clan of John Brown or perhaps the ancestor of Brown."[49] The Mother, who rises for the first time in the piece, prefaces the dance of the Citizen. "She walks down the steps and across the stage as though she were pacing the floor in disturbance of spirit and deep anger. She faces the CITIZEN as she starts to return to the porch, and speaks: 'TAKE THE WINE CUP OF THIS FURY AT MY HAND.'"[50] The Citizen "slowly rises into terrible action." Graham is very allusive as to the dramatic idea, but simply adds: "This dance has the qualities of the Harpers Ferry incident without being literally John Brown. It is an exhortation, the utterance of a fanatical man."[51] These last words concerning fanaticism could describe the Revivalist's sermon in the final version of the ballet, although for him wrath was generalized as a picture of religious fundamentalism. [Figure 2.3] As such, the Revivalist sermon, although it had no text, recalled the Jonathan Edwards sermon in *American Document* where the opposition to evil lost something of its humanitarian and social basis. Graham theorized each character, however, as embodying traits that could be found in all Americans, and as such, also in each other. "Hidden in every American is that fanatical strain . . . Sometimes it is good and sometimes it is misdirected, terrible and cruel with a ruthless selfishness."[52] Copland apparently did not object to the retention of the Fugitive or to the introduction of the Abolitionist. The score he delivered to Graham contained the music intended for these very characters and their scripted scenes. Copland's notes on the "outline of action" rename Fear in the Night as "Negro" and Day of Wrath as "John Brown." But, Graham deleted both of these roles before the premiere. As Howard Pollack relates: "Copland, who first saw the dance only days before the premiere, was surprised to find that 'music composed for one kind of actions has been used to accompany something else.'"[53]

Copland composed the score to the second of Graham's scripts. As Marta Elaine Robertson shows: "While the particulars of Graham's narrative changed significantly from script to choreography, her choreographic superstructure changed little in relation to Copland's score."[54] Thus, the music itself helps render the erased characters visible because it acts as a kind of sonic plumb line up through which they emerge when the choreography and the music together seem to point elsewhere. In these moments the movements of the characters dancing before us suggest other characters. Graham "derived" the Bride from the Daughter, the Husbandman from the Citizen, the Revivalist from the Fugitive, the Pioneer Woman from both the Mother and the Indian Girl, and the Followers from the two Children and the

Figure 2.3 Martha Graham and Erick Hawkins in the final moment of *Appalachian Spring* (1944). Hawkins's demeanor suggests the fanaticism of John Brown. Courtesy of the Music Division, Library of Congress

Neighbor.[55] But all of these characters can be turned back upon their origins. "The actual chronology of Graham's final choreographic narrative," adds Robertson, "[was] superimposed upon the score."[56] For this reason, one could also sense a certain dislocation between the narrative implied by the score and the narrative implied by the choreography. This dislocation set the stage for the emergence of the erased characters at a fairly subliminal level. One *saw* what was not present in that one *heard* what was composed for absent action. In theatrical parlance, Graham killed these characters, but she could not prevent their return from the dead in the score. They were encrypted in the score and fitfully brought to life each time the music intended for them corresponded by analogy to their intent and situation.

It is possible Graham decided that the Fugitive, the Indian Girl, and John Brown were too controversial for a patriotic ballet in time of war. The official setting of the premiere and the surrounding world events almost dictated a patriotic interpretation. John Brown was the most incendiary figure of all since he brought together the violence of social protest against slavery, which engaged simultaneously the case of the Kansas land grab that displaced the indigenous population of the state. Prior to Harpers Ferry, the Free State Kansas incident was an example of how the conflict over slavery prior to the Civil War concerned the theft of land that also affected Native Americans. As W.E.B. Du Bois wrote: "They [white Europeans] stole the land of America from the Indians, used its wealth of fruit and gave it over to the rape of aristocrat, Puritan, slave and immigrant. Kansas was the last chapter of this great theft."[57] From this perspective, the John Brown figure encapsulated the racial concerns of *American Document* by conflating the plight of the slave and that of the Native American.

John Brown may actually have been Erick Hawkins's idea since he presented his own choreography evoking John Brown—*Free Stater*—*Kansas*—in 1943 during rehearsals for *Appalachian Spring*. It was one of four solos that made up his *Liberty Tree*. Hawkins also presented his own *John Brown* in 1945.[58] He danced the role of John Brown himself, which had heroic and yet extremely direct and minimal dimensions with an unmistakable Graham vocabulary. Unlike his other work of this period, *John Brown* was extremely well received critically. Stark Young wrote: "His is an art beginning with character and manliness, a deep, ascetic, rigorous fineness of understanding and a constant search for what is clear and final."[59] Edwin Denby called *John Brown* "a fine example of Japanese Noh drama."[60] A year later Graham's *Cave of the Heart* would also evoke Noh to certain critics. Graham must have observed *John Brown* closely. With a text by Robert Richman, the work also featured an Interlocutor, as had *American Document*, although Hawkins also spoke text. It boasted a very percussive score by Charles Mills, and a suggestive and highly effective set by Isamu Noguchi. Although Hawkins subsequently said that none of his work of the 1940s was derivative of Graham *John Brown* surely was, but in the best sense. It was also politically more outspoken than Graham was willing or able to be during the war or anytime after the war. Granted Hawkins premiered *John Brown* after the armistice—several days after the declaration of VE Day—but he may have meant it as a corrective to Graham's final cuts in *Appalachian Spring*.

Character Compression

Let us return now to the question with which we started. Did *Appalachian Spring* contain a politics, and if so, what kind of a politics? Jacqueline Shea-Murphy has given insightful attention to the way the Indian Girl haunts the final version: "Graham envisioned the Indian Girl, from the start, as a haunting spectre—a kind of ghostly being present in her absence, suggested but never fully acknowledged, only visible in flits and moments, and then only to some of those watching."[61] Shea-Murphy convincingly describes how the Indian Girl is present not only through her affinity with the Pioneer Woman but in many dispersed visual details including the Followers thumping on the floor with their hands, the squash blossom hairdo of the Bride, and even motifs taken from the earlier *Primitive Mysteries*. By contrast, the Fugitive and John Brown, while visible in the choreography of the Revivalist as well as in the stern interpretation of the Husbandman as performed by Hawkins, are also audible in Copland's score. I do not agree with Crist, however, that "the Revivalist is not there as a preacher. . . He adopts the character of the Fugitive."[62] As Helen Thomas has pointed out, "Cotton Mather, who was the leader of the Boston ministers who wrote the tract against dancing, was a major point of reference for Graham's creation of the Revivalist."[63] Thomas shows that Graham went in a different direction after writing "NAME?," and conceived a wholly new character: the Revivalist. This character also suggests the eighteenth-century preacher Jonathan Edwards whose "Sinners in the Hands of an Angry God" sermon was quoted in *American Document*. A program note used at a Tokyo performance in 1955 clarifies: "These preachers, often fanatic in temper, preached a doctrine of austerity, condemned all earthly pleasures as evil, described the imagined horrors of hell and damnation and left, at the end of their sermons, very little comfort in everyday life."[64] The Revivalist is also called a Man of God. Edwards was known as the Revivalist or Awakener whose subject matter was hell. "Edwards knew that the indispensable emotional appeal in an awakening sermon was fear, even terror, and it knew no age limits."[65] The self-immolation Thomas describes in the Revivalist's movement begins to sound like the movement of the Fugitive overcome with terror, which makes him, as Graham says, almost clown-like. The Puritan, also evoked by Graham in "NAME?," overwhelmed the Abolitionist in the final version. Thomas continues: "The imagery that the movement connotes is that of a man who is trapped by the nature of his Puritan calling. Torn between the spirit and the flesh, he is not simply chastising the couple, but is also attempting to exorcise the flesh from himself."[66] The panic of the Slave and the fury of the Abolitionist mutated into, and were painted over by the self-exorcism of the Revivalist, which also recalls Hawkins's role as Flagellant in *El Penitente*, a work done in 1940. I am stressing the palimpsestic quality of the dance, which made *Appalachian Spring* a haunted number in more ways than one.

I think the adequate term for this is character compression and it leads to a working definition of the archetype in choreography. One can see within the Revivalist's gestures of panic and fear, movement that may have originally been choreographed for the Fugitive. Some of the Revivalist's movement vocabulary is evoked in Graham's original description of the Fugitive: "[the Fugitive] falls, rushes, hides, tumbles, lies still."[67] The Revivalist's floor work in particular— while easily considered integral to the choreographic representation of a fire and brimstone sermon from the modern dance perspective in which the floor is used without literal connotation—could also suggest the agonized panic of the escaped slave. At one point the Revivalist is cradled in the arms of his congregation like a Christ figure descended from the cross, which suggests the Fugitive's persecution. The Fugitive himself was to be cradled in a similar fashion in the arms of the Indian Girl. What reemerges here is not only a quality of movement proper to an erased character but visual composition originally intended for erased characters. It is the similarity of the Revivalist's movement to that of the Fugitive that allows the Revivalist to morph momentarily into the Fugitive. Archetypal movement for Graham is movement that justifies the momentary merger of two identities because it enlarges the range of expression from fear, to self-punishment, to fanaticism, while, at the same time, maintaining the premise that the dancer we see is anchored in a discrete identity. I think Marta Robertson had it right: "Graham condensed the haunted frenzy of the Fugitive and the fanatical personality of the Abolitionist into the convulsive sermon of the Revivalist."[68] But, if archetype is the result of such condensation, the closer one scrutinizes it the less one understands what it is about. To the degree that archetype blurs distinct character, it also blurs plot: archetype generalizes character and in so doing renders mimetic activity abstract. In other words, the character compression that results from encryption is an antinarrative strategy.

Paradoxically, the archetypal qualities of the characters in *Appalachian Spring* also render them complex and multiple. Archetypal movement—if that is what we may call movement in which character compression suggests itself—is movement in which encrypted identity surfaces from a body we had thought to be singular and unitary, revealing itself in a ghostly fashion while remaining under erasure. If the Fugitive emerges from but also recedes back into the Revivalist, the former is encrypted within the latter. Encrypted content implies the psychoanalytic distinction between latent and manifest content in dreams. The term used by Freud was condensation (*Verdichtung*) in which "a sole idea represents several associative chains at whose point of intersection it is located."[69] Laplanche and Pontalis point out that condensation is also common in joking, word errors, and neologisms; they note that in such contexts condensation "can be seen as a consequence of the censorship and as a means of avoiding it."[70] The encryption of the Fugitive and the Abolitionist in the Revivalist points to a social reading of the archetype in which the encrypted figures have been censored. Encrypted characters are nevertheless sensed and felt by the audience through the music combined with choreographic fragments originally set to that music.

One explanation for this is that Graham may have set choreography in the studio for characters that were subsequently dropped, and some of this choreography may have been conserved and applied to new figures. In other words, as she revised the scenario she did not start the choreography over from scratch.

The changed choreography was set to the same music, which may have induced Graham to adapt the choreography to a new character rather than entirely rewrite it. She may well have left choreographic traces of erased characters in those that replaced them. But, it is not simply a question of one character reminding us of another. The Revivalist presents a conflation of two absent figures: the Fugitive and the Abolitionist. The Husbandman, or The Citizen as he was at first called, recalling John Brown, is suggested in the fanaticism of the Revivalist, but no trace remains in the Revivalist of the Abolitionist's political orientation. Embodying John Brown's fanaticism as religious fundamentalism renders some of the Abolitionist's intensity, which was indeed religious as Brown considered himself an instrument of God, but keeps Brown's politics undetermined. Fanaticism as an archetype cannot be pinned down to any historical situation, let alone to a historical figure. In this sense, all the characters share the spectral qualities of the Indian Girl. But essential to their ghostliness is their ability to commute between two other beings, neither of which are themselves. Graham wrote of the Indian Girl: "I want to have her [the Indian Girl] always on the stage . . . By a mere crossing of the stage . . . she can so suspend time as we often do in our thoughts."[71] This quality is reminiscent of the Pioneer Woman as danced by Matt Turney in 1958 in Peter Glushanok's film of *Appalachian Spring*. On the other hand, the originator of the Pioneer Woman role, May O'Donnell, said of that role: "I was the older person. I was the person from other generations that was, you know, sitting and looking back, thinking back, appraising the future."[72] The Indian Girl and the Mother are positioned to suggest a kind of nostalgic reflection that is also present in Graham's own performance of the Bride in the Glushanok film. But, in O'Donnell's interpretation of the Pioneer Woman, the Mother rather than the Indian Girl fulfilled this function. For Robertson the Pioneer Woman is "largely drawn from the Mother in Graham's script."[73] "Her solidity, which Graham likened to a tree or a rock, was incorporated into the Pioneering Woman."[74] There is a contradiction between two erased characters preceding the Pioneer Woman: the solidity of the Mother and the spectral quality of the Indian Girl. [Figure 2.4] In addition, Graham thought of the Daughter in "House of Victory" as another precursor: "She is what one thinks of as the Pioneer Woman."[75] So, the Daughter, who in the final version becomes the Bride, seems bifurcated as well. In the end, each character seems to meet or fuse into another, and this is why I think the term "monstrous" is appropriate for what lies beneath the surface, and at the narrative and even simply visual limits of *Appalachian Spring*.

Erased characters subsist not only in other roles, but also in particular interpretations of other roles. In this sense the roles themselves seem designed to allow for radically different interpretations. For example, the movement qualities of both the Mother and the Daughter were later subsumed into those of

Figure 2.4 May O'Donnell as the Pioneer Woman in *Appalachian Spring* (1944). Courtesy of the Martha Graham Dance Foundation Archive

the Bride, the Pioneer Woman, or both, depending on who is dancing.[76] No character is unequivocally embodied. Not only the characters, but also the very kinesthetic qualities of their movement are passed through the crucible of the archetype. Just as Jung imagined Wotan as a variant of Dionysus—"a god of rage and frenzy who embodies the instinctual and emotional aspect of the unconscious"—so Graham imagined the characters of *Appalachian Spring* as embodiments of socially repressed energetic tendencies. Characters who are choreographed as archetypes cannot be mutually exclusive of one another. Compression implies not only palimpsest, but also assemblage; not merely a condensation but a construction outwards.

To support this archetypal presentation of character, *Appalachian Spring* resists both temporal and geographic determination. The original program mentions a "moment of Pennsylvania Spring" and one of Graham's early scripts calls for a Shaker rocking chair. But, as Howard Pollack points out, there were no Shaker communities in Pennsylvania.[77] The Shakers were in Boston as well as in parts of the Midwest. "The great Appalachian range and its abutting mountains," however, as W.E.B. Du Bois said in his biography of John Brown, "were long a rugged, lonely, but comparatively safe route to freedom."[78] In other words, the Appalachian route was a known path of the Underground Railroad, the path of escaped slaves to freedom in the north and in Canada. Within the Appalachian range, the Allegheny Mountains "swept from his [Brown's] Pennsylvania home down to the swamps of Virginia, Carolina, and Georgia."[79] Through the Alleghenies, Pennsylvania is linked geographically to the John Brown legend. The term Appalachian is itself a "spring" toward a different meaning concealed within the false alternative between Boston and Pennsylvania.

I am in agreement with Shea-Murphy about the ambiguities of the Indian Girl's invisibility, but I wish to make a slightly different although still related point. I do not wish to juxtapose visible to invisible figures as much as to posit them all as invisible, or in some sense, all as undetermined because of their archetypal status. This is not to deny that what we do see on the stage are white bodies. To imagine the eliminated characters only to erase them recalls the very historical process of oppression to which they were subject in historical time. To erase them in order to retain their imprint in sound and movement is an act of subtle but still rebellious although very sly political recuperation.

Appalachian Spring presents us, in other terms, with the historical bodies as what Hayden White calls monstrous bodies: monstrous because of their hybrid status as at once singular and multiple, historical and contemporary, archetypal and political. Monstrous bodies emerge not only from the awareness of how the past pressures the present, but also of how the compositional process pressures the final product. We could think of the process of discarded drafts as the genotext and the final product viewed on stage as the phenotext.[80] The genotext or erased draft is by definition not observable, yet it never entirely goes away either. Like a rewritten sentence it still contains the elements of a shadowy structure of an alternative wording. For this reason there is a discrepancy between movement per se and mimetic activity. The shadow life of the characters that appear to stand and move before us speaks to a more complex politics than is usually assumed.

"A chronological narrative" writes Robertson, "of the narrative from script to choreography shows Graham's compositional process as one of increasing abstraction."[81] As Graham eliminated particular figures as they were originally conceived in the scenarios, she replaced them with more conventional, but at the same time less specific, somewhat abstract figures. The dramatis personae—the Bride, the Husbandman, the Revivalist, his Followers, and the Pioneer Woman—are "abstractions" of more complex characters. Rather than abstraction, however, I prefer to speak of character compression. They are not reductions but accretions; not less, but more than what they seem. To develop this angle of analysis we should consider the relation of character to narrative in *Appalachian Spring*. For, it seems to me that abstraction occurs at the level of narrative more than at the level of character. The perception that *Appalachian Spring* tells a clear, and even a reassuring, story is an effect of emplotment. But, the characters' mimetic activity exceeds the plot's ability to contain its narrative meaning. The politics of *Appalachian Spring* should therefore be sought within the tension between emplotment and mimetic activity, a tension that undercuts the ballet's narrative clarity and thereby allows competing narratives to emerge.[82] The archetypal aspect of the characters does not derive therefore from their abstraction from other identities, but from that which they "contain" within themselves in the way of erased alternatives or by virtue of which these alternatives continue to pursue a shadowy existence. Put otherwise, abstraction is the ability of the danced personae to *stand for* the absent specificity of eliminated others. The compressed character is not a type or a prototype but what lies hidden behind a mask worn by another face and body. This is why I think monstrosity is a more precise term than either archetype or abstraction.

The second part of my argument, then, is that monstrous bodies are the expression of a sensed but barely visible politics—an *encrypted* politics—but a politics nonetheless. That is, they are the expression of a reaction to the repression of certain bodies in the national psyche, but they also emerge as a political dimension of Graham's work by virtue of having been encrypted in the fabric of the work through its compositional history. The haunting of characters by their numerous antecedents in *Appalachian Spring* indicates the presence of a choreographic political unconscious. This points to the fact that the Popular Front, although forced to abandon its antiwar stance after the outbreak of World War II, remained "a political and cultural charter for a generation."[83]

The Critique of Marriage

The very fact of Graham sharing the stage with two male dancers in *Appalachian Spring* was unusual, and registered as such in John Martin's review: "For overextended intervals the stage is taken away from Miss Graham in particular and from the emotional continuity of the work as a whole by the two characters known as the Husbandman and the Revivalist."[84] Hawkins as the Husbandman performed an exultant dance taking possession of the space of the frontier; Merce Cunningham as the Revivalist danced a violent and possessed sermon. The two male figures took aggressive possession of space. Graham's as the Bride, on the other hand, was frequently self-contained and circumscribed; she cut sharp corners with momentarily anxious and insecure directional changes. The contrasts between male and female movement in *Appalachian Spring* could not be more striking. Rebekah Kowal argues that through this role Graham expressed her doubts about marriage: "[T]hrough the Bride's plight, Graham performed a kind of public contemplation on the issues she found troubling about marriage, including female subordination and loss of autonomy."[85] Hawkins asked himself in a diary entry: "Is it true when she says that I would be content only with a wife who was completely subservient to me? I don't think so."[86] Whatever the case may be it seems clear that Graham thought he did.

That Graham had a critical view of marriage seems indisputable. Graham lambasted marriage in 1941 with *Punch and the Judy*. Graham and Hawkins were only married in 1948: he apparently began to think about marriage after their first estrangement in 1946. But there is no evidence Graham was considering marriage with him in 1943 or 1944 although the idea certainly may have occurred to her after the first four years of their relationship. Kowal's argument is credible given Graham's clandestine opposition to conventional feminine identity during the war. Kowal notes: "My retrospective reading of the piece, suggesting its feminist undertones . . . is not conveyed in contemporaneous accounts of the piece, which overlooked what I see as obvious references to the Bride's prenuptial anxiety."[87] Perhaps it passed unnoticed because the Bride's dependent quality in *Appalachian Spring* was also an evocation of WPA and Section Art representations of the frontier and companionate marriage prevalent in the late 1930s and early 1940s.

To "express a distinctive national culture" was the goal of American scene art, which the Treasury Section of Fine Arts supported in 1934 by fostering ideas of "the land as the source of American democracy" and of a "revolt against the city."[88] Despite the closure of Federal Arts programs by 1943, regionalism remained a prominent style in the United States through corporate sponsorship and mainstream press dissemination of the regionalist school. In companionate marriage, so often depicted in regionalism, we see the comradely ideal of shared labor in domesticating the frontier.[89] *Appalachian Spring* depicts just such a couple. Put otherwise, marriage in *Appalachian Spring* is a motif of regionalism, although it is safe to assume Graham was not entirely at ease with this motif.

If Kowal's point constitutes a retrospective reading, other aspects of *Appalachian Spring* present us with disappeared readings. "Moment of Crisis," Graham's second solo, was doubtless read by her 1944 audience as related to the panic of war; today, it is read as part of an expression of the Bride's personally conflicted experience. Even Pearl Lang who was present at the creation of the work later saw the solo as "the anticipation of a storm, of something dissonant in her life."[90] Lang does not see *Appalachian Spring* in a historical so much as in a personal or purely psychological perspective. But, the war context clarifies the solo's meaning, which would otherwise remain abstruse. Few today would consider Graham's enduring masterpiece a patriotic ballet, or even view it through the lens of World War II. The politics of *Appalachian Spring*, in other terms, is itself a *past* politics if not a politics of the past, a prewar anti-Fascist politics repressed by subsequent events.

Although the Indian Girl may not have suggested anti-Fascism, the Uncle Tom's Cabin scene most certainly did. But, cutting this scene and these characters may have been the safe thing to do in a work to premiere at the Library of Congress. There are some indications, however, that Graham made these changes against her better judgment. Of the Copland score she jotted in a notebook: "I am afraid of the lyrical line."[91] Melody was the musical counterpart to narrative. In the summer of 1944 while she was working on the choreography, she also wrote somewhat despairingly of the score's narrative qualities, which she felt did not correspond to her script: "I had made a script but the music brings another color and feeling to what I must do . . . There are times when we find no warmth in our culture."[92] Graham's hostility to narrative itself can be construed as a misgiving over nationalism. Another indication that Graham was thinking against the grain of narrative when she created *Appalachian Spring* lies in her intent "to reach through to people without the benefit of story and with as much freedom from superimposed meaning as possible."[93] In these comments, Graham's impatience with narrative, part and parcel of her impatience with patriotism, organized religion, and nationalism, emerges.

Movement Can and Does Lie

One begins to perceive a lie beneath the pattern, from the lie of the walk-around patterns of minstrelsy of *American Document* to the lie of the square dance patterns in *Appalachian Spring*. Graham described folk dancing as:

> Lively but sweet decorum which is unspoken physical understanding— a human courtesy, which is surely among the most invalidating flatteries invented by the human race. The geometrical ground plan is more felt than seen. The caller gives out the figures indicating their almost algebraic variants, and a chain of grasping, releasing.

What is "grasped" and "released" is also narrative linearity and melodic resolution. Is it possible that even "the American bone" moves in deceptive ways? To conclude with this quote, tucked away in one of Graham's black notebooks, is to recontextualize the saying most often enlisted to foreclose Graham: "movement never lies." Evidently, movement can, does, and even must, lie. Perhaps it is time to finally reconsider the old saw that Graham subscribed to such a naïve concept of the communicability of truth through movement. "To assume," writes Ramsay Burt, "that dancers' experiences while performing are in some way the same as those of the audience is to return to Graham's notion that the body never lies."[94] As of *Appalachian Spring* we should, I think, assume that this was no longer the case, if it ever had been. Graham's dramaturgical phase, which reached completion with *Appalachian Spring*, inaugurated a more complex practice in which the dancer and the audience would be in a dissymmetrical relationship. The copresence of monstrosity and wholesome pleasantness is the starting point of this dissymmetry that exists between ritual and myth in the mythographic works.

A regionalist image contains the knowledge of the national body as monstrous: the image of the land or the country functions ironically for the urban audience. The double audience required by irony is geopoliticized as the image of the heartland contains more than the "sweetness of manners" Virgil Thompson saw there.[95] The encrypted image is maintained *as* buried and thus it continues to raise questions as to its political effect, as well as continuing *not* to be seen. *Appalachian Spring* was originally conceived as, and has the potential to continue to be, choreographically polyphonic. That each body displays the imprint of multiple erasures accounts for the voice of a politics working against emplotment, or rather, displacing emplotment with the mimetic activity of bodies that convey a history under erasure.[96]

There was an edge to *Appalachian Spring* that made it more than just the ballet of sweetness that Virgil Thompson saw. One can perceive this edge in the photographs of the original production. Each character projects shadows against the set that float in different directions; each character projects a shadow with many edges in a somber atmosphere. These shadows themselves suggest that ghosts surround each character. The edge derives also from Graham's uneasiness about marriage, which one can even perceive in her eyes if one observes the film closely. The disquiet beneath the wholesome surface of *Appalachian Spring* disclosed the no-longer admissible contestations of the Popular Front that needed to be suppressed in 1944 because of the persistence of right-wing political tendencies within the United States despite the country's involvement in a war against Fascism.

3

The Invention of Martha Graham

Emergence and the Strictures

"One can say of the artist that he does not practice his calling, but *is* it,
himself, represents it ideologically."

—Otto Rank, *Art and Artist* (371)

By 1948 with *Night Journey*, writes Ramsay Burt, "Graham enjoyed unprecedented autonomy as a cultural producer and was thus able to articulate a feminine point of view that was inconceivable at that time in most other fields."[1] How
did Graham progress from her first large-scale success in 1938 with *American
Document*, which brought her the beginnings of national notoriety, to the kind of
autonomy Burt refers to only 10 years later and thanks to which she articulated a
feminine consciousness with virtually no cultural currency outside her own
dances? In this chapter I study the development and vicissitudes of her image
across the decade, and how her shift to mythical subjects in the immediate postwar years superseded the more conventional connotations of her prewar and
wartime celebrity identity.

At the war's end Graham was in a foundering relationship with Hawkins and she
turned to myth not as a symbol of national identity, but as a way to conceive of
woman in pre-patriarchal terms. She did not subscribe to Winkelmann's luminous
classicism adopted by the Nazis but to Harrison's dark classicism. The feminine
point of view to which Burt refers, and which is symptomatic of the vexed question
of Graham's "feminism," prefigured the intellectual critique of patriarchy that gained
visibility in US intellectual life of the early 1970s, thus coinciding ironically with
Graham's retirement from the stage. *Night Journey* was roughly contemporaneous
with the appearance of Simone de Beauvoir's *The Second Sex*, first published in
France in 1949. But Graham did not read French, and did not follow contemporary
continental philosophy. The psychoanalytic and personal significance of *Night Journey*, and of Graham's role in that ballet as Jocasta—the mother who is also the wife
of her own son—will be discussed in the next chapter.

Politics of the Image

Graham's choreographic and civic commitment to the Popular Front launched her reputation not only as a leading American dancer and choreographer, but also as a prominent public figure with a political dimension to be reckoned with. A cluster of editorial cartoons published in 1942 show Graham alongside caricatures of Mussolini and Hitler. She is pictured staring at a piece of fabric; the legend reads: "Strange Talisman. Dancer Martha Graham always carries with her a bit of 500-year-old cloth from the dress of a medieval Italian saint."[2] In this trio of images Graham forms a counterweight to Hitler and Mussolini under the auspices of what Toril Moi has identified, apropos of the critical reception of Simone de Beauvoir, as "the personality topos." "The implication," specifies Moi, "is that whatever a woman says, or writes, or thinks, is less important and less interesting than what she *is*."[3] Moi's analysis gives us a sense of the potential pitfalls of Graham's political visibility of which she was certainly most aware. This caricature of Graham's provided, nonetheless, a religiously oriented counterweight to the Fascist cult of personality; Graham's image invoked the civilizational values of Western culture under the threat of Fascism.

Since the 1936 invitation to dance at the Olympic Games, which she refused, Graham continued to hold the attention of the Third Reich. A radio broadcast directly addressed to her, transmitted in 1941, was recorded and transcribed by the NBC short-wave monitoring service. The transcript reads:

> Strange as it may seem, whenever I think of American, of specifically American art, I cannot help thinking of your art, Martha Graham. Is it perhaps because the United States depends far more on women than on men? The American boy is dominated by his mother; the American husband by his wife and the American father by his daughter. . . . Sometimes I am inclined to think that the great misunderstanding between the United States and Germany, long before Hitler, are rooted psychologically and not politically in the fact that Germany is a man ruled country while the United States is dominated by women more or less.[4]

As the voice identified her not only with America but also with the American woman, the patriarchal quality of Fascism cannot have escaped Graham. Bertram Ross remembers hearing her say she had received phone calls at night from the Nazi Party, and implying that she was involved with espionage, although this has never been confirmed.[5]

Yet, it was not long before American consumerist culture sought to feminize Graham, and thus to undercut some of her political clout. With the entry of the United States into World War II the outspoken defender of democratic values and traditions with a critical anti-Fascist subtext was being primed to sell products. Spot quizzes in newspapers tested the familiarity of the general public with her name, asking whether Martha Graham was a "Playwright, culinary expert, [or] dancer"?[6] Her handwriting was analyzed in newspaper columns: "Note the letter 'r' which is larger than any of the other small letters. That tells us that she takes unusual pride and interest in decoration—in jewelry, clothes, background, etc."[7] Human-interest columns associated Graham with cosmetics, jewelry, superstition, and grace. She was portrayed Garbo-like, as a mysterious star one might spot on the streets of New York: "Martha Graham, dancer, attracting attention as she opens her compact on Fifty-seventh street . . . it is exactly like a small red theatrical mask."[8] As Jackson Lear has argued, "by the 1920s and 1930s advertising had begun to assimilate the allegedly rebellious impulses of aesthetic 'modernism.'"[9]

Otto Rank's distinction between success and fame was prophetic of the challenges Graham's newly found celebrity would pose to her artistic and personal identity. "Success gives him [the artist] both, the individual justification of his work and its collective recognition, whereas fame stamps both himself and his work as a creature of the community."[10] Graham's celebrity image was bound toward fame, and she was being characterized as a woman of lavish tastes. In 1939 Graham was featured eyeing herself luxuriously in the mirror in a newspaper advertisement for mink coats. The banner read: "A Dancing Queen in Queenly Mink!"[11] One is tempted to rewrite Rank's phrase "creature of the community" as "creature of the commodity." That Graham was being associated with these luxury items indicates a popularly held view of dance itself as an upper-class luxury item; Graham's success had brought her to the attention of a broad public, but media outlets were eager to refashion her identity to match sexist stereotypes of the woman artist. Graham was opposed to this manipulation, but only expressed her resistance in private. "Each woman artist," she wrote to David Zellmer in 1943, "is a Cassandra who fights with the God Apollo and refuses to take upon herself the accepted role of woman."[12] In this case, the accepted role of woman was the consumer. To be an artist was not to be a woman in the conventionally accepted sense, but the artist, to achieve celebrity, had to submit to sexist stereotyping. If unwilling to accept this, as in the case of painter Georgia O'Keefe whose career bears some comparison with Graham's, the choreographer would have had no other choice than to withdraw from the urban milieu of the art market. Although Graham, like O'Keefe, was drawn to the American Southwest, Graham never retreated there permanently. Yet, despite the development of her celebrity image, there was nothing showy or opulent about Graham on stage in the 1940s. As Bertram Ross remarks: "Her costumes were never decorative. There was always some element that was a little bit wrong. She used to talk of divine awkwardness."[13] In this connection it is important to underline what Pearl Lang called the "austerity and simplicity" of Graham's aesthetic.[14]

The direction of this image construction changed, however, from that of a self-indulgent star to a spokeswoman for wartime femininity. The war years were bringing momentous changes in the economic and social status of American women. "In 1938," writes William H. Chafe, "over 80 percent of the American people strongly opposed work by married women. Five years later, over 60 percent approved of such employment."[15] As women replaced men in the workplace Graham's celebrity made her an icon of the industrious, but also jeopardized, femininity of the American woman. Graham herself was a woman of work—the arduous physical labor of dance—but at the same time she was a leader in a field traditionally marked as feminine. Graham's identity as a modernist was ignored to underline that she was instead a woman of work. But, the fact that her work was dance made her appear to be a woman of leisure. During the war Graham's image veered toward "productive" femininity.[16] Indifferent to, and indeed shockingly ignorant of, her iconoclastic dance aesthetic, fashion magazines enlisted Graham to advise working women on how to preserve their feminine beauty in the workplace. "Minute Sketches" featured a drawing of her face looking demurely down: "Martha Graham: it is said of her that she moves more beautifully than any woman of this generation."[17] Clearly, the press made some incongruous assumptions about Graham's artistic identity, but at another level she must still have welcomed the publicity. The price of her notoriety was the feminization of her image in terms of prevalent clichés. As she was a dancer, that image necessarily affected the image of herself in her art. This was in evident contrast to Graham's image of the 1930s, which I have called elsewhere "an imaginary feminine masculinity."[18] As film scholar Mary Ann Doane has observed, "The woman's new role in production was masked by an insistent emphasis on a narcissistic consumption. She was encouraged to view herself as engaged in a constant battle to protect her femininity from the ravages of the workplace with the aid of a host of products: hand lotions, facial creams, mattresses, tampons."[19] Doane might have added dance training to this list of beauty products. "Lovely Martha Graham believes that dancing gives a woman the poise and bodily grace that are so essential to charm."[20] Graham herself wrote a short piece for *Glamour* magazine entitled "As You Control Your Body So You Shape Your Life": "Good posture," she said, "makes you [women] feel well, poised, alert, serene."[21] Another nationally syndicated interview had Graham "coaching" women war workers on physical fitness.[22] Graham was doing her patriotic duty while reaping the benefits of the publicity.

What impact did this construction of Graham have on her productions between 1942 and 1945? The new accessibility heralded by the success of *American Document* was at risk of devolving into an unpalatable theatricalism. *Punch and the Judy* (1941), her first domestic comedy, had Graham and Hawkins portraying a married couple. [Figure 3.1]. *Land Be Bright*, her most overtly patriotic

Figure 3.1 Martha Graham and Erick Hawkins in *Punch and the Judy* (1941). Photo: Barbara Morgan Copyright Barbara Morgan/Barbara Morgan Archives Courtesy of the Dance Collection, New York Public Library

work, premiered in 1942. "Miss Graham played Betsy Ross, Erick Hawkins, Chingachgook (out of the Leather Stocking Tales), and Merce Cunningham, a Yankee orator."[23] It was only performed in Boston and Chicago, but quickly dropped. In these works Graham was attempting to comply with the role she had been assigned.

Publicity copy for bookings starts as follows: "As Timely as Today's Headlines is the Question: . . . What kind of spotlight attraction can you offer the public that will dispel the uneasiness caused by World War II? There is one safe answer!—MARTHA GRAHAM AND DANCE COMPANY. The great GRAHAM is a sure-fire bet!"[24] Dance Critic Walter Terry also complied with this rhetoric in a 1942 review:

If it is escape from the present that you seek in the theater Miss Graham makes the escape complete, for every one of your muscles is controlled by the imagery of dance. If you seek entertainment or stimulation, the Graham dance is again equally potent, for she entertains and stimulates not merely the eye of the beholder but his entire feeling being. . . . Such an all-out dance is surely the most powerful kind of war-time dance.[25]

Terry transforms John Martin's theory of kinetic transference through movement— metakinesis—into a means whereby the anxious bodies of the audience can be pac- ified rather than incited to action; the choreographer's will to perform anti-Fascist critique on the home front—action rather than reaction—was being replaced by a politically conservative and sexually normative image of the dancer. These uncharac- teristically accessible works did not, however, make up the entirety of Graham's rep- ertory, and paled before the more dramatic and poetic *Letter to the World* (1940), *Deaths and Entrances* (1943), and *Herodiade* (1944). But, they do represent a for- gotten tendency engendered by prewar and wartime publicity with which Graham was to a certain degree complicit.

The way Graham crossed the line into popular culture unveils the mechanism of her growing reputation across the 1940s as well as her own conflicted feelings about it. Framed as the spokeswoman of "narcissistic consumption" she also became a celebrity standard bearer of the average housewife in the sense defined by feminist film critics La Place and Doane. Theater critic Eric Bentley thought he saw a personality split in the image of Graham's face: "Sometimes, especially in photographs, she looks like the standard glamorous woman of these United States. Yet, above the standard American mouth, set in the unnaturally motion- less mask of her upper face, are the perturbed eyes of the American intelligentsia, luminous centers of un-American activities."[26] The tension between conven- tional glamour and potential subversion, in Bentley's terms, suggested radically discrepant levels of meaning in the interpretation of her facial features. There were serious fault lines between the politically outspoken woman artist of the prewar anti-Fascist moment and her new role as the patron saint of the American working woman. The invention of Martha Graham's celebrity image bears di- rectly on the choreographic mechanisms of encryption and emergence that played an important role in her choreography starting with *Appalachian Spring*.

Media attention to Graham in this vein peaked in the late 1940s, when she appeared as Miss Hush for eight weeks on the radio program "Truth or Conse- quences."[27] The 1947 radio spots were designed to raise money for the March of Dimes Fund.[28] Each caller who guessed at her identity based on hints broadcast each week contributed 10 cents for polio research. [Figure 3.2]. A housewife from Fort Worth, Texas, Ruth Annette Subie, ultimately guessed the identity of Miss Hush, and won $21,500 in prizes, which included a Canadian beaver coat, a gas refrigerator, a house-painting job, a kitchen range, a home freezer, a $1,000 diamond ring, a vacuum cleaner, electric blankets, and venetian blinds. A photo in *Life* showed Subie collapsing at the news, and also noted that $100,000 was earned for the March of Dimes. For her part, Graham—"the grim practitioner"—earned "the huge publicity which the modern dance could never have brought"[29] This denigration of modern dance for having no economic power led to the title conferred upon Graham by *Life* in 1947: "priestess of the intellectual ballet."[30] The dancer, like the intellectual, paid no attention to the marketplace and could only be driven by "grim" concentration and fanatical devotion. Modern dance was presented as a strange blend of quasi-religious commitment and intellectualized physical labor.

In this new environment of postwar consumerism Graham no longer stood for the Popular Front artist, the budding starlet, or the working woman; she certainly could not be made to speak for the consumerist housewife. Instead, she was cast as the "grim practitioner" who stood for something more perverse and incomprehensible. The discrepancy between the image of Graham the media fabricated since the beginning of the decade and her evolving postwar stage personality reached something of a breaking point in 1949 when her agent Isadora Bennett conveyed to her a publicity offer: ". . . You are about to be asked to entertain a proposition from the advertising firm of Proctor and Gamble to say something sweet about Ivory Soap in connection with costumes—or, preferably, face-washing."[31] Graham was close to the premiere of *Night Journey*. One can hardly imagine a more surrealist juxtaposition than Jocasta endorsing soap to housewives. In 10 years the media had progressed from testing the public with questions such as: "Who is Martha Graham?"

Figure 3.2 Martha Graham at the NBC microphone (1947). Copyright Bettmann/Corbis

and eliciting the answer: "a famous dancer," to the-fill-in-the-blank, produce-the-name brand label: *Martha Graham*. Intellectuality suggested a profundity that one would normally not find in popular culture. In the postwar era her image projected irreconcilable contradictions, and Graham banked on this to project a more deviant and anxiety-ridden identity. As poet Ben Belitt put it: "That's what she has the courage to penetrate, the sexual morass in which she enters quite as much as Freud, and comes back from that dripping with filth and with some insight."[32] That an insider would view Graham's work this way indicates how transgressive it must have been for the general public. Myth, after all, was not situation comedy fare.

The underground or insider discourse of Graham showed her awareness of the necessity to play with images as Bertram Ross has noted:

> Martha is the great image-maker. She makes images all the time. She makes an image to fit, to suit, the particular need of the particular situation and time. I do not know if she has a genuine response in her. Everything is totally calculated. She has said "I do not lose my temper. I use my temper." Or "no-one has ever seen me cry." Or, "Truth . . . What is so wonderful about telling the truth? Anyone can tell the truth. It's boring."[33]

As Maria La Place has pointed out, Bette Davis was one of the few artists able to control her own image as an independent woman and movie star throughout the 1930s and 1940s. "Davis came to signify rebellion against male authority, the demand for control over her work, the struggle for autonomy and artistic integrity."[34] It is not by chance, then, that Davis studied with Graham, and that aspects of the actresses's physical characterization in woman's film of the 1940s recalled Graham's stage persona. Many of Davis's most dramatic moments in films of the 1940s contain extremely economical and incisive movement choices that recall moments of Graham's performances. "Every time I climbed a flight of stairs in films," wrote Davis in her autobiography, "—and I spend half my life on them—it was Graham step by step."[35] Film scholar Richard Dyer makes a distinction between publicity and promotion, the latter of which in film constitutes "*deliberate* image making."[36] Graham did not have a studio system behind her for promotion purposes, yet contradictions between her artistic identity and the manipulation of her image in the press are legible. Dyer perceives such tensions as "themselves crucial to the image."[37] By the late 1940s Graham cut a far more transgressive figure than she had in the prewar and wartime era, and the contradictory tensions within this figure now aided and abetted her sense of theatricality to rejoin the artistic project it had initially threatened to compromise.

In her private relationship with Hawkins in the early 1940s Graham nevertheless appears to have experienced a more conventional identity. In a letter to Hawkins of July 27, 1943, she reflected: "I think I have a great need to be simply and biologically

a woman . . . I suppose any woman who is active in an art or some such creative activity must feel that need to return at times simply to her function."[38] The reflection of
a new lyricism in her stage presence along with its well-timed political intervention
on behalf of the Popular Front may have been responsible for the success of *American
Document*. But, Graham's distinction between the woman artist and the "biological"
woman is telling.[39] Unpublished notes by Frances Wickes—later to be Graham's analyst—paint a portrait of "*the impersonal woman* who follows an independent spirit
that moves within her."[40] Although the notes are undated, Wickes may have taken
Graham as one of the models for this type. Impersonality is a term that resonates
with Anglo-American modernism where poetic impersonality is most closely associated with T.S. Eliot.[41] For Wickes, the impersonal artist was one who "portrays the
myth or the inner mysteries perhaps in dance or histrionic form, or her own life embodies it so that it becomes manifest to others."[42] She was also the Sibyl capable of
communication with others at a subliminal level: "If she can mould these perceptions into form, she activates these images *in the unconscious* of others."[43] The negative
pole of "the sybil, the prophetess, and the mystic" was, for Wickes, Cassandra: "She
activates the evil potentials in those she fascinates, so becoming a factor in personal
strife."[44] Wickes's archetypal conception of a double personality chimes with Bentley's analysis of the contradictions in Graham's facial expression, with my analysis of
character condensation in the previous chapter, and with the bifurcation of the postwar image of the dancer become profound intellectual and obsessive mythmaker. It
is almost as if a psychoanalytic discourse of the mid-1940s was becoming a tool for
Graham to fashion a new countercultural image of herself in Jungian terms.

Another Jungian theorist, Esther Harding, spoke of the conflict of modern
woman in terms of bisexuality:

> So long as the masculine side of woman's nature was allowed to remain,
> as it was in the past, undeveloped and unconscious, it either slept unrec-
> ognized or it functioned in a purely instinctive fashion. . . . These changes
> have produced for woman an unavoidable inner conflict between the
> urge to express herself through work, as a man does, and the inner ne-
> cessity to live in accordance with her own ancient feminine nature.[45]

Woman's consciousness of her dual nature, for Harding, is both a modern and an
ancient phenomenon whereas for Wickes the archetypes were uniquely housed
in ancient literary discourse on "the second sex." For Harding it was a question
of the return of an ancient conflict to the modern world. This return was
prompted by twentieth-century challenges to gender roles. Graham's interest in
Rank and Fromm was complemented by her discovery of Harding.

From the early 1940s Graham was concerned with the *emergence* of
"untamed" aspects of her own character projected in ideas for new roles that she

would create after the war. Apropos of Salvador Dali's aesthetics, for example, she noted: "(W)e all are not alone in that struggle for *emergence* and that constant battle against the strictures. . . . I do think we can keep an inner desperateness that creates form eventually if the concentration on that emergence is strong enough."[46] The emergence from unconscious to conscious was depicted by what I think it is safe to call modern woman literature—here again Harding—as an emergence from the primitive to the modern state under the sign of the psychological.

> The problem is no longer one of the twentieth century alone. It is one which has concerned women from the most primitive times. I do not mean to imply, however, that women of the past have been consciously occupied with the problem as an intellectual question. Psychological consciousness of that kind is a phenomenon peculiar, perhaps, to today.[47]

Harding presents in a nutshell the project of exploring new options for woman's personality through myth— return to something archaic that nevertheless has currency only in the present-day world—and new insight afforded to modern self-consciousness by the psychoanalytic treatment of myth.

More than Jung it was Harding who provided the blueprint for the transformations Graham's work would undergo in the postwar period. For this reason, Hawkins, despite his excellent performances, began to cut a discordant figure alongside the mutable Graham because he still assumed the necessity to play the conventional male role after the war. He knew that his arrival on the scene in the late 1930s had placed Graham in a different light before the public: "It was only when she had somebody like me who had weight, could she be herself and be a woman and not be a kind of a half-man. She was always a half-man to the other girls. . . . She didn't stay that way, but at least for a time."[48] Although he too changed with the times, Hawkins seems to have been unsympathetic to some aspects of Graham's postwar shift.

Postwar Productions

By 1946 Graham abandoned the Americana themes of the prewar and war periods to undertake a mythographic phase, which would be exemplified in her next four works: *Dark Meadow, Cave of the Heart, Errand into the Maze,* and *Night Journey.* The meadow (that was also a grave), the cave, the maze or labyrinth, and the nocturnal undersea passage became the symbolic décors (all designed by Noguchi) of Graham's postwar mythical narratives. They invoke counterpatriarchal imagery of the 1920s that were vaguely associated with Bachofen, but subsequently revisited by Jane Harrison, Helen Diner, and, later, by Robert Graves in *The White Goddess* (1948) and Erich Neumann in *The Great Mother: An Analysis of an Archetype* (1955). In the late 1940s and early 1950s Graham explored the symbolic life of pre-patriarchal images of woman that had emerged in archaeology and anthropology of the 1920s. She reclaimed the symbolic relationship of woman with the chthonic and tellurian.[49] Carl Kerényi noted that "the divine marriage of Plouton and Kore was celebrated on 'the Meadow'—here the word is employed as a place name."[50] The meadow, in other terms, signifies the underworld, and *Dark Meadow* seems to assemble these diverse references to Demeter and Persephone, the collective unconscious, death and rebirth.

This Jungian reading of myth extended from *Dark Meadow* (1946) through *Canticle for Innocent Comedians* (1952). The postwar moment freed Graham to explore roles engaging with aspects of her personality that the gendered normalcy of the anti-Fascist cause and the conventional gender roles enforced by wartime patriotism (in spite of Rosie the Riveter) had held in check. She introduced the character of the Hetaera who lays waste to conjugal harmony—associated with the powerful and vengeful concubine Herodiade, whose daughter Salome claims the head of John the Baptist—and who rejects harmonious coexistence with men. This character, exemplified in Graham's repertory by her portrayal of Medea (or, The Sorceress) in *Cave of the Heart*, was more monster than heroine. As Judith in 1950 she would claim the head of Holofernes.

The psychoanalytic basis of all these variations—the chthonic, the monstrous, or the Great Goddess that Harding referred to as the feminine principle—was a quest for personal rebirth or renewal.[51] In Jungian terms, Graham sought *individuation* in a "process by which a person becomes a psychological 'in-dividual', that is, a separate, indivisible unity or 'whole.'"[52] In notes on individuation, Wickes states: "the self is not a reality that is given but a reality that seeks itself."[53] Graham's role in *Dark Meadow* was One Who Seeks. The archetypal sets and props in *Dark Meadow*, being mostly phallic shapes with a series of references to fertility as well as to life and death, are suggestive of sexual difference. The work was referred to by some critics as a fertility ritual, the cue having been given by Weston, who associated the mourning of the god Adonis with "the reproductive energy of the god upon whose virile activity vegetable life directly, and human life indirectly, depended."[54] This is the first work in which Graham, with the help of Noguchi, displays the archetype as a visual symbol, but simultaneously positions the archetype within an environment that impedes the protagonist's quest for individuation. These elements of decor gradually become reappropriated as symbols of woman as divine being, "as the source of vegetation, fertility, fruition of every kind."[55] Individuation was a process of either overcoming or appropriating the archetype.

But, Graham's role as Medea in *Cave of the Heart* (1946) is the prototype of the Hetaera role.[56] Graham became interested in dancing the mad and possessive woman as early as 1941. The postwar period may have provided the condition of possibility for this emergence, but it did not supply its raison d'être. Prior to the Coolidge Commission Graham had asked Aaron Copland to write the score for "The Daughter of Colchis," which later became *Cave of the Heart*. On February 7, 1941, she wrote Copland: "She [Medea] possesses the animality of the undisciplined being wherever found. This is almost like a Japanese Noh drama piece called 'a revenge piece.' Someplace I read it might be any wife's letter to her husband. It is bitter, sardonic, murderous, despairing."[57] She thought of Medea as essentially "unhuman," but also called her an archetype, and attributed her feelings of murderous revenge to the average American housewife, all in the same letter.[58] Graham saw all women as trapped in the patriarchal prison of marriage leading to childbirth. Her resistance to marriage was a life and death struggle for her own artistic identity. Moreover, she was contemplating Medea at the time she was performing *Punch and the Judy*, a satire on the bourgeois couple.

Graham dates her own awareness of theater as such to the discovery of puppets: "[A] day when I saw a puppet show in my hotel drawing room—lace curtains resting on the floor—a green pouf in the center of the room—the puppets— 'Punch and Judy' in a corner—my first amazed awakening to the fact of theatre."[59] In the *Notebooks* she remarked that puppets gave her a deeper understanding of theater, indicating she may have perceived bourgeois marriage itself as a kind of theater. Hawkins thought of *Punch and the Judy* as "social satire": "[W]hen you got into the puppets you went under the thumb of the marriage convention."[60] On July 7, 1942, Graham sent Copland a scenario for "The Daughter of Colchis." But, on August 12, 1942, she wrote thanking him for accepting the Coolidge commission, and proposed another idea. "I am working on an idea which I hope you may like better than the script you have. At least I remember you said it might be nice to be less severe. . . . Have you any objections if I take the script 'The Daughter of Colchis' and rework it to submit to [Carlos] Chavez?"[61] He did not object, and the Medea ballet was temporarily shelved.

In spite of her romance with Hawkins, Graham was virulently antimarriage. In fact, her resistance to marriage may have been a basic cause of disagreement between them. Hawkins was conflicted about his dependency on Graham and his need to assert his own autonomy as an artist. He wanted to be more than Graham's personal and professional partner; he wished to be an artist who matched her in stature. "Say I was independence (*sic*) and yet want to lean on M's *security* and so I have conflict, resentments, anxiety and guilt . . . I want to be able to perform completely on my own and as an equal in M's company."[62] Hawkins's view of his relationship with Graham was entangled with his own identity as an artist. In a diary entry of August 21, 1946, he notes: "How can I live except by being independent . . . By disassociating myself from a closeness and a certain dependency on MG will I fail, i.e. Have to start over? . . ."[63] Hawkins's answer to his own dependence was to make Graham dependent in turn. He may have expected marriage to make him the dominant figure in the relationship because it would cast Graham in the role of the docile wife.

Hawkins had done independent performances and even tours. In 1944 he performed a solo program in Decatur, Georgia, where, in addition to his own choreography, he danced the Flagellant solo from Graham's *El Penitente*. Although Muriel Brenner accompanied him in four pieces, this program had the ambitious feel to it of a Kreutzberg solo recital in which the soloist was all-important. Hawkins wished to break through on his own not only as a choreographer, but as a soloist. In 1942 he toured a similar Americana program with Pearl Lang for which Austin Wilder Management printed a handsome brochure. Although Lang performed two of her own solos on the program, the program was clearly designed to showcase Hawkins. He did a similar tour with May O'Donnell in 1945.[64] In a quandary over his own identity, Hawkins separated from Graham. She wrote him on August 28, 1946, that she was nevertheless pleased he would continue to work with the company.[65] Hawkins found his own studio and started work that fall on *Stephen Acrobat*.

The situation was fraught because Hawkins had made substantial contributions to Graham's success. He was her disciple, most important male exponent, teacher, fundraiser, helpmate, advisor, accountant, producer, rehearsal director, technical assistant, company manager, and even for a time her booking agent. As Ethel Winter pointed out: "He took care of a lot of her dirty laundry, so to speak."[66] Hawkins referred to it in 1949 as "The problem of being handyman for Martha."[67] He was always in the line of fire fronting for her. His goal, however, was not only to support her work of which he was a part but also to gain recognition as a dancer and a choreographer himself. "I was ambitious, I had lots of energy and I wanted to use it. I suppose it was impossible that I should work just for your career alone and forfeit all desire to serve my own ends of wanting to be a fine dancer and create rich, exciting, wise, meaningful works of art."[68] A mutually supportive relationship modulated into a competitive one. How two artists share ideas, projects, and a life once competition enters the picture is never simple. "I mistakenly believed," explained Hawkins after their second separation, "that in all this construction for your work I would realize my own potentialities too—that there was some process working whereby in working for a good outside myself I would cover the ground I needed for my own career."[69] The impossibility of coordinating these distinct if intertwined goals became increasingly compromising for their relationship. "Seemingly I skipped or tried to skip some rungs of the ladder. And now I find that rungs cannot be skipped or they aren't there, and the ladder crumbles."[70] This was his analysis of the relationship four years later at the time of the final separation, but he must have had analogous thoughts in 1946.

When Graham finally did receive a score from Chavez who was in Mexico—the second of the Coolidge commissions—she found it insufficiently dramatic for Medea. Once again, she shelved Medea to work directly with the quietly contemplative mood of Chavez's score.[71] Helen McGehee has remarked that there is still a lot of Medea in *Dark Meadow*.[72] Nevertheless, the work is unique for its nondramatic and intentionally esoteric qualities. Encryption gains a Jungian psychoanalytic dimension with Graham's first postwar and most obscure work. No longer a strategy of political cover, encryption allowed Graham to display, but also to bury in plain sight, a personal discourse on love, desire, and isolation. As Hawkins said: "I don't know if Martha was ever that specific about what the idea was. You see, that's the great problem with something very poetic. It has images but can't specify them in words easily. I think you have to look at it as a poem."[73] It is not only the poetic aspects of *Dark Meadow*, but the fact that Graham may have aspired to address the audience at a collectively unconscious level, which removes dramatic momentum from it. Its symbols are, to quote Maud Ellman on Eliot's *The Waste Land*, "of the symbolic itself."[74] "I get the feeling," said Sears of *Dark Meadow*, "that both he and she are challenging you to take this journey and they know that you'll never get through it. If you were to *really* understand these dances, you'd have to be some sort of genius because it's calling on world mythology for a complete understanding of these things."[75] *Dark Meadow* utterly confounded dance critic John Martin although he claimed eventually to come to terms with it.[76] It seems to inhabit a dramatic vacuum through which it exerts a fascination by expecting the audience to supply a great deal of meaning. [Figure 3.3].

The meta-symbolic level of the piece also points ahead to the personal rituals that would underlie Graham's subsequent use of myth. Only, in *Dark Meadow* there is no myth within which to shroud the ritual. The title corresponds uncannily to Jung's much later account of a dream that led to his "conviction that there are archaic psychic components that have entered the individual psyche without any direct line of tradition": the dream of a meadow that is also a dark grave.[77] The dream's imagery distinguished between earthly and psychic depth in that the dreamer discovers a crypt beneath the meadow's layer of earth.[78] *Dark Meadow* comes across as meta-theoretical because Jung's dark meadow dream spurred his personal realization that the unconscious had a "social" or collective nature.[79] *Dark Meadow*, like Jung's dream, is about archetypes. Unlike *Appalachian Spring* where archetypes are based on national mythology, in *Dark Meadow* they have no explicit context. Graham reasserted the high modernist qualities that had apparently been abandoned in the drive to theatrical accessibility of her dramaturgical phase in the prewar and war periods.

Figure 3.3 Martha Graham and Erick Hawkins in *Dark Meadow* (1946). Photo: Philippe
Halsman Courtesy of Magnum Photos.

Jessie L. Weston's *From Ritual to Romance* (1920) influenced *Dark Meadow* as
it had Eliot's *The Wasteland*. Initially titled *Dark Meadow of the Soul*, Graham
worked for the first time with the conceit of the psychic landscape. Although
Graham's role for herself was not properly mythological she does appropriate for
herself "the position of the mythical subject."[80] Moving through a symbolically
laden landscape—in fact a natural landscape (a meadow) that is preternaturally
dark, hence capable of sinking into and/or becoming a tomb—Graham plays
the role of the Quester whose own identity will be wrested from the landscape
or monster. For Teresa de Lauretis, the woman's role with respect to the male
hero of myth is that of landscape or monster.[81] This has also been observed by

Erich Neumann: "[C]onsciousness is identified with the male hero, while the devouring unconscious is identified with the figure of the female monster."[82] Graham splits herself off from the identification of the woman with the obstacle in myth to make the landscape itself the obstacle encountered by the woman-as-hero.

Bertram Ross noted of *Dark Meadow*: "I saw that all the death images were turned into life images by the "she of the Ground" earth figure—and I began to see a legend not unlike the Persephone Myth being unfolded."[83] The meadow was dark both because it encrypted the "underworld" and because it was a sterile land beset with the anxiety of death. As Weston wrote: "[T]he land is restored to fruitfulness . . . [T]he effect upon the land appears to be the primary result of the Quest."[84] Although barrenness can suggest childlessness, in this case the sought after fertility has nothing to do with the literal birth of a child, but with the birth of the self. The return to fruitfulness was signaled toward the end of the work by a leaf being tilted out from the top of a set piece upstage center called "tree with green leaves." Hawkins remembered: "when I first pulled the string and the branch came up I . . . could tell it was a very poetic moment . . ."[85] As Adrienne Rich wrote later: "In pre-patriarchal life the phallus (*herm*) had a quite different significance from the one it has acquired in androcentric (or phallocentric) culture. . . . It existed as an adjunct to the Goddess . . . The tree in leaf is not phallic; it is a female symbol."[86] The landscape is filled with polyvalent objects, at once potential obstacles and environments containing their own inherent promise. As Gaston Bachelard has pointed out, there is no unity to archetypes, only dominant qualities and "imaginary dialectics."[87] If myth was present in *Dark Meadow*, it was present as a landscape rather than as a narrative. "I can remember," said Hawkins, "having a very specific notion that when that set was on the stage and you were on stage you were in another place. You were not just on the stage. You were in another mythic place."[88] Hawkins's testimony is valuable because it indicates *Dark Meadow* is a precursor of the myth works. The myth was that of the unconscious itself as a landscape for the crypt of personal secrets—those of the choreographer and the audience. *Dark Meadow* was a kind of postwar "call to order."

Dark Meadow seems to have exasperated left-wing dance critic Edna Ocko, writing for *New Masses* under one of the pseudonyms she used, Frances Steuben:

> Miss Graham's use of esoteric objects—little beribboned darts, angular branches shooting out from behind scenes—undoubtedly mystify the innocent and titillate the initiate, but I find it inartistic and old-fashioned, in addition to being distracting. "Dark Meadow" makes a fetish of fetishes.[89]

Ocko implies with the phrase "a fetish of fetishes" that Graham commoditizes depth. *Dark Meadow* is the most esoteric and least accessible of Graham's works, but Ocko's critical judgment contained an insight. As an audacious attempt to channel primary process *Dark Meadow* could be considered pretentious. The very project is to render depth superficial in the strict sense of at the (visual) surface. But, *Dark Meadow* also takes a position on feminine identity in the context of the world of images and commodities that Ocko was unable to read. Far from identifying herself with the landscape of *Dark Meadow*, which Graham nevertheless characterized as being "of the soul," One Who Seeks confronts this landscape as a potential adversary. In this sense, Graham appropriated the "journey" of woman's film and transformed it into a quest for an independent subject position. Although aspects of the construction of her celebrity image follow the logic of woman's film in Hollywood narrative cinema of the 1940s, I would nevertheless argue that, with Graham, there is not "the passive feminine identification with the image (body, landscape)."[90] For this reason, it is problematic to speak as Koritz does of Graham's work as a commodity in the 1940s because one must take account of the radical differences in her self-positioning with respect to narrative cinema and myth narrative. There is a hidden drama in the notion of the landscape of the soul, but woman is not to be identified with the landscape and hence the landscape takes on the narrative function of the adversary.

In addition to the choreography Hawkins "wrote" throughout his time with Graham during the 1940s, he choreographed many of his own solos in Graham's dances. His choreographic output of the 1940s could be extended to his solos in Graham's *El Penitente*, *Appalachian Spring*, and *Dark Meadow*. Hawkins was going through an Americana phase with Ballet Caravan before he met Graham. This was, of course, a Popular Front cultural moment in which Kirstein, de Mille, and others were also involved. In addition to performing in Lew Christensen's *Filling Station* and in Eugene Loring's *Pochahontas* and *Yankee Clipper*, Hawkins also understudied several roles in de Mille's Broadway musical *Oklahoma*. This was the context within which Hawkins choreographed *Liberty Tree* and *Yankee Bluebritches* in 1940, *Trickster Coyote* in 1941, *Yankee Doodle* and *Free Stater— Kansas* in 1943, and finally *John Brown* in 1945. Hawkins left behind the Americana theme with its folksy undertones in 1946—the year of his first separation from Graham—and that year he choreographed *Stephen Acrobat*, a portrait of the artist as a young dancer. This work nods to Joyce's study for *Portrait of the Artist as a Young Man*, *Stephen Hero*. Hawkins also took the same step Graham had away from Americana toward Anglo-American modernism.

Hawkins played the Acrobat and Stuart Hodes the Trainer. A program note explained, "The theme of the drama is the myth of the Fall."[91] There were four sections: Paradise, The Fall, Hell, and Paradise. The Acrobat is a male Eve who eats of the Tree of Knowledge. Hawkins used the apple as a prop. [Figure 3.4].

Knowledge will "destroy the freedom and fearlessness of the Acrobat's perform-ing life."[92] In Hell, the Acrobat says: "Where golden air did you turn this black?" And the Trainer responds: "O Stephen you fool, you ate from the logical tree."[93] A note reads: "Fantasies of sin burden Acrobat with guilt as heavily as actual sin. Stephen's hell is the war his guilt has declared against him."[94] The ending, how-ever, was happy: "For all his agony, Acrobat's will to live lets him hear Trainer call him back to that Paradise where there is no good or evil, and where Acrobat is at one with himself and his trainer."[95] Hawkins was reversing Graham's procedure of feminizing male heroes by masculinizing Eve. The work was received as too intellectual. Hawkins's use of text—and his frequent insistence on speaking

Figure 3.4 Erick Hawkins and Stuart Hodes in Hawkins's *Stephen Acrobat* (1946). Cour-tesy of the Erick Hawkins Dance Foundation and the Music Division, Library of Congress

parts of the text himself—must certainly have come across as strange at the time. It was almost as if Ted Hughes's characterization of Sylvia Plath's early writing as "impurities thrown off from the various stages of the inner transformation" applied to Hawkins.[96] Hawkins's impurities might have been seen to be ahead of their time if viewed with a more open mind. They are lost works.

Hawkins's own mythic phase, however, began choreographically with Graham's *Dark Meadow*. He saw his own role as He Who Summons as a kind of leader: "[I]t could be a divinity or a mythological character who leads the souls to the underworld (Pluto and Persephone)."[97] "He's a psychopompous," relates Sears. "He's supposed to be a Hermes kind of character but Erick threw at me the idea of Dagon [a fish god]"[98] Sears did not pursue this lead, but because Samson was held captive in the temple of Dagon, Erich Neumann interprets it as follows: "Samson's captivity is therefore an expression of the servitude of the conquered male under the Great Mother, just as were the labors of Herakles under Omphale, when he wore woman's clothes."[99] The long and remarkable solo Hawkins danced in *Dark Meadow* was entirely of his own creation, as was the skirt costume. But, the fertility imagery of *Dark Meadow* does have an Egyptian component in which the issue of whether the tree is a phallic symbol or a matriarchal fertility symbol is raised.[100] This relates to the ambiguities of the landscape's sexual symbolism.

Hawkins' solos within Graham's works are perhaps a more impressive achievement than the solos he did independently during the decade; however, they are not recognized as individual achievements because Hawkins did not sign them. In later conversations, Hawkins tended to credit himself only with the choreography he signed during the 1940s, which is common practice, and thus to limit the record of his own creative output. Yet, the way Hawkins objectified his artistic aspirations to himself in his journals from 1929 to 1949 makes it appear that he sought validation by equaling Graham as a performer and as a choreographer. This was in no way a mean-spirited competition. Graham was the first among other names he aspired to emulate. Parity with Graham came to mean equal critical notice—something Graham had great difficulty with— equal billing (which he acquired in January 1949), and more space to present his own work on her programs, which he never actually achieved because of the generally poor critical reception his own work received in the 1940s. But, it also meant equality in the relationship, something Hawkins said he only experienced once on a camping trip with her in the Santa Fe area in 1939. Since their entire relationship was based around her work and his participation in her work as a dancer, dance partner, and producer, this form of equality was not easy to achieve. This issue was at the heart of their first separation. The interviews Agnes de Mille recorded for her biography of Graham are full of titters and muttering about the love that dare not speak its name. Yet, the Graham-Hawkins correspondence shows an intense erotic relationship between them. "[A] double bed has never had the significance it now has," she wrote him at the start of their relationship.[101] Although there are no similar confessions made by Hawkins in the correspondence, sexual preference may not have been the deal breaker in 1946. Hawkins did note in his diary: "Did I not find Martha more exciting as a person than anyone else I knew either man or woman—a keener penetration into the aspects of loving, a greater appreciator (?)—and more exciting as a sexual partner than any I had known?"[102] She seems to have used him to experience an alternative feminine identity, but paradoxically prevented him from accessing a parallel masculine identity in equally conventional terms. It was convenient for Graham's champions to blame everything on Hawkins once he withdrew his support.

From this perspective, *Cave of the Heart* may not have been about Graham's reaction to Hawkins's withdrawal as much as about the difficulties she was having with herself. Some of Graham's letters allude to problems of self-control. It is perhaps telling that the Woman she was to play in the scenario for *Cave of the Heart—The Daughter of Colchis*—is paired with a Fury: "The real conflict takes place not between the Man and her, but between the Woman and her Fury, herself."[103] In the original version, *Serpent Heart*, Graham played One Like Medea and Hawkins, One Like Jason. Yuriko was the Daughter of a King and May O'Donnell the Chorus. The program note read: "This is a dance of possessive and destroying love, a love which feeds upon itself, and when it is overthrown, is fulfilled only in revenge."[104] In her analysis of the collapse of their marriage in 1950, Graham reflected to Hawkins: "I wanted to be the Deathless One and there is no way to be that except through others when the time comes. In some strange way it is like an animal eating its young."[105] This is a negative view of rebirth. The love that feeds upon itself is also the love that is possessed by possessiveness. The rest of the note does indicate, however, that One Like Medea felt betrayed: "The One Like Medea destroys that which she has been unable to possess and brings upon herself and her beloved the inhuman wrath of one who has been betrayed."[106] It is unclear whether that betrayal existed in actual fact or was a phantasm. [Figure 3.5]

During the first separation Graham consulted with Erich Fromm, whom she had met in Bennington where he taught in 1943. (Ethel Winter took Fromm's course on Freud when she attended Bennington).[107] In a letter to Hawkins of October 19, 1946, Graham wrote: "I am not being analyzed as you know. I have just seen Fromm twice to help me to see things as they are . . ."[108] It is possible Graham saw Fromm more than twice since it is thought in psychoanalytic circles that they were having an affair.[109] If true, this would help explain why Graham retained a distance from Hawkins during their first estrangement. On October 14, 1946, she wrote to Hawkins:

This [the separation] may not have to be permanent—but I must have the same privilege you have—which is freedom from what seems like a harmful association until I can work it out. Fromm made me see when I said I wanted to do what would help you and myself most that I must consider myself only—because you would not want help if I could give it—so please let us sever all connections until if ever, it is possible again through my inner control and freedom from this compulsion—obsession, whatever it may be.[110]

What the compulsion is to which Graham refers in this letter we can only guess, but it had a self-destructive character. Graham's involvement with

Figure 3.5 Martha Graham and Erick Hawkins in *Cave of the Heart* (1946). Courtesy of the Music Division, Library of Congress

Fromm supports the possibility, however, that the character of He Who Summons danced by Hawkins in *Dark Meadow* may, unbeknownst to him, have been modeled on Fromm who was summoning Graham to self-realization without Hawkins. If the second separation with Hawkins in 1950 devastated Graham, the first apparently did not. If Fromm did take advantage of Graham sexually his unethical conduct may have compromised her ability to negotiate her difficulties with Hawkins at a crucial time. Hawkins, for his part, was seeing the analyst Ruth Foster. In 1948 Hawkins would briefly be in the care of Wickes, whom he ended up despising for undisclosed reasons.

The Labyrinth

Despite the importance of *Dark Meadow*, the pivotal work between Graham's prewar anti-Fascism and her postwar mythographic period was *Errand into the Maze*. Graham took the title from a poem by Ben Belitt, whom she had met at Bennington in 1939 where he was working with set designer Arch Lauterer, who did the original set for *American Document*. Belitt wrote *Dance Piece* as a homage to Graham.[111] He remembers that Graham told him *Errand* was a way to deal with a stressful period in her life. She wrote him letters in which she would "talk of her personal state, her anguish at the time."[112]

Belitt saw *Errand* above all as "a poetic response to the image" encapsulated in the word errand itself: "She had the sense of the image as an entire disclosure, as whole script."[113] Belitt did not actively collaborate with Graham; he simply provided the catalytic word. Unlike the earlier procedure in which Graham had provided dense poetic texts to composers, here a poet provided Graham with one densely poetic word: "Her genius is to be able to conceive of a total dance within the range of a single encompassing image."[114] Such images came in the form of words:

> She was satisfied with the particular appropriateness of an operative word: errand. It was her excitement about the word errand, which involves a choice of will and into an area or element of peril in an encounter out of some expressive need from which the participant fully intended to return. Graham as a female Theseus enters the maze to do battle with the Minotaur.[115]

Performed to a score by Gian Carlo Menotti, Graham structured *Errand* in a viscerally dramatic way. The psychological dimension is powerful since the maze itself can be an allegory of inner conflict, and the Minotaur is a nightmarish figure. Indeed, the Minotaur is a monstrosity of the heroine's own making, and perhaps for this reason, like Minos, she created the Maze to imprison him. With

Errand into the Maze, the operative motif of encryption is charted as if on a map: what is encrypted and the search to understand it becomes the piece's theme. What started in 1944 as a choreographic technique for encoding concealed meaning became a way to invite the spectator to an active investigation of this concealment. There is an increasing exteriorization of encryption in Graham's work of the late 1940s and early 1950s such that the crypt itself becomes a choreographic figure. The crypt as Derrida characterized it is an inaccessible place located at such inwardness that the location becomes indistinguishable from an excluded exteriority. With *Errand* the fact of the crypt itself becomes visible and dramatic. Graham ventures into the maze and risks being trapped there. She advertises depth. Just as Graham was creating roles for herself through which she worked out clandestine interior monologues about her own identity, cryptology was no longer so much a technique for sublimating meaning as a stylistic motif that positions the audience as meaning seeker. This is not to say that her work after 1946 served no psychological purpose for Graham, but that, to the contrary, the works began themselves to become formal equivalents of introspection. As Penelope Reed Doob writes of the labyrinthine idea, it can convey both complex artistry and inextricability.[116] They were also a means with which Graham could contemplate the notion of the trap and how to get out of it. In her letters to Hawkins about their first separation she mentions the problem of "a deeper trap than I knew," which she finds herself in. It is "a trap of the past—and not of our relationship."[117] She does not elaborate.

Belitt's sense that Graham developed the entire work by unpacking one word, although it certainly speaks to Graham's vital relation to literature, may have also been a bit of wishful modernist thinking. *Errand into the Maze* was no doubt also inspired by Hawkins's earlier idea for a Minotaur ballet with Ballet Caravan. "There's no question in my mind," remarked Hawkins in conversation with Sears, "that my having talked about this [the Minotaur] . . . intrigued her as an image, too."[118] Although Graham's postwar Minotaur cannot be identified unequivocally as an allegory of fascism as Hawkins's prewar idea for *The Minotaur* would have had it, she did repeatedly refer to the Minotaur as a Creature of Fear, and to *Errand into the Maze* as a work about overcoming fear. A program note from the Asian tour in 1954 sets the stage for this high modernist abstraction:

> The story has been transformed into a drama about the conquest of fear itself. The heroine enters like the maze of her own heart, goes along the frail thread of her courage to find the fear which lurks like a Monster, a Minotaur, within her. She encounters it, conquers it, and emerges to freedom.[119]

Overcoming fear, from a psychoanalytic perspective, entailed overcoming doubt. Erich Fromm was developing a theory of individual psychological freedom, independence, and productivity based on a comparison with the irrational faith that Fascism required. His *Escape from Freedom* was published in 1941. It posited that to live without faith in the face of the existence of Fascism necessitated a nonreligious reconceptualization of faith as rational. Without rational faith one is "sterile, hopeless, and afraid."[120] In a letter to Zellmer of July 28, 1943, Graham quoted from an offprint Fromm had given her, "Faith as a Character Trait." "[He] speaks so vividly of doubt, also. And that is where I learned a great deal about myself. Principally, that I am given to irrational doubt."[121] *Errand into the Maze* is about overcoming irrational doubt, which can also be expressed as fear. Issues of anxiety even in the postwar period cannot be separated from the historical emergence of Fascism itself and the association of the unconscious with the "primitive" side of man's nature capable of laying waste to civilization.

In the preface to the first edition of M. Esther Harding's *Psychic Energy*, a book "conceived during the war years, amid the din of a world cataclysm," the author asks: "Is it not possible that the primitive and unconscious side of man's nature might be more effectively tamed, even radically transformed? If not, civilization is doomed."[122] Harding makes no appeal to democracy, but instead to Christian archetypes, and she lumps Communism with Fascism as psychological stumbling blocks, which means she makes no appeal to Socialism, either. The end of the war does not presage the end of the threat Fascism represents: "It does not look as if it could be repressed once more into the unconscious. It has come to stay."[123] For sociologically oriented psychoanalytic theory, the defeat of Fascism had left civilization with a new burden of the unconscious.

The objective political correlative of Fascism in the 1930s and 1940s was fear. The very fact of Fascism instilled fear. Louis Mumford wrote: "Fear enters the door with the daily newspaper, and the last radio report in the evening creates a waking nightmare which slips unnoticed into the horrors of sleep."[124] President Franklin Delano Roosevelt said in his first inaugural address of March 4, 1933, "The only thing we have to fear is fear itself," thereby evoking the fear of the Great Depression in an attempt to tame it.[125] Graham first encountered the expression of fear as part of the political landscape through her work on Archibald MacLeish's *Panic*, a verse play for which she choreographed the Chorus in 1935. "What arms can defend the/ Evening—the night hours—/When fear: faceless: devours us?"[126] The emergence of Fascism as what Mumford called barbarism was an equally frightening experience affecting people's lives in a psychologically disturbing way. By the same token, the analysis of Fascism as a political, social, and cultural phenomenon was inseparable from the recognition of its *psychological* basis. Mumford wrote: "[T]he true sources of Fascism are to be found in the human soul, not in economics."[127] To be a subject of irrational doubt, as Fromm put it, was a requirement of anyone about to subordinate him- or herself to Fascism, that is, to an irrational authority on the basis of what Fromm called "a conflict between love and hatred."[128] The political and so-ciological stakes Fascism raised were crucially psychological in that they spoke to far-reaching affective conflicts. Doing battle with Fascism was doing battle with one's own fear. Fascism was itself the insertion into the mind of an unconscious, if still conflicted, mandate to submit. When Graham shared the stage with Professor George S. Counts of Columbia University in an event hosted by the Committee for Anti-Nazi Literature in 1937, Counts testified to "madness rampant in Germany—the people doing, saying, and writing things they do not themselves believe in, because they are terrorized." The account of this talk published in *The Dance Ob-server* underlines his warning "that Fascism arose out of our western world and is therefore not entirely removed from this country." Graham's approach to this prob-lem was reflected in her call for dancers to be "watchful of their world and sincere in their art."[129] To effectively resist Fascism would seem to require a self-vigilance: the quality of one's movement could be a litmus test. It is also very likely that Graham understood patriarchy not only as historically synonymous with irrational political authority, but also Fascism as a large-scale historical instantiation of patriarchy. Fromm would likely have confirmed this perception since his research exposed the workings of patriarchal authority in the modern family as well as in political author-itarianism. Fromm wrote an essay in 1936 for the anthology *Autorität und Familie* (*Authority and Family*) edited by Max Horkheimer. Parts of this anthology were translated into English as *Cultural Aspects of National Socialism* (February 24, 1941) and distributed in mimeographed form as a "research project" pamphlet produced by the Institute of Social Research in New York. Other parts were translated under the auspices of the Works Progress Administration.[130] Although this work by the International Institute for Social Research in collaboration with Columbia Univer-sity placed the study of Fascism in sociological terms, its references to the uncon-scious also place it squarely in the realm of psychology. As an example, one can read: "it appears that the consciousness of a people had been modified to such an extent that they voted against their own rights, thus inducing collapse of all that democracy stands for." The goal of the study of "Literature, Music, and Art" in the project is to "analyze the powers that threaten to pervert the consciousness of a democratic people into its opposite."[131] The problem of Fascism, in other terms, was presented as a psychological complex.

It is thus not surprising that when Graham choreographed the battle with fear in the immediate postwar years Fascism still hung in the air as a compelling point of reference for irrational violence. The transition between anti-Fascism and myth in Graham's work can be understood as the unrecognized continuity between the social-psychological analysis of Fascism and the post-Freudian theory that took aim at patriarchal authoritarianism. It is my contention that Graham was operating quite precisely in this nexus. To overcome fear was a prerequisite of self-realization in vanguard thinking and hence became related to the Jungian concept of rebirth. Just as in his *Escape from Freedom* Fromm had undertaken a social psychology of Nazism, Graham located her fear of the authoritarian character of patriarchy in a political context.[132] The Minotaur carried that political meaning. The first battle against Fascism was a battle against one's own fear to act, against the unconscious tendency to submit. Hence it becomes clearer how a transition from anti-Fascism to myth could have taken place in Graham's work in such a brief timeframe. Issues of psychological freedom and the political will to act had personal as well as political ramifications, and were part of the legacy of the political and psychic history of Fascism.

At the end of *Errand* Graham triumphs over the Minotaur who lies dead at her feet, and the final image is of the heroine stepping through an imaginary gate, a Noguchi set that has been called the pelvic bone, an unmistakable symbol of the birth canal.

> The creature returns, and, mounting on his forefront, the protagonist seizes his nostrils and forces him to the ground—a daring stroke of choreography which is superbly justified in performance. The final passage takes place between two branches of an object resembling a forked tree, which not only defines the stage space, but also makes the emergence physically as well as mentally apparent.[133]

The original costume for the Minotaur enabled Graham to seize hold of his nostrils as mentioned in the review, thus rendering the struggle more palpable, violent, and horrifying. The pelvic bone set, in Graham's terms, was the "doorway from which the child I never had comes forth, but the only child that comes forth is myself."[134] [Figures 3.6, 3.7, and 3.8]. The work is psychologized because the result of the struggle is the rebirth of the self. But, for the audience in 1947 the allegory of Fascism was still clear. The transition at the work's end from victory in battle to self-realization makes the struggle itself appear in retrospect to have been entirely psychological. Graham's self-birth or rebirth makes of the heroine what Harding would call a "Moon Mother," "the woman who belongs to herself" or "She-who-will-not-have-a-husband."[135] A connection is thus established between *Dark Meadow* and *Errand into the Maze*. In these Graham defines herself as her own daughter. Both works were created during her first separation from Hawkins, and they are attempts to individuate herself not only with respect to an earlier self, but with respect to her relationship with him. *Errand*, however, is not about a quest but a battle, and her adversary is the fearful patriarchal figure itself. The price of failure to individuate is the loss of freedom itself. The universalizing of her personal drama is here justified through recent world events.

Rank enables us to reconsider Graham's rhetoric of fear, which, although meaningful in the anti-Fascist context, was replaced by anxiety in the postwar context. "[T]he anxiety of birth forms the basis of every anxiety or fear."[136] More than the Creature of Fear, the Minotaur is the Creature of Anxiety, which anxiety, according to Rank, is rooted in the experience of birth itself. Rank claimed "[T]he psychoses are closely related to the mythological world view" and "[T]he human problem of birth stands actually at the centre of mythical as of infantile interest and determines conclusively the content of fantasy formations."[137] Rank's insight was that anxiety was not converted into physical symptoms—as with hysteria—because it was itself always already physically experienced in the trauma of birth

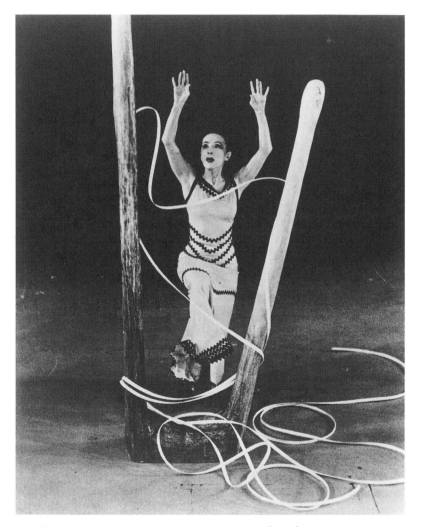

Figure 3.6 Martha Graham in her *Errand into the Maze* (1947). Courtesy of the Dance Collection, New York Public Library for the Performing Arts

Figure 3.7 Martha Graham and Mark Ryder in Graham's *Errand into the Maze* (1947).
Photo: Michael Ochs Courtesy of Michael Ochs Archive/Getty Images

itself. Graham's rebirth in *Errand* is thus both beset with anxiety and trauma. But, it would be a mistake to divorce it entirely from the Fascist context both because of the links of patriarchy to Fascism and because Graham's sense of her own tendency toward irrational doubt made her a potential subject of Fascism, which she most likely recognized. This was what instilled in her anxiety, and it is difficult to pry apart the political and personal concerns of the 1940s in a way that splits the decade in two. It is much more likely that these concerns survived in altered form across the decade. Graham's drama, which also contributed to her iconic status in the 1940s, was precisely *not* to reinvent herself after the war, but to continue to grow from the person she had been. It is this so little recognized fact that lends her the authenticity that galvanized audiences in the postwar era.

Hawkins did not care for *Errand Into the Maze* and never danced the Minotaur role opposite Graham: "[S]he somehow put her own interpretation which is I think a little silly myself. . . . Fear of sexuality is a kind of a strange notion."[138] These comments also enable us to see that *Errand into the Maze* may have been about the fear of attraction to Fascism couched in the most visceral, hence sexualized, terms.[139] Certainly, the sparse language Graham used for this work matches up

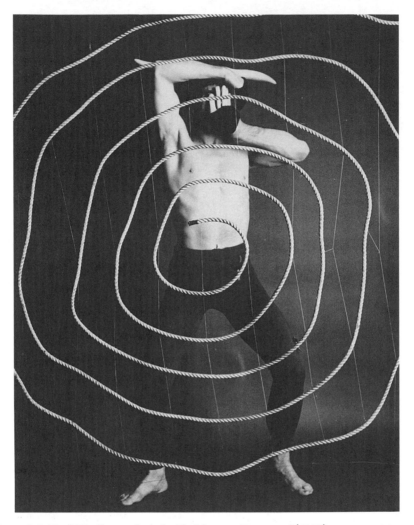

Figure 3.8 Erick Hawkins in his solo *The Minotaur Discovered* (1952). Courtesy of the Erick Hawkins Dance Foundation and the Music Division, Library of Congress

with the rhetoric of fear. During the war Graham characterized Nazi society as a society of fear. Graham's main critique of Nazi culture was that it engendered fearful movement. "How can the dance," she said a 1939 interview, "which is free- dom of thought and expression, exist in countries dominated by hate and fear?"[140] But the choreography for *Errand*, coming as it does after the war, more readily suggested an inward psychological and particularly sexual anxiety. Just as Fascist imagery can commute to anti-Fascist imagery, prewar anti-Fascist aesthetics easily commuted to a discourse of postwar psychological anxiety. Marcia Siegel has written: "I think *Errand into the Maze* is a dance about sexuality, although a case could be made that the Creature of Fear is a personification of death, oppression, madness, even censorship—anything that threatens the individual's identity and that it takes courage to turn away from."[141] By adopting a more historically informed context Siegel could have added Fascism.

What makes the protagonist's relationship to the Minotaur in Graham's *Errand* complex is her simultaneous attraction and repulsion to the creature. In 1942 Graham wrote of Hitler as a "creature," not a human being: "I believe that Hitler is made by us. He is all our carelessness, our lack of civil responsibility. It is as though we had made this man and foisted him upon the world and that is what makes him so horrible. He is so much *the creature* we are too."[142] In these comments, Graham admits the continuity that can exist between Democracy and Fascism. Frankfurt School theorist Herbert Marcuse, who worked for the CIA during the war to analyze Nazi culture, remarked on the connections between liberal democracy and totalitarianism:

> Totalitarian violence and totalitarian reason came from the structure of existing society, which was in the act of overcoming its liberal past and incorporating its historical negation. . . . This abolition was not restricted at all to the totalitarian states and since then has become reality in many democracies (and especially in the most developed ones).[143]

Since Graham spoke of the Nazi regime as a regime of fear it would follow that she construed Hitler as the Creature of Fear. It is possible that the sexuality of *Errand* is designed to convey an attraction or bond that escapes conscious control. Repressed sexuality, in other terms, could refer back to the unconscious attraction to Fascism itself. Interestingly, Hawkins also related the Minotaur figure to the unconscious: "It's unconscious in the sense that you are attracted to it in the first place."[144] Jung identified the Minotaur, with reference to a 1935 Picasso etching, as "a symbol of man's uncontrollable instinctive forces" and interpreted Nazism in the same light as an excrescence of the unconscious at a broad social level.[145] The labyrinth of these theories leads us to the conclusion that, for these theorists, Fascism not only emerges from the unconscious, but remains part of the unconscious of the Western subject. *Errand into the Maze* is a post-Fascist anti-Fascist work. The question of Fascism through Fromm's work had become one of independence and autonomy from unconscious psychological motivation. To be unavailable to Fascism was to be a productive personality. In this way, politics and psychology merged just as a sociopolitical phenomenon could be conceived as an individual psychological problem. The transition from Graham's anti-Fascist politics of the first half of the decade to her immersion in psychoanalytic thinking after the war belongs to this cultural phenomenon. Graham was very much a part of her own time, although we barely recognize such features in her work today.

With *Dark Meadow* (1946) Graham eschewed accessibility by eradicating narrative intelligibility and replacing it with archetype; in *Cave of the Heart* (1946) she staged the Medea legend to counteract the conventional feminine image constructed for her during the war years; in *Errand into the Maze* she used the labyrinth to resist patriarchal power and express distrust of men by identifying them with the arbitrary authority of Fascism; and, in *Night Journey* she developed an elaborate meditation on her failing relationship with Hawkins, and encrypted an anticipatory ritual of separation. All these works were forms of self-analysis, which Rank envisaged as the hallmark of the modern artist. Rank linked the artist to immortality-ideologies: ". . . [W]e find the immortality-ideology which appears in mythic form as rebirth of the self (incest) and artistically as eternalization of the self (in the work)."[146] The themes of *Dark Meadow* and *Errand into the Maze* were rebirth of the artist's self, and, through rebirth, the artist myth of immortality as dynamic and alive. "Naturally," remarked Rank somewhat prophetically, "spiritual self-representation in the work is always one essential element in artistic creativity and in art, but it is only in modern artists that it becomes a conscious, introspective, psychological self-analysis."[147] Hawkins read Rank's *Art and Artist* when it came out in 1932, and both Graham and Hawkins were reading Jung since their meeting with Campbell in 1938; Fromm would be another important influence on both since at least 1943. They were imbued with contemporary psychoanalytic literature and applied it equally to life and art.

Art historian Stephen Polcari has made the case for a connection between Graham and the New York School of Abstract Expressionist painters on the basis of the common tendency to "psychological introspection."[148] The choreographic question for Graham was how to structure introspection in and through choreography such that her dance could function as introspection for the audience rather than as voyeurism. The audience, that is, had to engage with a parallel yet equally private introspective process made possible only by the spectacle it beheld. *Dark Meadow* attempted this, but assumed a collective unconscious in the raw state. What I mean here by collective unconscious is the sum total of private experiences that can be applied to a symbol deprived of plot, *mythos*. The question of how to induce introspection in the audience would only be answered, however, with *Night Journey*, about which Graham was thinking already in 1946. Interestingly, Belitt remembers Graham also associated this work with the war: "I remember Martha was in the midst of *Night Journey* in 1946. She began to talk to me about it with the utmost earnestness, responding very strongly to the poignancy of all things connected with fatality and sacrifice and war."[149] The personal and the political seem to merge in an indistinguishable dread: "It was the violence of the whole ambiance of the 1940s that attracted us both, I suppose, brought us each to dwell on the 'nocturnal': night journeys, night marches, unknowns, blood pieties."[150]

|| 4 ||

Jocasta at Colonus

Post-Freudian Landscapes

"To me to live means to act on the stage, and to act on the stage means to live."

—Martha Graham (*Every Soul is a Circus*, Notebook)

The landscapes in my chapter title are two works of the postwar period: *Night Journey* (1947), a recognized masterpiece adapted from Sophocles' *Oedipus the King*, and *Voyage* (1953/1955), a relatively unknown and, by most critical accounts, failed dance.[1] *Night Journey* has remained active in the Graham repertory and Graham's own performance of Jocasta survives in a 1961 film directed by Maya Deren's cinematographer Alexander Hammid.[2] The critical disparagement of *Voyage* in the early 1950s was unfortunately myopic: Graham herself believed strongly in the work and continued to revise it under different titles—*Theater for a Voyage* and *Theater for Voyage*—up to and through the 1955 New York season. William Schuman composed original scores for both dances, but *Voyage* was never filmed, and few photographs remain. Although I reserve the bulk of my discussion of the latter work for the next chapter, I introduce it here in order to suggest a comparative view of these works.

Although they shared such different fates—one being her most famous and the other her least famous work—there is still a legitimate basis for comparison. Both *Night Journey* and *Voyage*, intertwined with Graham's personal life, belong to a period extending from her first separation with Hawkins in 1946 to the couple's decisive breakup in 1950 and its aftermath in Graham's effort to come to terms through Jungian analysis with the deeply regretted loss of Hawkins.[3] For this reason, myth and psychoanalysis are critical categories for understanding Graham's work of the immediate postwar period, but the very different approaches *Journey* and *Voyage* take to myth, and the relation of psychoanalytic theory to mythmaking, can only be fully explained with respect to the before and after of the Graham-Hawkins breakup. Hence, the idea of dances as landscapes—a conceit I adapt here from Graham herself who often spoke of the soul's journey—refers not to the 'soul' in a timeless or mystical sense—but to a life and its events in relation to the space of the stage.[4]

Mythic Heroism

Graham's use of myth had both professional and personal ramifications. From a professional standpoint, her adaptations of myth projected a heroic image of herself. This was particularly true of Jocasta in *Night Journey*, the only one of her roles she herself singled out as heroic. "I feel this character will be different from any other I have done," she wrote to William Schuman, "because she is of heroic stature."[5] *Dark Meadow* (1946) and *Errand into the Maze* (1947) had already positioned Graham's *self* as the subject of her art in a way similar to that of Abstract Expressionist painters—mostly male—who fostered images of themselves both on and off the canvas as heroic figures confronting their own and, by extension, humanity's unconscious drives. The idea that art practice could access and comment on unconscious impulses originated with surrealism and has also been associated with the Abstract Expressionists.[6] "The subject of artists," observed Art Historian Michael Leja in his discussion of the New York School, "was the artist as subject."[7] The iconography of myth was reconciled with personal complexes and obsessions in the mode of the dream. Conversely, dreams—images of highly subjective fantasy—could be manipulated as a species of publicly shared myth once they were connected to some kind of narrative form. The participation of the archetype in the life of the psyche was not far off. By the time we see her in the dressing room applying her makeup as Jocasta in the 1957 film *A Dancer's World* Graham seems to have become herself a mythical figure of the dance world: the dancer archetype. Graham's figure by the 1950s exuded the aura of classical mythology—transgression, celebrity, godlike distance, and perversity—and suggested that the modern dancer might be to an even greater degree than any visual artist the postwar artist-hero par excellence. But, this kind of image also constituted a commodification of Graham's stage personality, and she knew it. "I am now a commodity like Lux or Ivory soap" she has been cited as saying.[8]

Myth and Accessibility

The idea that bodies should communicate with the audience in uniquely corporeal terms—let us take the cue from Gay Morris and call this idea *embodiment*—indicated a distrust of narrative in dance modernism since its inception.[9] By embodiment in this context I do not mean the transference of physicality and corporeality to other media (as described in Chapter One), but instead the artistic use of the body itself as its own medium. If bodies adhered to the well-established patterns of textual representation, the libratory potential of dance's vanguard mission would be irrevocably compromised. Hence the dilemma of the 1940s when narrative, character, and psychological motivation, as Morris has shown, emerged in modern dance to jeopardize the vanguard status it had acquired in the 1930s. Morris sees in Graham, nevertheless, an exception: ". . . Graham's dances were still seen as vanguard productions that in their concern with myth and the unconscious revealed universal aspects of human existence."[10] Despite the fact that myth is rendered in narrative terms, which would presumably make it both accessible and theatrical, it also enlists "exalted nonrational, intuitive, 'poetic' ways of knowing."[11] Graham's work escaped the pitfalls of commercialization even as it introduced a new form of accessibility to the concert stage. Her solution to the problem of how to reach a wider audience with esoteric material that required of the public a special sensitivity to the body as a means of communication was quite original. Graham did not betray the ideals of embodiment she herself had so strongly championed in the 1930s, but found instead a new conceptual venue for embodiment. Myth, one might say, is narrative embodied. Graham's use of myth evoked very modern approaches to understanding human behavior from anthropology and psychoanalysis to innovations in modern theatrical practice. Although theatrical, Graham's mythic works of the late 1940s were certainly not accessible in the way of commercial musical theater or even of ballet: they presupposed erudition.[12] Yet, even without a sufficient background to plumb the depths of the most complex references in her work, the audience could follow the story while maintaining an awareness that the actual task at hand was to contemplate the effects of the unconscious. The reputation for depth—both intellectual and psychological—followed Graham throughout the 1950s. As dance critic Robert Sabin expressed it to Bertram Ross, "when he heard Martha was doing the Oresteia, he immediately started reading the three plays over and over again. And anything he could get his hands on. He didn't want to miss a thing. 'And you know Martha,' he said, 'she'll do one hand gesture that will be based on a hundred pages.'"[13]

Yet, Graham's works of the 1940s, it should also be noted, were not all mythic nor were they all especially accessible. Some works of the early 1940s in the comic and satiric mode—*Every Soul is a Circus* and *Punch and the Judy*—did lay claim to an uncharacteristic theatricality and accessibility. But, *Deaths and Entrances* (1943), despite its recognizable characters—the Bronte sisters—lacked a legible narrative.[14] "The three of us, Jane [Dudley], Sophie [Maslow] and I wore dresses with tiny trains but wide skirts reminiscent of the bustle period. The movements at times looked like mad birds moving."[15] Even the historical references of *Deaths and Entrances* were unsettled by formal and expressive qualities. After its premiere Graham reported: "The public seems baffled but moved in some way they do not understand."[16] But, she added: "I think the dancing is some of the most articulate and significant I have done but the idea is another thing. Perhaps the two do not need to go together or perhaps the material assumes a meaning of its own fashioning."[17] Graham's investment in embodiment betrays itself even when her conscious intent leads her toward a discursively conceived structure. Reflecting further on *Deaths and Entrances* Graham described her search as one for "[T]he instinctive suchness of body that is body."[18] As a nondance example of suchness she invoked the MGM lion, which implies she was concerned to express the idea of embodiment accessibly or at least with reference to popular culture, however paradoxical that may sound. Nevertheless, *suchness* suggests embodiment rather than narrative.[19] Similarly, Graham's preliminary thinking on *Herodiade* (1944) reveals a fundamental disinterest in the narrative premise, not only because *Herodiade* was based on a poem by Mallarmé, but because its premise was highly subjective. In a letter to David Zellmer of June 12, 1944, Graham wrote of "a return to the exact, the existing, the precise moment" that she had become aware of in the writing of poet Ben Belitt. "It is not the study of abstraction but it will become so exact from the individual moment that it will be general."[20]

Nevertheless, there is evidence of Graham's growing appeal in the course of the 1940s both with the general public and the intelligentsia. The Company's Broadway seasons were extended first to two consecutive Sunday nights in 1943, then to a one-week run in 1944, and finally to a two-week run in 1946–47.[21] A memo by her press agent Isadora Bennett states: "Her dances have always made history as theatre and as dance. But in the past three seasons she has been making *box-office history*, quite as much as dance history."[22] Drama critic Stark Young would not have identified Graham as "the most important lesson for our theatre" in 1948 without the phenomenon of the two-week Broadway season. The popular success of her uncompromising modernism was anomalous, and it resonates with the contradictions of the Graham image itself.

Graham's Style

Graham's remarkable success during this decade hinged partially on her choice of collaborators—above all set and property designer Isamu Noguchi but also certain of her dancers whose crucial roles in production areas has gone largely unsung. In addition to his dancing, Erick Hawkins's perspicacious and effective efforts to commission musical scores of prominent composers, his insistence that they be played live—not merely on piano, but by a small orchestra—his original initiatives to find major funding through individual donations (something Graham had never before attempted or even considered and was reluctant to even try), not to mention his role in the professionalization of her school, all these contributions were essential to "upgrading" the Company's production values amidst the economic austerities of war time.[23] Notwithstanding all this, Graham's success hinged first and foremost on her own qualities as a performer, which crystallized in a new way during that decade. Any responsible historical and critical account needs to describe these qualities.

By the mid- to late 1940s Graham's choreography matched the evocative level of her on-stage interpretation such that she was becoming the visual talisman of her own choreographic imagination. Graham's choreographic gifts all but disappeared within her own performance even as the powers of suggestion the performer unleashed nuanced the dramaturgical frameworks the choreographer devised.[24] As William Schuman, the composer of both *Night Journey* and *Voyage*, said: "The dancer created the choreographer; the choreographer created the dancer. I am certain of this: there was an interplay."[25] If her dances were coming to be called *theater* this only indicates how the interplay of dance and choreography created something that was neither one nor the other taken in isolation. Her work was theatrical but this is *not* to say that her movement or the choreographic conception subtending the movement—with a few isolated exceptions—were mimetic or pantomimic. In fact, she had only disparaging things to say of "the bodily-inarticulate respectability of theatre" [26] even as she struggled at times against her own "unintentional obscurity."[27] As Bertram Ross has testified on first seeing Graham perform in the late 1940s: "I couldn't believe what I had seen and felt Martha somehow through movement made vivid—was able to show—all those feelings you have inside you—that you can't even put into words."[28] The point is that Graham not only portrayed feelings, but she did so in a way that protected their status as indefinable.

There are some indications Graham was aware of what had emerged in her as a performer by the early 1950s when she recognized similar qualities in Bertram Ross and became interested in formalizing them. After the first performance of *Voyage* in 1953 she wrote to Ross about how he might teach a new approach to feeling in dance:

> I do not mean that this would take the place of any of the technic but it would take the place of the old mime in earlier or classical dance education. But worked out in a different way. It would be taught . . . say one lesson a week as a special approach to communication. I believe that so many do not know what 'feeling' is. They confuse it with emotion or meaning in a literary sense and it is none of these things really and yet all of them.[29]

Graham's thoughts on the teaching of feeling "as a special approach to communication" were addressed to Ross since his performing revealed a special understanding of this approach. Ethel Winter called him "a poetic actor."[30] (Later in Ross's career he began to develop his voice.) Ross collaborated intensively with Graham throughout the 1950s in rehearsal and by phone on the development of her work, something there is not evidence Hawkins did.[31] This collaboration reached a crescendo with *Clytemnestra* (1958) for which there was talk that he should be credited as the co-choreographer. "Martha and I scripted *Clytemnestra*," one reads in his manuscript notes. "There were meetings in her apartment and long phone conversations."[32] Another manuscript page contains the notation: "I created *Clytemnestra*."[33] The correspondence between Hawkins and Graham in the early 1940s shows the mentor encouraging and guiding the younger dancer through insecurity and self-doubt. Ross, on the other hand, came with a ready-made enthusiasm and alacrity seemingly unclouded by the sort of insecurity that plagued Hawkins, although it should also be noted that Ross did not entertain the choreographic ambitions that Hawkins did. Ross, however, was not the sexual partner Graham wanted, but only what he called the "fantasy lover."[34]

Hawkins, too, was aware of the unique qualities that made up Graham's stage persona. Of her performance in *Appalachian Spring* he said:

> I remember standing there and watching Martha. I had a beautiful insight that came to my mind. I saw that what Martha was doing was in her expression, in *her feeling*, making more things happen per minute than the ordinary green dancers can do . . . I had a beautiful apprenticeship with Martha that way and so I was able to watch and these times of insight would come to me because I was watching a great artist work.[35]

Modern dance needed to retain the primacy of embodiment even as it strove to reach a larger audience to survive economically. What both Ross and Hawkins call "feeling" is not storytelling but, rather, something more like embodiment. The images produced by feeling emerge from behind, beneath, and through story or character—when these are present—in a way that disrupts, undermines, or renders ambivalent the information narrative imparts while still relying upon it.[36] The images Graham's work disseminated on stage, unlike those of Abstract Expressionist painters, were not representations *of* the unconscious but communications *with, from, and to* the unconscious. The visual and literary framework of the productions—particularly the mythical ones—helped to convey the premise that the unconscious was a modern corollary of mythic consciousness. One might say that the mythic framework itself constituted a deliberate and calculated appeal to the audience's primary process. The audience was not expected to focus on plot, but called upon to see through the plot to the feelings the dancer embroidered around it. This was the paradoxical form of accessibility Graham practiced in the second half of the decade.

Myth did enable Graham to express a distrust of the rationality *of* language proper to the principle of embodiment *through* the evocation of narrative rather than through its rejection. Narrative logic, whether of classical or personal myth, opened onto the irrational rather than onto the presumably transparent world of means-ends rationality. Myth, in her work, presupposed the fracturing of narrative structures through montage and flashback. But, a critical dimension also emerges here: the critique of language by gesture, and the possibility of social critique embedded in "unconscious" thought. One might think of the critique of organized religion in the tense, abrupt, driven, and highly repetitive pious gestures of the Revivalist and his followers in *Appalachian Spring*. If such gestures referred to certain obsessions related to religious fanaticism, their ability to suggest the unconscious motivation of religious sentiment points to a subtly critical gaze cast on organized religion through movement. And, in *Night Journey*, although Jocasta cannot escape punishment at the end of the ballet for her transgression of the incest taboo, her agency in the consciousness of her predicament belies this ending and has greater ramifications than the daring move to place her character instead of Oedipus at the center of the action.[37]

Embodiment and Theatricality—Showing and Telling

It cannot be denied Graham's work became highly theatrical as of 1938 when in *American Document* it took the direction of dance theatre. But we are entitled to ask how the presence of theatre developed in her work.[38] What are the historical roots of this term as it is applied to her? The space between dance and theatre had been explored in William Butler Yeats's *At the Hawk's Well*, a poetic drama or play for dancers interpreted in London by the Japanese modern dancer Michio Ito in 1916. Influenced by Ezra Pound's editing of Fenollosa's translations of Japanese Noh Plays, Yeats introduced Irish elements. "I have asked Mr. Pound for these beautiful plays," wrote Yeats in the Introduction to the 1916 edition, "because I think they will help me to explain a certain possibility of the Irish dramatic movement."[39] Graham's future collaborator Isamu Noguchi created a mask for Ito's production of *At the Hawk's Well* in the late 1920s. Although the year is disputed, Noguchi and Graham first met through Ito.[40] She subsequently performed in Ito's choreography in the Greenwich Village Follies. Horst's biographer Janet Soares relates that Graham received a great deal of information about Ito's aesthetic from Horst when the latter served as Ito's accompanist for classes in New York.[41] Thus a certain modernist "Celtic" conception of Noh traveled through Ito to Graham, mediated as well by Isamu Noguchi.[42] In fact, the 1916 production of *At the Hawk's Well*, at which T.S. Eliot was present, took Yeats, as Helen Carr explains, out of the category of éminence grise for the younger generation of imagist poets. "The qualities which Pound and Eliot would soon be insisting should be found in what Eliot called 'the modern movement in poetry' were defined through that encounter with the Noh; it would be esoteric, erudite, elitist, returning to the past in order to speak of the present."[43] The influence on Graham of the Yeats-Pound-Eliot-Joyce branch of Anglo-American modernism cannot be underestimated. It tends to be, however, perhaps because it was only by the second half of the 1940s that Graham's work fully manifested it. The relation of *Cave of the Heart* to Noh theater harks back to the interest of Yeats and Pound in Ernest Fenollosa's discovery of Noh.[44] Graham seems to have been reading Yeats well into the 1940s: when she sought the title for *Night Journey* in 1946 she sent Schuman a list of possibilities, all taken from "the Yeats version of the play."[45] Another important influence on Graham in the later 1920s was the German modern dancer Harald Kreutzberg. Soares provides evidence that Graham observed Kreutzberg rehearsing in New York in 1928.[46] Since Horst was also serving as Kreutzberg's accompanist in New York, the German dancer rehearsed in Graham's studio where she was able to observe him at work. Soares adds: "His abstract dancing, distinctive costuming, and professional theatricality were the stiffest competition Martha faced because they were most akin to her own developing style."[47] As a citizen of the Third Reich, however, Kreutzberg was no longer touring the United States by 1936, and Ito—who had since moved to California—was interned by the US government by 1942, and then deported back to Japan.[48] Because of the war Graham was not pressed to acknowledge the influence of these prominent artists on her work.

In 1941 John Martin noted of Graham's performance in *Letter to the World* "a style which can no longer be called dance, as that term is conventionally used, but must be described as a kind of surrealist theatre."[49] She herself perceived this quality in Hawkins when she observed that his dancing "seems to have become theatricalized to a point of speech in terms of theater."[50] The "point of speech" to which she refers was, however, not a representational equivalent of speech, but rather a rendering of impulse as the substratum of speech. The central medium of theater—the spoken text—is both acknowledged and displaced in these formulations. Modern dance was theater by other means. Martin called it surrealistic. To be theatrical in a surrealist sense was to reach a degree of transparency that, while suggestive, had little to do with the conventional forms of theatrical expression. Frances Wickes commented on surrealism in this way:

Surrealism, with its effort to give validity to the inner realities and the irrational, is a revolt against the limitations of the conscious, a protest against the absurd pretense that we can limit reality to that which consciousness decides to accept.[51]

This tension between the conscious and the unconscious in surrealism allowed for dancing itself to be the bearer of irrationality whereas choreography allowed for the positioning of the body in a representation of the unconscious that had, of necessity, a dramaturgical dimension, just as, in Abstract Expressionist painting, the unconscious had a pictorial dimension. Graham displaced the tension Morris identifies between embodiment and narrative onto the structural relation between dancing and choreography. Dancing shows, but choreography tells. Showing and telling become both differentiated and conjoined in Graham's theory even as they became interlaced in her practice. It was the interplay between them—the structural support and tension they lent to one another—that must have fascinated her audience from the 1940s well into the 1950s.[52]

In an undated letter to Hawkins Graham elaborated on the difference between dance as showing and choreography as telling:

> But what is needed—wanted—is the superman again—not dancing incidents of life or times in history—but dancing that reveals—not interprets or comments—. From certain moments of listening to the heart there issue moments that hold security for people for a little space—It is as tho' a loved one's hand rested on you coolly, simply for an instant. Fear leaves you. In dancing it brings security to an audience to see a person possessed, integrated, impassioned, disciplined, beautiful with a radiance that belongs to integration—Humanity becomes potentially divine for an instant—that is enough . . . Choreography is secondary. The emergence of the life, of person, is primal.[53]

Graham makes a claim in this letter for the highly personal function of dancing in its proximity to life as opposed to the storytelling properties commonly associated with the syntax of choreography. Graham envisions the union of the personal, the superhuman, and the divine in dancing—this union simulating the emotional security of requited love—and she contrasts all the above to choreography, which communicates with its audience through narrative form ("incidents of life or times in history").

This letter is directly relevant to Graham's production aesthetic because in it she makes an argument for the superiority of dance over choreography: in dancing the function of revealing trumps interpreting: showing trumps telling. Graham's remarks in this letter starkly oppose the way dancing reveals the "person" to the use of plot and roles with which to *impersonate*. But, if revealing and showing are to take precedence, interpreting and telling cannot be wholly expunged. Narrative is secondary to dance as "participation in an event," and the finished work is secondary to any particular instance of its performance.[54] Graham adapted the idea of "participation in an event" from T.S. Eliot, who wrote that literature is "a presentation of thought, or a presentation of feeling by a statement of events in human action or objects in the external world."[55] By substituting *participation* for Eliot's use of the term *statement*, Graham played with the relation of showing to telling discussed above. That this relation was much on her mind is also indicated by a note she wrote about it: "In the beginning was the Word": She calls the word "The act of statement"; she asks: "What is the beginning?" The implication is that from the perspective of the beginning of the world in the word, a statement of events is itself an act.[56]

The Chorus

From the perspective I am developing here in which Graham transforms a problem for modern dance into a working method, it is noteworthy that two works of the late 1940s were adaptations of Greek tragedies. The ancient theater tradition offered a model for permutations between showing and telling (dancing and acting) on the part of chorus and dramatis personae, respectively.[57] The references to Greek tragedy in *Cave of the Heart* and *Night Journey* in particular allowed Graham to shift audience attention back and forth between emphases on dancing and on acting. In *Cave of the Heart* one dancer performs the Chorus as a lone figure. We have the impression she would like to stop the action, and she does punctuate it forcefully, but she is powerless to affect it. Rather, she looks upon the action stoically, and her final gesture of covering her face with her cape is powerful in its simplicity. Her movements are the more forceful for being brief and simple [Figure 4.1]. In *Night Journey*, on the other hand, where the Chorus frequently occupies the center of the stage, especially during the tryst between mother and son, it is given more vigorous choreography to perform than either Jocasta or Oedipus as they repair to the marriage bed wrapping themselves and each other in a length of rope by which they become both united and entangled. The switch in focus from the Chorus dancing center stage to a more figural representation of passion as an entanglement upstage, allows the eight chorus members—Daughters of the Night—dancing directly in front of Oedipus and Jocasta, to show passion in its complexity as both desired and feared.

The Daughters of the Night are not a chorus in the traditional sense—and they are certainly not the male chorus of Sophocles's play—but Moirai: embodiments of fate.[58] As such, they are also extensions of Jocasta herself: "Just as she (Jocasta)," noted Graham, "is an aspect of them so they (the Chorus) are of her." The Chorus exemplifies the complex interaction between present and past in *Night Journey*, or what Graham also called actual and dream. As she noted: "There are two areas of action: what might be called the actual and the dream. There is a thread linking the whole and that is the chorus action."[59] The Chorus manages to inject Jocasta's present consciousness into her memories of the past just as the past itself is represented in the ballet as a kind of dream or virtual reality of the stage whose consequences nonetheless cannot be escaped through any presumed "return to reality." As Gay Morris has noted: "Graham disrupted a linear, cause-and-effect kind of time in a way that differentiated itself from the usual mode of making dances."[60] John Gould notes that the Chorus of Greek tragedy is "the locus of an unresolvable tension between intense emotional involvement in, and exclusion from, tragic action: the chorus are both the prisoners and the passionately engaged witnesses of tragic experience."[61] In identifying Jocasta with the Chorus, Graham had them share an involvement in the action. But, it was a surrealist exclusion in that the action itself was presented as already in the past, and of the order of the dream.

Figure 4.1 May O'Donnell as the Chorus in *Cave of the Heart* (1946) with Yuriko, Erick Hawkins, and Martha Graham. Courtesy of the Martha Graham Dance Foundation Archive

Poetics of the Program Note

Morris focuses on Graham's use of program notes in the 1940s as an indication that her choreography was becoming increasingly narrative in that decade. Morris distinguishes *Night Journey*, however, from conventional narrative ballet because it disrupts a linear presentation of events: "Graham's use of time would have put *Night Journey* on the side of the vanguard as opposed to traditional methods of treating time and plot structure in the theatre."[62] *Night Journey* takes place in Jocasta's memory as in a dream where the characters from her life return to haunt her. "The dream can be her weakness," she wrote Schuman, "very beautiful and very tragic, I think."[63] Graham was successful in conveying this conceit largely thanks to Noguchi's set, which did not localize the action in a single representational space, thus contributing to a modernist aesthetic. All this, it should be noted, was clarified by the 1948 program note: "The action takes place in Jocasta's heart at the moment when she recognizes the ultimate terms of her destiny . . . The Daughters of the Night, Oedipus in his inescapable role, and the Seer pursue themselves across her heart in that instant of agony."[64] The idea is that time is compressed into an instant. The program note is not limited to a realist interpretation of the action, but it can and did clarify the choreographer's intention.

Program notes for Graham's domestic performances were symptomatic of her desire to reach a large audience. They became problematic in Asia, however, when the overly simplistic nature of the notes caused some audiences to find them patronizing. In a review of December 15, 1955, from a Rangoon newspaper during Graham's Asian tour, "We Understand Too" by Po Toke, the author takes a tongue-in-cheek approach to the program notes, which he finds both unnecessary and offensive: "If they had not told us over the loud speaker before the show started we wouldn't know what it was all about. As for me I listened carefully. So I knew the story. Once I knew the story I knew what the people of the stage were doing."[65] The reviewer then goes on to describe how the program note clarified his viewing of *Night Journey*:

> The last is a Greek play. I didn't remember the name of the king. He doesn't know his mother and marries her. First of all a blind man comes out with a staff. The queen is sitting on a funny looking couch. The dance is about her reflection on how she met and married her son. The king wears a slip like Tarzan and he tries to take off the shawl wrapped around his body. I think it depicts his attempt to answer the riddle of the sphinx. After that he pats a cloak around the queen and they walk about which means they are crowned as king and queen. The two of them pull a piece of string as if in a tug O'war. Then they get on to the

couch and tie one another. It means they are in conjugal marital bliss. At this time the blind man comes along, gets on the couch and kicks the string which tied them together. Both fall down. The king pierces his eyes and blinds himself. And when the blind man tells the queen that the king is her son she strangles herself with the string. The blind man then walks across the stage.[66]

This review implies that Graham's program notes were patronizing to Burmese audiences.

Although it is hard to generalize, Graham's program notes did not, in my view, so much glue American audiences to the narrative content, as they served the opposite purpose: they relieved the audience of the necessity to explain movements to themselves in narrative terms. Program notes put things clear in order to get beyond clarity. The disruptions of narrative time and the abstract decors induced the audience to observe movement not for the plot but for subjective resonances associated with Jocasta's dream state. Morris stresses the mimetic qualities of Graham's gesture, especially in her first solo where she covers her breasts and genital area with her hands and recoils in horror at the sight of the bed.[67] Graham's mimetic gesture, while it did carry clear meaning, was not pedestrian but highly histrionic—in a "'grand style." Graham was representing the modern dancer as tragedienne, but this was also in keeping with the idea that the deep psychological investigation tragedy contained was anthropological in that it belonged to a realm of universal behavior that salvaged myth from the depths of history. The flexed foot extended boldly in the air, the tense and hieratic bearing, the tragic fall to the floor take on new meaning in this "Greek" context as essential rather than merely as mimetic gestures. That is, they are brought back to the origin of tragedy in ritual even as they move the story forward with psychological connotations that are distinctly modern.

I would also argue that Graham's innovations in the telling of the story made mimetic gesture almost inevitable from a craft standpoint because gesture focuses audience attention on the myth itself, which risked disappearing amongst the modernist spatial and temporal uncertainties. Dance Critic Robert Sabin confided in Bertram Ross that he found the opening night of *Clytemnestra* "hair raising, too real, too personal."[68] One should not underestimate that Graham ran the risk of myth material appearing too personal. Inasmuch as the narrative is based on kinship roles, the Oedipus legend disrupts the conventional attributes of these roles: the mother is the wife, the husband is the son. The character compression and its monstrous consequences, already noted in *Appalachian Spring*, are achieved in *Night Journey* by virtue of the narrative itself. Hence, they are much more visible. To counteract this impression, modernist stage design evokes the archaic, and theatricality rejoins the essential origin of tragedy. But, what is proper to Graham's mythographic phase, and what most distinguishes it from the earlier dramaturgical phase, is the double role played by myth and ritual. I am not so much interested in the contrast between narrative and abstraction as in the ways that narrative and abstract devices work both to coordinate and disjoin myth and ritual. The mimetic presentation of the story and the ballet's function as a ritualized "showing" struck a precarious balance that lent the piece its particular energy.

Mythic roles, like dancing itself in Graham's terms, can be "superhuman"—divine—at the same time as they portray the devolution of human individual life into tragic consciousness. Mythic roles can either serve to embody personal experience without too much explanation (as in *Dark Meadow* and *Errand into the Maze*) or to retell a story with personal resonance (as in *Cave of the Heart* and *Night Journey*). Or, they can do both. Ted Hughes discusses myth as both "something fundamentally internal and subjective . . . a self-validating world," and as "a step-up transformer" in which the "private, subjective situation . . . has become the drama of a god or goddess."[69] It is this "double session" inherent to myth that Graham explores on multiple levels in *Night Journey*. Her manipulation of myth and ritual in this work is perhaps the most sophisticated of her oeuvre, and it is carried out through an intermeshing of present and past that has a marked psychological dimension. The action is staged as though it were taking place in the mind of Jocasta—that is, with all the affective charge that accompanies memory with its layers of regret and desire, in sum, as a very subjective impression of events. Despite this fact, because it is already part of the past, one senses that nothing Jocasta does in revisiting these events can in any way change or alter them. We perceive her agency as that of someone who foresees the future only because she is a ghostly presence in the past she relives. Consequently, through identification with Jocasta, the audience is induced to view the events of her life from an equally subjective perspective. In other terms, the audience is induced to free associate. The interplay of past and present—action and reminiscence (with the paradox that action is in the past and reminiscence in the present)—lends itself to the impression that *Night Journey* is a vast metaphor for psychological introspection in the service of private ritual.

"The secret of her scholarship," said Schuman, "is that it is never divorced from emotional urgency."[70] Ritual lends urgency to myth. Or, as Ben Belitt put it in discussing Graham's use of myth: "A myth is the enigmatizing of vision. What you are creating is an enigma as a mode of knowledge."[71] The enigmas Graham shared with her audiences incorporated personal secrets and rituals not available to them except as a spectacle from which they might retrieve and meditate on their own secrets. The personal as well as the political secret were both encrypted in Graham's works of the 1940s. Graham used myth not only as a step-up transformer, but also, and more importantly, as a step-*down* transformer.

The archetype is the hinge that connects but also crucially separates public myth and private ritual.

The View from the Sixties

Although this psychoanalytic-cum-mythic aura of Graham's work was defini-tive for its avant-gardism in the 1940s, David Vaughan challenged Graham's avant-garde laurels in a letter published in 1958 in *Dance Magazine*. Vaughan claimed Graham's choreography had relinquished a direct creative involvement with the body as primary material. The breaking point was *Clytemnestra* although Vaughan attempted to discredit Graham's work in general as purely psycholog-ical.[72] By the late 1950s Graham's interest in myth and the unconscious led to the accusation on the part of younger artists drawn to minimalism that her work had devolved into theatricalism.[73] "It is hardly possible to relate her work to anything outside of theatre," said Yvonne Rainer in 1966, "since it was usually dramatic and psychological necessity that determined it."[74] The twin charges of psychologism and theatricalism certainly exposed role-playing in 1940s and 1950s modern dance to scrutiny. "The problem with modern dance" returned to haunt Graham in the 1960s when her work looked all too legible and all too dramatic as well as all too emotional and, hence, excessively theatrical. But, this judgment was also erroneously applied to the 1940s. "By the mid-1940s," wrote Jill Johnston in 1968, "I imagine Graham was already a bit exhausted."[75] When alcoholism began to impede her ability to choreograph, Graham underwent a precipitous decline that began to show its effects with *Phaedra* in 1962. But her works of the 1940s and 1950s need not be viewed exclusively through this lens, but should also be considered from within their original aesthetic, and in their historical context.[76]

Vaughan's charge relies on a decidedly pejorative use of the term *theater* to indicate a pantomimic relation to movement. While this may have been the case with *Clytemnestra*, it was not applicable to her work of the 1940s. But, the charge against the amalgam of psychology and theater implies not only the existence of danced characters who behave and move according to a psychological logic, but also the exploration of personal affects based on private psychoanalytic experi-ence: "The atmosphere of the dances," in Gay Morris's gloss of Vaughan's cri-tique, "was reminiscent of what 'prevails in an analyst's consulting-room.'"[77] Even though Vaughan's assessment of Graham was not objective in that it advo-cated for Merce Cunningham's aesthetic turn, Vaughan was correct about the direct link between Graham's choreography and psychoanalysis.

It is worth speculating, however, that an unspoken link between dance and psychoanalysis may have simply gone underground in the 1960s. Rainer recently wrote: "[M]y performance for my shrink, with its concealments and confessions, can be likened to my performance of *Trio A*, which demands a comparable juggling of suppression, or censorship, and the exposure of energy investment and sexuality, no less than expression of self."[78] Rainer's statement on the relation of minimalist dance to psychoanalysis 44 years after Graham's decline hints that avant-garde innovation, when all is said and done, might have its own unspoken relationship to the consulting room.[79]

One cannot discuss evocations of the unconscious in choreography and communication at an unconscious level between performer and audience—with or without the use of mythical characters—if one does not accept that the artist's life and living play a significant role in the genesis of creative work. As Yuriko said: "All her work in some way she felt as a person, either experiencing or experienced by herself or someone else (a member of her company)."[80] It is appropriate and indeed necessary to bring biography into relation with the analysis of production work. I wish to stress, however, that my interest is neither in psychoanalyzing the choreographer nor in psychoanalyzing the choreographer's work in the hermeneutic tradition of psychoanalysis itself. My interest is to pinpoint how Graham's use of psychoanalytic theory coordinated—both suppressed and revealed in Rainer's terms—the relation between life and work. This is a biography of choreography.

Hawkins entered Graham's life before she had conceived the idea of the Greek cycle as a full-fledged project. She had experimented with the relation of dance to choral movement much earlier in *Dithyrambic* (1931) and *Tragic Patterns* (1933)—a work subtitled "Three Choric Dances for an Antique Greek Tragedy"—but when it came to Greek myth and culture, Graham the autodidact gained much from Hawkins the classics scholar.[81] Hawkins deepened the presence of myth in Graham's thinking, although she derived the psychoanalytic aspects of it from other sources. Both Graham and Hawkins knew the Cambridge School had been engaged since the 1890s with the cultural and archaeological aspects of ancient Greek ritual. They both read Jane Harrison religiously and must both have been compelled by the continuity of a project that had brought classical studies, particularly archaeology, into the sphere of comparative anthropology and modernism in the early twentieth century.[82] This was a first step in the realization that myth could be (re)lived, which is a particularly modern concept.[83] Also to be found in Harrison was the chthonic focus of Greek culture so often referred to by critics of Graham's work. Mary Beard writes of Harrison:

> Her view that ritual must always come first, that the *things done* have precedence over the *things said*, has had a complicated afterlife ... But the basic message of her work—that somewhere underneath the calm, shining, rational exterior of the classical world is a mass of weird,

seething irrationality—is a tenet that almost everyone working in the history of Greek culture would now take for granted.[84]

Through these studies Graham realized the potential of myth as a vehicle with which to express contemporary experience, although her work may not have been systematic enough for Campbell's taste. "Joe (Campbell) never felt," remembers Erdman, "that she treated them [the stories] mythologically. What she did was to enact the stories, the myths themselves . . . It wasn't so much mythological as human . . . "[85] Hawkins, who continued to be inspired by mythology after his association with Graham, also felt that her use of myth was overpersonalized. He later differentiated his own choreographic use of myth from that of Graham: "I was using generic Greek mythic ideas in their generic terms and not translating them into personal experience . . . "[86] In the 1950s as his own work became a meditation on poetic-philosophical concepts Hawkins rejected the link between myth and psychoanalysis.[87] His work became increasingly abstract, and he considered it to be poetic as distinguished from Graham's, which he considered psychological. Hawkins was in the process of separating myth from psychology. One can detect here the beginnings of the notion that Graham's work was dominated by psychology, an idea that took hold in the 1960s. It is in some sense a curious distinction since the genesis of her work was so related to literary, and especially to poetic, texts. In any case, both artists were deeply involved throughout the 1940s in modern and ancient literature, and in psychological theory and psychoanalysis.

James Frazer's *The Golden Bough* was as influential on Graham as it had been on Joyce and Eliot.[88] In her literary biography of Ezra Pound and H.D., Helen Carr wrote that Frazer gave those artists "new metaphors by which to frame their art, and from which to form a very specifically modernist aesthetics."[89] Perhaps Frazer's most marked influence on Graham is to be found in the recurrent theme of a ritual of rebirth. One can imagine the combined impact of Frazer and Harrison on Graham and Hawkins. Harrison insisted on the irrational side of Greek ritual and the female principle in early Greek culture, ideas that would be carried forward into the mid-twentieth century by Jungians such as M. Esther Harding in *Women's Mysteries* (1935). But perhaps more important than Frazer's themes was his emphasis on a natural cycle of death and rebirth that suggested a two-tiered spatial topology of the visible and the invisible, of what lies above the ground and what lies below it. Graham's innovative use of the floor (known as floor work) in her technique has often been interpreted as an expression of succumbing to gravity in the humanistic (and anti-balletic) sense—e.g., accepting one's humanity as gravity bound. But it could equally well be considered as a quasi-religious recognition of what lies beneath the earth and a dialogue with that fearsome hidden space. This might be the chthonic and tellurian aspect of her work that fit well with her interest in ritual and Greek sources. Hawkins related that Graham had a phobia about traveling underground and refused to use the New York subway. I am proposing that Graham's use of the floor be considered more for its mythological than for its uniquely realist and humanist connotations. As in the myth of Demeter and Kore (Persephone), there is always the above and the below, the primary visual surface and the world beneath acting as a force field.

It is also from Frazer that Graham may have derived the notion of the crypt and encryption. She was to transform the sense of what lies hidden beneath the earth into a dramaturgy where actions, positions, and attitudes infer an invisible opposite or complement. Henri Lefebvre's idea of absolute space—if transferred to a logic of the stage—captures the idea of what Graham was after because it points to the presence of both the visible and the invisible: "[A]bsolute space condenses, harbours (at any rate seems to harbour) all the diffuse forces in play.... Absolute space is thus also and above all the space of death, the space of death's absolute power over the living...."[90] This awareness of plural spaces of action brought with it the psychological complexity of what is hidden beneath the surface, which is also a metaphor for the unconscious. The dead and the unconscious are seen to commune when the past reinhabits the present, as in *American Document* and *Appalachian Spring*. But, it also finds an analogy in one of Graham's technical and expressive innovations: the contraction and release. When the dancer contracts the concavity of the spine creates the feeling in him or herself and for the observer of retreating beneath or below or into the body's surface structure; the release, on the other hand, reasserts that structure by stretching it outward into space toward its corporeal limits. Absolute space is also structurally present in the antinomy between the desert and the city—two landscapes of importance to Graham's life and work. Although she lived and worked in the urban environment of New York City, a needed contrast was provided by the desert landscape around Santa Fe where she sought rejuvenation beginning in 1937 at the invitation of Merle Armitage, and later, at the home of Cady Wells, a painter to whom Armitage had introduced her.[91] It was also in the desert that she had her most harmonious moments with Hawkins on a camping trip in 1939.[92] This geographic polarity corresponds to what musicologist Nadine Hubbs refers to in Copland's work as the "pastoral and urban industrial."[93]

Frazer also made possible for Joyce, in Eliot's estimation, "the mythical method." Eliot understood the mythical method as "a continuous parallel between contemporaneity and antiquity," which was "... a way of controlling, or ordering, of giving a shape and significance to the immense panorama of futility and anarchy which is contemporary history."[94] As Eliot also indicates, it is psychology that allows for myth, archaeology, and ethnology to coalesce in modernist art.[95] He opposes the mythical method to narrative: "Instead of narrative method, we may now use the mythical method." From Eliot's classicizing modernist perspective, myth and narrative were hardly compatible. There is no doubt that by 1946 Graham was employing her own version of the mythical method as pioneered by Yeats, Joyce, and Eliot. Psychology was the glue that held myth, archaeology, and anthropology together as modern dance. If we are to reassess Graham's work from within its own intellectual and historical context, neither narrative nor truth can be considered the operative terms. Yet, these are exactly the terms with which her work has been attacked and foreclosed since the 1960s.

Johann Bachofen's discussion of mother right—*Das Mutterrecht* (1861)— contained a sociohistorical insight that influenced Graham, and was certainly transmitted to her through Fromm, who wrote "The Theory of Mother Right and its Relevance for Social Psychology" in 1934.[96] Fromm's reworking of Freud's interpretation of the Oedipus legend in the light of Bachofen maintained that " . . . [T]he hostility between father and son, which is the theme running through Sophocles's trilogy, is to be understood as an attack against the victorious patriarchal order by the representatives of the defeated matriarchal system."[97] This amounts to a rereading of Oedipal conflict in which the son's desire for the mother signals his identification with her instead of his competition with the father. This is the theory that underwrites the ascendance of Jocasta as the pivotal figure of the Oedipus legend. Anthropologist Bronislaw Malinowski had discussed mother right as early as 1924 in terms of a historical-sociological advance over the Oedipus complex.[98] According to Malinowski's Biographer Michael W. Young "the family theory of the origin of human society was challenged."[99] When anthropology recognized the cultural relativism introduced by the mother right theory, the Oedipus complex could no longer be held up as universally valid.

The influence of Bachofen seems to have been present as early as the 1930 solo *Lamentation* in which the solo figure suggests Demeter the Mother, whose mourning induces the barrenness of the earth. The lateral pulls of Graham's body enhanced by the stretch of the tubular costume emulate the horizontal expanses of the earth by contrast with her reach down through the fabric as if to the underworld where Persephone resides. *Lamentation* introduces the relation of mother to daughter in Graham's choreography quite early. I shall claim that this relation was more fundamental to Graham's philosophy than the fate of solitude. Bachofen also seems present in Graham's "Mothers of the Hungry Dead and Living" toward the end of *American Document*. These are indications that the contested category of Graham's feminism might be better understood with respect to the anthropological, and sociological rediscovery of mother right as a contemporary phenomenon that was destabilizing for Freudian psychoanalytic theory.[100] But, it is only with Graham's myth works of the second half of the 1940s that she gets to the heart of the matter.

Bachofen situates mother right in an Orientalist context: "[T]he first great encounter between the Asiatic and Greek worlds is represented as a struggle between the hetaerism of Aphrodite and the conjugal principle of Hera."[101] He also posits "the relation between matriarchy and hetaerism" as the archaic precursor to "the progress from matriarchy to the patriarchal system."[102] The use made of Eastern influences by female soloists of historical modern dance in the early twentieth century is echoed in the 1940s by what some scholars refer to as Graham's feminism.[103] The Asia-Greece binary is structural and, hence, productive of (dramatic) conflict. Graham injected the mother right complex into the presentation of space, and thus created a subtle visual tension between metaphors for Asia and Greece in particular characters and/or situations. It was this ability to realize literary, anthropological, and psychoanalytic discourses visually and spatially—thanks in large part to Noguchi's contribution—that made Graham's work of the mid- to late 1940s appear daring and attractively perverse. When this conflict became embodied in one person—Jocasta who is both mother and wife of her son—it allowed Graham to psychologize patterns of early twentieth-century modern dance in the postwar era.

Preludes to *Night Journey*

Frederick Hawkins is listed as acting the role of Tiresias in *The Antigone of Sophocles* on Friday, November 21, 1924, at the Northeast High School Auditorium, in Kansas City, Missouri. In May 1941 Hawkins coached actors in *Oedipus Tyrannus*, with choral score by Virgil Thomson, at Fordham University Theater, New York City. It is as if he were preparing for an Oedipus ballet since childhood. In 1947 he originated the role of Oedipus in Graham's *Night Journey*. It is lesser known that he also choreographed and danced Oedipus in *The Strangler*, a ballet he presented on a mixed bill in August 1948 alongside Graham's premiere of *Wilderness Stair* (later titled *Diversion of Angels*) in New London, Connecticut.[104] Hawkins wrote Copland: "Martha and I unbeknownst to each other were working on an Oedipus." This ignorance seems implausible given that Hawkins himself could have been in rehearsal for *Night Journey* in late 1946 or early 1947.

Graham began preparations for *Night Journey* in 1946. She wrote William Schuman on August 30, 1946, that she was working on the script, which she then sent him on October 28, 1946. The script, which to my knowledge has never before been discussed, was included in the letter on eight numbered typewritten pages.[105] Graham's basic idea for *Night Journey* was worked out, at least on paper, between August and October 1946, right after the premiere of *Dark Meadow*, and well before *Cave of the Heart* and *Errand into the Maze*. It is striking how closely together these works were choreographed but also how nonsequential they were in their development, a situation that almost places them in the sort of psychic space-time that the works themselves depict. Eight months after the *Night Journey* script was sent to Schuman, it premiered in Cambridge. In the very midst of writing the libretto—to be precise, on September 21, 1946—Hawkins announced to Graham that he was leaving her. Her changing relation to the younger Hawkins had to influence Graham's vision of Jocasta in relation to Oedipus. Their personal separation lasted approximately one year, during which time they continued working together. It was during this separation that he choreographed *Stephen Acrobat*, and left behind his Americana solos of the early 1940s.

After *Stephen Acrobat*, and once he returned to Graham, Hawkins took on *The Strangler* of which he wrote to Copland: "My piece is like a fore-piece to Martha's, being Oedipus as a young man before the Sphinx. It is really a rite of initiation into manhood."[106] The purpose of his letter to Copland was to request an original score for a projected ballet on Melville's *Moby Dick* in which Hawkins would portray Ahab. Copland demurred because he did not think Melville's novel was in the realm of possibility from a musical perspective, especially for a small instrumental ensemble of the sort Graham was using. Hawkins was thinking of large-scale psychological portraits of male figures à la Graham. The future would show this was not really his cup of tea, but his image of himself at this time was conceived very much in her terms. Whereas she had used him effectively as a foil for her own persona, he wanted to become a male version of that persona without a foil. Both Graham and Hawkins conceived of Oedipus projects in ways directly relevant to their life at that time: Graham needed to contemplate the raison d'être of why she had become involved with Hawkins; Hawkins needed to free himself from Graham in order to assert his artistic independence.

Ethel Winter said that in 1946 "when he [Erick] came back, it was obvious that she gave in to helping him with his own choreography and really pushing him."[107] However, he never asked Graham to dance in his own choreography, nor did she ever advise him on it. An unprecedented satellite group of the Graham Company (Erick Hawkins, Ethel Winter, and Stuart Hodes) toured the Midwest in 1947 with a repertory of Hawkins and Graham works. This was an effort on Graham's part to share the Company with Hawkins, and to lend her imprimatur to Hawkins as a choreographer and a dancer. Isadora Bennett's press copy announced a "new type of streamlined company . . . which carries its own technicians, numbers six with Stuart Gescheidt (Hodes) and Ethel Winter in important supporting assignments."[108] With the repertory of Graham's *Salem Shore*, and *El Penitente* alongside Hawkins's own choreography of *Stephen Acrobat*, and *John Brown*, among other of Hawkins's works, the satellite group toured Illinois, Ohio, Indiana, Iowa, Kansas, Nebraska, and Louisiana. In New York, Graham presented Hawkins's choreography on her programs. Reviews of his work were, with the exception of *John Brown*, generally poor. As he himself admitted, he was finding himself then, but he was proud that his work was never judged to resemble hers. Despite these difficulties, Hawkins remained extremely keen on establishing his own identity as a choreographer. On March 29, 1949, Hawkins wrote William Schuman that he was planning to turn the satellite group into an independent company showing his own work:

> Because of my future plans of touring in my own concerts on a different scale from Martha's company . . . I am pretty desperate at this moment since I have let myself be frustrated so long from proceeding to get out my ideas. My success on this past short tour has encouraged me very much and the time is ripe for me to move fast.[109]

Complete artistic autonomy, however, would only take place once Hawkins and Graham severed their personal relationship.

Jocasta

"Mythology is actuality, as we now know."
—H.D.[110]

Night Journey begins with the dramatic premise of Jocasta looking back on her life at the moment before the decision to commit suicide, through which act she atones for her incestuous relationship with her son, Oedipus, whose children she has borne. In the *Notebooks* Graham calls it: "a seeing as in retrospect her past—a reenactment of her life . . ."[111] Seeing and reenactment constitute the fulcrum on which the work's dramaturgy is structured. The entire work is suspended within this psychic loop between memory and action, contemplation and decision. It begins with Jocasta alone on stage holding a length of rope above her head with which she will ultimately hang herself, although the action she will perform at the work's end is more precisely that of strangulation (a point that shall have its significance): she will twist the rope about her neck and subside backward to the ground. The substitution of strangulation for hanging is noteworthy for suggesting a connection between Jocasta and the Sphinx—the Strangler.

Graham stands at the center of the action from beginning to end, and the action is itself presented as her own memory of events. She lives through them again as she contemplates them for the last time. But, there is always an ambiguity between living and contemplating that lends all the other characters the quality of being phantoms. *Night Journey* transpires as an internal monologue in which all the characters are projections of Jocasta's psychic activity, figments of her imagination, as in a dream. In the libretto she notes: "This is what might be imagined as occurring in JOCASTA'S heart when, behind the door of her room, she faces her death."[112] Ethel Winter referred to "the piece of gauze lit upstage like a window" as "the only thing light on the stage," reminding us that Jocasta is in her bedroom, or in "a space reminiscent of a room where love has been lived."[113]

As Jocasta contemplates the rope, instrument of her own suicide—twisting from the upper torso as if already dangling in its noose—the blind Seer Tiresias enters from the opposite side of the stage, and travels a long diagonal toward her using a staff carefully tapped on the ground to guide each deliberate step. As he comes nearer to her, he extends his staff in the air to lift the rope from off her hands, much as he will do later when he disengages Oedipus and Jocasta from their entanglement in the rope, which has become the symbol of their ill-fated wedlock [Figure 4.2]. Throughout *Night Journey*, gestures are repeated with varying meanings: props and objects have what one could call a polymorphous perverse relation to meaning. As the Seer ultimately lifts the tangled rope from the erotically engaged bodies to send them falling away from each other to the floor, he might almost be the missing father/husband of this triangle—Laius. The Seer's ghostliness is underlined in the way he later repeats his diagonal path across the stage after Jocasta's death, this time beating his staff into the ground more strongly as a haunting memory. Tiresias almost seems to be Laius's Erinyes as defined by Jane Harrison: ". . . vengeful souls of murdered men."[114] Tiresias is not present in the original libretto, but the role of the Oracle was initially to be cast as a woman.

Tiresias's first intervention with the rope triggers Jocasta's journey into memory as the stage action itself becomes a symbolic return to the past. The Chorus enters precipitously, relegating Tiresias to the background. They rush in and freeze in place. In her notes Graham refers to "Women standing silently like granite on stage."[115] Ethel Winter spoke to me of the two-dimensional style of the Chorus, which reminded her of Indonesian shadow puppets. Because of the twist in the upper body there is a pull through the shoulders in two opposite directions that she called "going and leaving."[116] "You are in the center" of this pull. As Winter explained, the Chorus always foresees what is about to happen. Like the energy of the choric shoulders pulled in two opposite directions simultaneously, time itself in *Night Journey* expands in two directions: In the same instant in time, Jocasta reminisces as the Chorus foretells.

Graham's Jocasta is someone who, by looking back at past events already sees the future in that past. That is, she lives and relives simultaneously. Jocasta is both the subject of a memory projection to be seen by the audience and a real presence *re*living those very events as they are enacted before us. Hence

Figure 4.2 Mark Ryder as Tiresias, with Martha Graham and Erick Hawkins in *Night Journey* (1948). Courtesy of the Martha Graham Dance Foundation Archive

her retrospection has the effect of increasing the consciousness of tragedy in the very replaying of events. The Chorus is an extension of Jocasta in precisely the sense that she herself relives events even as she foretells by remembering. Jocasta is at the center of the drama in more ways than one, and her knowledge thus outpaces that of Oedipus. The long agonizing coming to realization of Oedipus is not part of this work. *Night Journey* is not the drama of Oedipus's search for the truth ending in self-blinding; it is the drama of Jocasta's abiding possession of knowledge as the contemplation of the coming catastrophe. According to Graham's original conception: "When she dances it is in full tragedy because the truth is known to her and to all. She faces the trap sequences have laid for her and she faces her memories in all their beauty and bitterness."[117] In light of these words, Hawkins's preoccupation with the tragedy of Oedipus seems misplaced. "When you have true tragedy then is when Oedipus has torn out his eyes. He says: 'Now I see.' He had to convey that very exactly in the work, if that's what you're going to say."[118] This concern for the meaning of Oedipus's blindness on Hawkins's part may be the reason for the literal image of the eye that was used at the moment of his blinding in the first performance, but was later cut. Margaret Lloyd reported the presence of "a large, surrealistic pasteboard eye with heavily fringed lids, a pale blue pupil on one side, a red one on the reverse, which Oedipus carried about at the end to tell us what we all knew."[119] Hawkins did not share Graham's enthusiasm for Mother Right. But, he was ideally cast as Oedipus precisely because he was blind to this difference.

The paradox of Oedipus seeing the truth only once blinded is secondary to the paradox of Jocasta who experiences and understands simultaneously. The dynamism of the moment is captured at the center of this double direction—a backward and forward pull—that Jocasta epitomizes. As Schuman expressed it: "That is the thing that goes through all the work: 'at that moment.' A moment. She is a woman who captures a moment."[120] Schuman's very accurate perception chimes with Joseph Frank's study of the importance of spatial form to imagism: "All these writers [Eliot, Pound, Proust, and Joyce] ideally intend the reader to apprehend their work spatially, in a moment of time, rather than as a sequence."[121] Graham's very conception of time lends itself to spatial representation and hence is ideally suited to choreography that reveals the hidden in the visible. Although Schuman spoke from a direct working knowledge of Graham, his words also echo Ernst Cassirer's characterization of myth as timeless:

> Whatever duration may be imputed to it [myth], can only be regarded
> as a moment, i.e. as time in which the end is like the beginning and the
> beginning like the end, a kind of eternity . . . [122]

More significant to Graham's dramaturgy than myth as story—*mythos*—was the peculiar relation of mythic experience itself to spatiality. Graham's emphasis on the character played as persona fit well with Ezra Pound's poetic interest in "moments of being" enacted through historical or legendary characters without plot (the plot was boring).[123] As Joseph Frank characterized Pound's concept of Imagism: "[An] image is defined not as a pictorial reproduction but as a unification of disparate ideas and emotions into a complex presented spatially in an instant of time."[124]

Myth was more than just a narrative premise: it enabled the reliving of a "psychological moment" that is definitive of the persona. Large chunks of the plot are simply excised. The focus of narrative temporality gives way to performative spatiality: mythic choreography condenses time into space. The dancer steps, as it were, outside of time to become the mythical figure, but that very figure condenses itself into a time that has no continuum but is all self-contemplation. Cassirer said: "It is no mere play that the dancer in a mythical drama is enacting: the dancer *is* the god, he *becomes* the god."[125] Graham fulfills this dictum by creating what Pound called "moments of being." More formally pertinent than the status of myth as story was its relation to temporality, which Pound also referred to as the "delicate pause of life." Myth allowed for a reliving of a psychological moment through which the artist's self could be expressed as a mythological persona. Graham theatricalized these literary concepts to the point where they no longer seemed literary, but fundamentally choreographic. In this sense, her faithfulness to Anglo-American modernism was also, and more significantly, an extension of its ideas into a dimension it had not known, or had only begun to probe in Yeats's theatrical experiments with Ito.

The moment of choice was dramatically and kinesthetically rendered in *Night Journey* as a tension between two opposing forces: the past and the future. This is a more visceral paradox than that of Tiresias's seeing blindness, or later, of Oedipus's. Schuman reports Graham gave him this assignment in writing the score: "Can you imagine Jocasta first realizing that she is lover and mother? What does this mean in music?"[126] This realization is seen, heard, and consciously realized all at once. The simultaneous and contradictory registers of time and experience are rendered by the score's dissonance, which supports a dramaturgy of condensation in and of the moment. The Chorus holds what Yeats referred to as "the branches of suppliants" when, at the start of his adaptation of the play, the city of Thebes seeks an answer to the plague "[w]hile the city smokes with incense and murmurs with prayer and lamentation."[127] The presence of the branches places the beginning of *Night Journey* in a contradictory present: both the moment before the entrance of Oedipus into Thebes after his triumph over the Sphinx and the moment when the plague besets Thebes and leads to discovery of the true identity of King Oedipus. Jocasta will hold the branches in their courtship duet, thus also suggesting how the end is prefigured in the beginning. Again, the situation of Jocasta itself is conceived as not only a crossfire of temporalities, but as a subjectivity caught within two contrary vectors of energy.

Jocasta's first solo is of "a woman besieged by memories," but who resists them. "Up to this point it has been tragic but with the quality of the tale told. No conflict takes place. Even the dance of JOCASTA has an element of the poetic telling about it."[128] In the script Jocasta is first seen as a 'poetic' teller, which is the level Graham identifies with what she called "actuality." As the dance was actually staged, however, there was nothing remote about Jocasta once she began to move. As Doris Hering remarked in 1948 of Graham's opening moments: "Jocasta . . . lunges desperately one way then another like some frantic caged creature who knows there is no escape, yet seeks it almost as a reflex."[129] Once the tale is no longer told, but relived, the actuality of the world gives way to the dream-like quality of reexperiencing: memory becomes indistinguishable from dream. Memory, in this way, supports the idea of showing, which Graham always preferred to telling. Yet, showing also gains a memorial dimension here:

> When she fell and entered the condition of dream the movement of the bodies should have another quality. There comes the realm of MEMORY with its exaggerations, its distortions. Incidents and movements telescope into each other. Nothing is too strange because it has the irrational logic of a dream.[130]

Although the script was written prior to working out the choreography in the studio, much of it faithfully reflects the dance as it was performed. Graham's mimetic movements at the start of the work are in the service of the telling she wished the audience to differentiate from the phantasmagoric dream of memory that would follow. Once having entered the realm of memory, however, there is not only temporal distortion, but "the irrational logic of a dream."

One critic favorably inclined to Graham's work nonetheless commented in *Dance Observer* on the unreal quality of the stage action as merely a reflection of her superior strength as a performer:

> So expressive in their violence, so provocative in their implication, so moving in their emotional content are these expressions of Jocasta's realization, that Miss Graham indicates she might easily be able to tell the entire story without benefit of the actual appearance of Oedipus, or the Seer, or the Daughters of the Night. Actually these figures become little more than objects which are related to Jocasta's life. Only her character becomes truly convincing choreographically.[131]

While it is possible that the dancers had not yet found themselves in their roles at the premiere, this description seems to underline Graham's artistic intent in foregrounding herself as the subject of memory. This tends to render the choreographic space abstract with relation to the events of the narrative, whether told or shown.

What Graham calls "the realm of Memory" in which Jocasta's past is reenacted begins through a kind of flashback that shows the triumphant entrance of Oedipus into Thebes [Figure 4.3]. He walks up a series of what Noguchi calls "stepping objects . . . a kind of architecture you walk over." "Architecture," further specifies Noguchi, "turns out to be a symbol of imperialism for the conquering hero, Oedipus."[132] It is with Oedipus that Jocasta's double consciousness becomes evident: she is simultaneously inside and outside of the dreamed memory that is her own past. From her position outside she realizes the reality of the relationship she is living to be impossible. The past, even as it is being relived in the virtual present of performance, is only available in/as a mournful recollection.

These events are depicted to the exclusion of Oedipus's encounter with Laius at the crossroads and his encounter with the Sphinx. *The Odyssey*, as Graham probably knew, contains a precedent for the Oedipus myth as Jocasta's story:

> He [Oedipus] took the prize
> from a slain father; presently the gods
> brought all to light that made the famous story.
> But, by their fearsome wills he kept his throne
> In dearest Thebes, all through his evil days,
> While she descended to the place of Death,
> God of the locked and iron door. Steep down
> From a high rafter, throttled in her noose,
> She swung, carried away by pain, and left him
> Endless agony from a mother's Furies.[133]

Figure 4.3 Hawkins's entrance as Oedipus in *Night Journey* (1948) (Pearl Lang in foreground) Courtesy of the Music Division, Library of Congress

For Homer, Jocasta assumes all the guilt. For, after her suicide, Oedipus continues to rule. In order for Graham to place Jocasta at the center of the action as the tragic protagonist, it did not suffice merely to eliminate Laius and the Sphinx. It was above all important that Jocasta assume the guilt for the relationship with Oedipus—that is, that she assume the tragic consciousness of her own responsibility for the relationship. This also means that she acknowledges her own desire as engine of the tragedy. Graham's personal and encrypted ritual in *Night Journey* was to weigh her own guilt for the relationship with Hawkins, and for its failure. But, in more positive terms, the fault also means the acceptance of the burden of choice. Jocasta is at the center of *Night Journey* because she acknowledges her own choices. Part of this recognition entails an acceptance of her own destructive agency: her hetaerism. She realized the necessity for this in 1946 when they first separated, and she relived it a second time—as anticipation—during the actual making and first performances of *Night Journey* in 1947. As she wrote to Hawkins after their final separation in 1950, "I realize that I lost my life by my own means and that I must recognize the fact."[134]

Autobiographical Rite

To understand *Night Journey* as a ritualized form of coming to terms with personal guilt for personal loss—in itself arguably a heroic quality—might remain purely conjectural without seeking Graham's own understanding of the relationship's failure. In a letter to Hawkins of September 3, 1950, Graham analyzed her own role in the relationship's failure and took responsibility for it:

> This goes back, I believe to the matter of age. . . . I was born May 11, 1894. That makes a great gap between us. . . . The only way I knew to work was through myself and I made of myself a kind of goddess with the fetish of my power of youth, the changelessness I wanted. I was curious in that I preached life and talked of life and yet in some inner way I refused to recognize the laws of life. That growth in all its phases is life, not a static revelation of some individual being . . . I had built up the attitude from a time I could not remember and cannot now that I was an instrument of God, or creative force, and was being used by that and that was my function. In so doing I lost sight of reality. I wanted to be the Deathless One and there is no way to be that except through others when the time comes. In some strange way it is like an animal eating its young.[135]

Graham's self-analysis in this letter is an avowal of her own narcissism. She also pinpoints the role played by their age difference in the relationship's difficulties.

And, she impugns her own fixation on the power of the dancer as "death-less"—outside of time—which had led to a misguided belief in her own immortality. Needless to say, others reinforced this belief by considering her a goddess.

Graham's words here are key to understanding the myth of Oedipus and Jocasta in *Night Journey* as an autobiographical rite. As Hawkins himself wrote in a 1947 article, borrowing from the poet Louise Bogan: "It is the rite which enables the individual to participate in the myth. The myth can be lived only through the rite."[136] Hawkins did not specify what he meant by *rite* beyond the fact that it was the "theatrical embodiment" of myth, but he did add that ". . . men need symbols of integration in the inner drama (life) today more than ever."[137] I would take him to mean that the individual dancer's rite, because it remains private, is offered to the audience as a *symbol* with which to construct their own personal rite—one unique to each audience member and also surely nonidentical with that of the choreographer and the dancers. Hawkins was later to think of ritual as metaphysical, and shared as a revelation by both the dancer and the audience in equal measure. But this was not Graham's concept. For her, audience and performer participate in rites of an essentially different, even incommensurable, nature. The presence of myth resolves them into one performative ritual. In this way, the term *rite* acquires psychodramatic connotations for Graham. The social function of performance would be to bring myth and ritual together, to allow them to coexist in the shared social space of the theater. That Graham and Hawkins were thinking in these terms appears to be confirmed by the libretto: "I use this name for her [Jocasta] at this time but if I can avoid using it on the program I should like to because it confuses people who are looking for aspects of the play action."[138] The term symbol, as Hawkins uses it, indicates a threshold between autobiography and cultural pattern, or perhaps more pertinently, a transformer. Encryption presupposes a double session within one work that relies on the interplay between two scores: the myth as symbol unleashes the performer's rite, but also unleashes the separate rite of each audience member.[139] These rites are paradoxically sealed off from each other—private—although they exist in spatial proximity.

The Question of Incest

Fiona Macintosh has noted of *Night Journey* "its un-Sophoclean insistence upon the erotic nature of the incestuous encounter between mother and son, and its concern with the act of incest to the exclusion of parricide."[140] Why Graham chose to work on the incest theme in the first place is a question seldom, if ever, asked. The original critical reception of *Night Journey* was more cognizant of the incest theme than later reactions to the work. At the premiere, Walter Terry wrote: "Her [Graham's] characterization is a compelling one which generates sympathy because of its honesty and which, at times, almost evokes a feeling of disgust because of its unglossed presentation of human passion."[141] This sense of disgust and perversity in the original critical reaction to *Night Journey* was undoubtedly much stronger in 1947 than it is today.

Psychoanalysis explains disgust before the representation of incestuous relations as a symptom of the repression of the unconscious urges associated with incest. But, according to Otto Rank, the artist is unique in being able to unlock this repressed material and allow the unconscious some relief from lifelong repression. This is precisely, for Rank, the social function of the artist and why the artist's engagement with incest is a socially positive force. Freud himself noted that the play *Oedipus Rex* "can be likened to the work of a psychoanalysis" because it deals with repression and the lifting of repression.[142] As Sally Banes remarked, Graham on Noguchi's bed resembles "nothing so much as a psychoanalytic patient on the couch, ready to delve into the depths of the unconscious in order to dredge up painful, ancient buried memories. The reference to the popularity of Freudian and Jungian psychoanalysis in the 1940s is unmistakable."[143] [Figure 4.4].

Figure 4.4 Graham as Jocasta in *Night Journey* (1948). Courtesy of the Martha Graham Dance Foundation Archive

Dance scholars have since debated whether *Night Journey* is Freudian or Jungian. The question of Freud versus Jung may hinge upon whether Graham presented the Oedipus complex as universally valid, since Jung broke with Freud because the former rejected the foundational validity of the sexual drives. "What I seek," wrote Jung, "is to set bounds to the rampant terminology of sex which threatens to vitiate all discussion of the human psyche; I wish to put sexuality itself in its proper place."[144] The hallmark of *Night Journey* for Banes was sex: "All they have together is sex—on the floor, in bed, walking, and indeed, wherever and whenever they can."[145] This emphasis placed on sex in the choreography by Banes would seem to make her interpretation of *Night Journey* Freudian. The title, however, was probably suggested by Jung's "night sea journey," a phrase he attributes to Frobenius in *The Psychology of the Unconscious*.[146] Graham, for her part, was reading Esther Harding's *Psychic Energy*, first published in 1947, which elaborates on the night sea journey. In *Psychic Energy* it becomes clear that Jocasta's tragic end is a requirement of the myth of Oedipus, but not of the night sea journey concept itself, which is one of rebirth.

> . . . Jonah's sojourn in the belly of the whale can be taken as representing not only Christ's descent to the underworld in the days between the crucifixion and the resurrection, but also the night sea journey that is an almost constant feature of the hero ordeal, as Frobenius clearly demonstrated.[147]

It is the unconscious status of incest that allies the night sea journey with a story of compulsive desire, but the end of the journey is liberation from such desire. Graham signified this rebirth by disrobing and thus essentially changing garments symbolic of different psychic states before the end. A process of transformation was indicated at the end of *Night Journey* even though this process was completed by her suicide. Graham was interested, however, in the ambivalences of transformation, which is why she placed the crux of *Clytemnestra* in the question "why?": ". . . I go dishonored among . . . the dead . . . And yet, I suffered, too . . . It is the eternal question we ask in face of what appears to be punishment . . . "WHY?" . . . "[148] This is also why Graham experimented in her next solo, *Judith*, with garments as states of transformation: "The dresses which constitute the garments for the various parts will be on the stage arranged as part of the scene itself. They will be in color and will be replaced as I see it when she finished with them as though they were to wait to be worn again by some one else."[149] Graham also used this theatrical device effectively at the end of *Seraphic Dialogue*. When Saint Joan becomes beatified she enters in a different dress.

Neither Freud nor Jung, But Rank

Graham's knowledge of Jung is certainly better documented than is her knowledge of Freud, notwithstanding the latter's pervasive cultural influence making it unlikely that any modern artist in the West could have avoided him.[150] Thanks to Freud, the tragedy of Oedipus claims pride of place for its theoretical importance to the psychoanalytic movement. Sophocles's tragedy combines the quest for truth as a metaphor of psychological introspection with a myth that became "the touchstone of psychoanalytic truth."[151] Of Oedipus himself, Otto Rank said: "He knows that he will do so, but he does so without knowing it. There is no more instructive example of the effects of unconscious forces and of repression."[152] The gradual discovery of the truth—*recognition* in Aristotle's terms[153]—is tantamount to the desublimation of unconscious desires that otherwise only surface in dream images. For these reasons, *Night Journey* can be aligned with Freud. The Freud-Jung alternative, however, may be a distraction from more crucial issues. The more important question is how Graham shifts the importance of the Oedipal relationship from the father to the mother. And, the relation of the Sphinx to both Oedipus and Jocasta— something never discussed in the context of Graham—is one key to the important shift in Freudian theory associated with Rank, Reik, and Fromm.[154] As we shall see, the Sphinx has a place in the thinking of both Graham and Hawkins on *Night Journey*. My position is that *Night Journey* is, first of all, neither Freudian nor Jungian, but Rankean, in that it is Rank who allows for theater and, by extension, dance, to accomplish the social equivalent of dream work.

Graham purposely situates *Night Journey* between theater and dream in order, I would argue, to suggest the possibility of desublimation for the audience, and thus to ensure the dance reads as psychoanalytically fraught. Graham's manipulation of the dream state is in no way an indulgence of the irrational. As Rank observed: "the reference of creation to the unconscious, if nothing else, is a conscious act."[155] In fact, just as Freud said that *Oedipus* is like an analysis, Graham fashioned the choreography of *Night Journey* itself as an analysis for, and of, the spectator. In *The Incest Theme in Literature and Legend* Rank claims that art, and particularly theater, can fulfill the social function of desublimation of unconscious desires otherwise only to be noticed in dreams. If the author, particularly the playwright in Rank's discussion, can render his own incest fantasy in sufficiently universal terms, s/he endows theater with "social value."[156] The incest theme as it surfaces in theater has, for Rank, a social and therapeutic value. He links theater with what I would call social dream-work. One could say that theater for Rank, and by extension dance, is a form of social dreaming that temporarily suspends repression.

The fact that *Night Journey* is dance and not theater made it closer in 1947 to the unspeakable subject of incest, and it could evoke disgust all the more readily because it was the danced adaptation of a play. In drama critic Eric Bentley's 1953 essay on Graham he said: ". . . dance is of itself more primitive than literature or opera."[157] Bentley's perception gives us a hint of how Graham's mythic narratives were seen in the late 1940s and early 1950s to bypass the conventional trappings of theatrical narrative even as they conveyed stories. Graham's retelling of Greek myth, especially in *Cave of the Heart* and *Night Journey*, suggested the origins of Greek tragedy. That is, the narrative was secondary to the perception that dance offered us the essence of tragedy in a ritual sense that theater could only approximate. The impression created by these works was reminiscent of Jane Harrison's vision of the prehistory of theater in dance.[158] Bringing Bentley together with Rank one can say that the transference of unconscious artistic activity from the dramatic author to the dancer, and from the dramatic text to choreography—all qualities of the so-called primitive nature of dance— had the effect of making any dance about unconscious drives iconic of the unconscious itself. It was also a culturally coded invitation to the audience to desublimate—to get beyond its disgust and accept what it beholds as an engagement with the unconscious. Dance, like theater, provides the missing content of the form of psychoanalytic insight. With *Night Journey*, the spectator is invited to take on the role of *analysand*, and in this way the collaboration between audience and choreographer is established. "The artist, in short, must become a psychoanalyst," said Rank.[159]

In *On the History of the Psychoanalytic Movement*, Freud wrote: "Dreams are only a form of thinking; one can never reach an understanding of this form by reference to the content of the thoughts; only an appreciation of the dream-work will lead to that understanding."[160] This brings us back to the role of theater in Graham's work. *Night Journey* posits that dance is to theater as dream is to myth. Dance is the latter-day analysis of theater, which recuperates the archaic representation as a modern phenomenon by itself appearing more primitive than that which it recuperates. Unlike the Abstract Expressionist renderings of the unconscious, Graham's rendering of it is mediated and theoretical, deriving as it does from a *conscious* positioning of dance and choreography in relation to dramatic literature and psychoanalysis as both more primitive and, paradoxically, more theoretically sophisticated. At the same time, Graham draws on the tradition of the chorus as an acting agency within dance, and a danced agency within acting. It is this kind of work—in the Freudian sense—that dance can do, which distinguishes Graham's dance theater from theater *tout court*, and illuminates its relation to dream and myth simultaneously while never losing sight of theater through which it reasserts its self-conscious and calculated position as a psychoanalytically informed performance.

Night Journey's structure of memory that frames a future moment of fateful decision is also appropriate to the historical circumstances of the Graham-Hawkins relationship in 1947. *Night Journey* prefigures this relationship's end, which both must have been contemplating since 1946. As Jane Harrison had said, *dromenon,* the Greek term for action, is

> not simply a thing done, not even a thing excitedly and socially done. . . . It is a thing *re*-done and *pre*-done, a thing enacted or represented. . . . It is sometimes *re*-done, commemorative, sometimes *pre*-done, anticipatory, and both elements seem to go to its religiousness.[161]

For Graham, the introspective subject of *Night Journey* was the least symbolic and most obvious (yet still hidden) part of the choreography: the anticipatory action on stage of Graham and Hawkins as doomed lovers. Rather than containing repressed material of significance to the artist and the audience, the role of the Oedipus myth in *Night Journey* is, in one sense, to displace the autobiographical content while still exposing it to plain sight. As Eliot had pointed out: " . . . [T]he meaning of the series of acts is to the performers themselves an interpretation."[162] This action is cloaked in myth. What Rank would call the subjective artist here fulfills the need for self-analysis by cloaking the work in objective terms. It is precisely in this sense that myth could be thought to fulfill the function of narrative as long as we assume that the function of narrative is an objectivity to be grasped by the audience. In 1947 Graham was 53 and Hawkins 38. Graham came to see the failure of their relationship as a result of her own insecurities about aging. In a letter to Hawkins of September 3, 1950, she wrote: "I think I resented the fact that you were younger than I. I did things, such as the jealousy things, to make myself out a martyr to time."[163] This was in response to Hawkins's remark: "[Y]ou have allowed yourself to keep a neurotic irrationality which has constantly broken the tender shoots of what you seemingly wanted to grow."[164] These insights are prefigured in *Night Journey,* which is, in another sense, the ritual prefiguration of their separation.

Through Jocasta, Graham could experience the self-accusation she would later express to Hawkins, and assume guilt for the relationship's failure. "[W]hy did I do what I did to destroy or corrupt our relationship?" she asked in a letter to Hawkins in 1950.[165] To choose to destroy a relationship can be a way to maintain control over it. What becomes desublimated in *Night Journey* is Graham's realization of the loss of her relationship to Hawkins. This is done in the tragic mode of realization that it was an inherently destructive relationship. "When the incest taboo works to foreclose a love that is not incestuous," writes Judith Butler, "what is produced is a shadowy realm of love . . . What emerges is a melancholia that attends living and loving outside the livable and outside the field of love."[166] The incest theme served this purpose for Graham: it justified the end of the relationship, albeit in the form of tragic realization.

The marriage of Bride and Husbandman in 1944 in *Appalachian Spring* is represented three years later in *Night Journey* as an incipient reality, but one that contains the seed of its own destruction. *Night Journey* inverts *Appalachian Spring* in that marriage no longer suggests the roughhewn American couple but the incest fantasy. The Husbandman is transformed into a figure evoking more complex emotions in Jocasta: "There is anger for the son, anguish for the lover and longing for the security of the husband."[167] But, significant choreographic details also indicate that Hawkins embodied for Graham the brutal opportunism often associated with the character of Oedipus. Although each caress and kiss in their long duet is mimed, and thereby highlighted in a stylized manner, whenever Oedipus places his foot on Jocasta's body the physical contact, by contrast with the stylization, has a literal impact, and its energy is cruel. [Figure 4.5] When Ross took over the Oedipus role some of the cruelty of the relationship was softened:

> There was a movement in the dance where Martha was sitting on the stool and Erick quite a distance away from her, with leg straight just fell with all his weight catching himself on Martha's shoulders with his hands. I did ask Martha if we could change that—I saw no excuse for it being unnecessarily cruel. I think that was replaced by a rude embrace— like somebody getting rudely familiar with a person you didn't know. Martha said "It is as if a perfect stranger pinched the queen's behind."[168]

The version we see in the film may no longer contain all of the cruel details of the original. But, an artificial presentation of tenderness of the mimed kiss is the foil against which the cruelty of Ross as Oedipus stands forth. Ben Belitt noted of *Night Journey*: "It's the violence that comes through in such an enormously constructed way that makes this a very contemporaneous piece: not the erotics of Freud."[169] Graham was, in this sense, Hawkins's Laius, or, put otherwise, he was out to kill the mother just as he had vanquished the Sphinx. It is probably for this reason that later, in *Clytemnestra*, Graham had the idea of casting one male dancer (Bertram Ross) in the roles of both Agamemnon and Orestes—father and son.

The Missing Sphinx

The rope used to such a variety of effects in *Night Journey* was called the umbilical cord, an image that links not only the depiction of the relationship to its kinship ties, but also links Jocasta to the Sphinx through the latter's threat of strangulation. Rank theorized the strangulation threat of the mother at the

Figure 4.5 Hawkins and Graham in *Night Journey* (1948). Courtesy of the Music Division, Library of Congress

child's birth to be more psychically significant than the fear of castration at the hands of the father (incest prohibition) in retribution for the son's incestuous desire for the mother.[170] If the Sphinx is another figure of Jocasta, then her destructive agency in relation to her son-lover stands revealed as does his to her. Through a switch in emphasis from the father-son to the mother-son relationship *Night Journey* foregrounds not so much a lifting of repression as a realization of aggression. Oedipus's encounter with the Sphinx prefigures his later encounter with Jocasta in more ways than one: when Oedipus kills the Sphinx, he effectively kills the mother who might otherwise have strangled him. We find ourselves here in Rank's theory of the birth trauma.

Before Fromm, Rank was critical of Freud's emphasis on the father in the Oedipus complex; it was Rank who suggested the relation to the mother might be more primary. By shifting attention from the father-son to the mother-son relationship, Rank sacrificed his close relationship to Freud by 1926. Rank discusses the maternal character of the Sphinx in *The Trauma of Birth* (1924) where he attributes the destructive tendencies of the relation to the mother to "birth anxiety." The Sphinx designates the primary relationship to the mother as being the life-threatening trauma of birth. On this view, the Sphinx becomes a substitute for Jocasta, and calls attention to the fact that Oedipus also has a destructive relationship to the mother. ". . . [T]he mixed figure of the Sphinx representing the anxiety experience as such has been recognized by Psychoanalysis as a mother symbol, and her character as 'strangler' makes this reference to the birth anxiety unambiguous."[171]

"[T]he myth [of Oedipus] is always stated in terms of a man," Hawkins told David Sears. "And so it's not the story of Jocasta; it's the story of Oedipus."[172] This, of course, is the polar opposite of Fromm's position. Given that Hawkins disapproved of the way Graham diverted the focus from Oedipus to Jocasta it is not surprising that, as she was contemplating *Night Journey*, he took up the project of his own choreography about Oedipus and the Sphinx, *The Strangler*.[173] Hawkins drew upon *The Riddle of the Sphinx* by the Hungarian psychoanalyst Geza Roheim. In a diary entry for August 16, 1946, Hawkins wrote: "Yesterday in visiting Geza Roheim he told me that the answering of the Sphinx's riddle was a sign of growing up."[174] "After Oedipus had killed Laius," wrote Roheim, "he hurried to Thebes, where lived the Sphinx, a cannibalistic monster with a woman's head, wings, and the body of a lion . . . She used to set every passer-by a riddle and if he could not answer it she sprang upon him and either strangled him, carried him off into the air, or ate him."[175] Hawkins subtitled *The Strangler* "A Rite of Passage." In a program note to the 1950 performances in New York he wrote: "The Sphinx, half-lion and half-woman, represents the father and mother in the primal scene; her wings are a symbol of physical ecstasy of the parents and her name, in Greek, meaning the Strangler, refers to the danger of parental fixation of domination."[176]

Hawkins commissioned the text for *The Strangler* from Robert Fitzgerald, a poet whom he knew from his classics days at Harvard. The text, which he likened to one of Yeats' dance plays, was read by actor Joseph Wiseman (Pearl Lang's husband) and Hawkins himself, and the silent Sphinx was played by actress Anne Meacham at the premiere in Connecticut, and later, in New York, by Marian Seldes. At the New York premiere the negative press crushed Hawkins. Walter Terry called it "a pretentious, barren and dull staging of the legend of Oedipus and the Sphinx."[177] Although no photographs of the work survive, it apparently consisted mostly in a discussion between Oedipus and the Sphinx with very sparse passages of movement. Robert Sabin wrote in *Dance Observer*: ". . . [T]he central figure turned out to be Oedipus and the argument was the hero's discovery of his own manhood and victory over the Sphinx and her riddles."[178] Hawkins was even more crushed by Graham, who was in favor of withdrawing it from the New York season after its first three performances. *The Strangler* may have been an embarrassment to her, but this was not only because of its critical failure. The first words of *The Strangler* were "Night, night, night." The commentary on *Night Journey* had to be unmistakable. As Don McDonagh said: "Graham saw tragedy and Hawkins rebirth" in the same legend.[179] One could add: not only in the same legend, but in the same relationship. Hawkins's focus on the same myth blew the cover of Graham's private ritual. That Hawkins wanted *The Strangler* to be read by the audience in relation to *Night Journey* seems clear from a 1949 program note: "It treats the portion of the Oedipus myth preceding *Night Journey*."[180]

Graham had originally considered including the character of the Sphinx in *Night Journey*. She wrote of the Sphinx in her scenario: "She is Youth personified and she speaks to youth in him [Oedipus]. She has about her the eternal quality of the prostitute, the object of desire and she never ages because he sees in her all the desires frozen into one instant by his imagination."[181] In the *Notebooks* Graham imagines a scene between Jocasta and the Sphinx: "Jocasta trapped by agingness/moment of worship at the feet of the young girl— the Sphinx—Youth—."[182] But she also imagined the Sphinx as a double of Jocasta: "She is also an aspect of JOCASTA in that he sees in JOCASTA at some instant those same qualities." Graham injected the seductive qualities of the Sphinx into Jocasta, making the Oedipus complex the Jocasta complex. "This ambiguous creature," wrote Roheim of the Sphinx, "enticing and dangerous, who loves but to devour, is, therefore, the mother of the hero."[183] And, Roheim adds that despite all the forms she may take—woman, lion, "wanton strangler" demon—". . . ultimately she is identical with Jocasta herself."[184] The fact that Graham dropped the Sphinx from *Night Journey*—it is a role somewhat analogous to the Princess, also called the Victim, who is Medea's rival for Jason's affection in *Cave of the Heart*—indicates that she did not want jealousy to be the dominant theme of *Night Journey*.[185] But, the Sphinx also potentially contained a vision of Jocasta herself as monstrous. If Graham decided against using the Sphinx in *Night Journey* it is perhaps also because she had already reconfigured the Sphinx as the Minotaur in *Errand into the Maze*. Just as the Sphinx is part woman, part animal, so the Minotaur is part man, part animal. The Minotaur is, in other terms, a male Sphinx with whom Graham did battle to emancipate herself from binding relationships with men. Hawkins was using the Sphinx to assert his emancipation from Graham as a kind of coming of age but this emancipation remained purely symbolic as it did not catalyze the artistic recognition that would have distinguished him from her and either made their separation more legitimate, or obviated the very need for separation as she bowed to his greater artistic destiny. In this sense, their rivalry was reciprocal. Hawkins was attempting to hold on to his relationship with Graham by doing precisely what made that relationship impossible for her to sustain. And, Graham realized that in not strangling Hawkins, she was destroying herself. In that sense Jocasta's suicide in *Night Journey* is a mechanical ending that covers up the ritual tracks of its more intimate meaning. But, as mentioned earlier, Graham's Jocasta does not hang herself: she strangles herself.

Hawkins and Lear

In his last New York season with Graham in 1950 Hawkins danced the Husbandman in *Appalachian Spring,* Jason in *Cave of the Heart,* and Lear in *Eye of Anguish,* this last a premiere Graham choreographed especially for him.[186] Graham had been contemplating a work on Lear since 1944: "It is essentially a piece to be played physically," she wrote to Zellmer, "and not structured in the usual 'buskin' manner. It demands the thing theatre folk are afraid of, a physicality of staging and playing, a searching into the language of body to really reveal the nature of it."[187] *Eye of Anguish* was the third of Graham's company works of the 1940s—the first was *Imagined* Wing, and the second *Wilderness Stair* (*Diversion of Angels*)—that is, works she choreographed without using herself. The question of how to choreograph *King Lear* pertained to the dialectic between dance and theater that preoccupied Graham throughout the 1940s.

Vincent Persichetti, who composed the original score for *Eye of Anguish,* remarked: "It [*Eye of Anguish*] was a real present to Erick Hawkins—and he didn't behave too well. There were emotional scenes."[188] Persichetti remembers violent altercations between Graham and Hawkins: ". . . [H]e had a crazy wig that really wasn't—I didn't think was right. But either Martha thought it was right or he thought it was right, but they disagreed about the wig and other things I know."[189] In a letter written to Helen McGehee on October 16, 1949, Graham mentioned that "Erick has a beautiful headdress wig which Yugi Ito made . . ."[190] A photo of Hawkins in costume as Lear shows that his face is almost entirely obscured. [Figure 4.6]

But, this was not the only problem. Although it was performed 186 times according to Persichetti (most frequently on tour) *Eye of Anguish* was a critical failure in New York. Graham had never before created the role of a tragic hero on a male dancer. It required giving the male's point of view central focus. Walter Terry laid the work's failure at Graham's feet as choreographer:

Figure 4.6 Hawkins as Lear in Martha Graham's *Eye of Anguish* (1950). Photo: Philippe Halsman Courtesy of Magnum Photos

He [Hawkins] is both dramatically effective and appealing while elsewhere his ranting agonies seem strangely superficial and contrived. This, I think, is due partly to choreographic troubles, for Miss Graham has permitted the focus of her work to shift away from Lear from time to time and only toward the close does she keep the movement progressing with Lear as the constant center.[191]

Hawkins became convinced that Graham was unable to create tragic roles for men.[192] As Graham generally allowed him to do his own choreography in her work, she may not have coordinated his movement with the larger picture, and thus caused discrepancies he was unaware of. He was on stage with the full cast rather than sharing the stage with her or alternating solos with her. Graham seems to have left him to his own devices as she attended to group effects. One critic noted: "There are magnificent moments of theatricality, one in which the entire group wraps itself in a tremendous red cloth, becoming a sculptural whole, identified as a group for a moment."[193] According to Hodes, who found it "full of ingenious moments," *Eye of Anguish* was well received on tour in the United States with regional audiences. The *Dance Observer* thought Hawkins was miscast. "He substitutes an actual ranting and raving dashing around the stage and stumbling manner, for a profound study of madness which would take great histrionic artistry as well as a powerful physique to achieve."[194] Hawkins apparently spoke on stage without a text.[195] Persichetti also thought the role of Lear did not suit Hawkins, and his comments reveal an understanding that Hawkins's own style had not yet emerged: "It looked like somebody . . . not up to being a big person like Lear. . . . It was just something not honest . . . He is a different and separate kind of artist. It was perhaps too much to ask for a total merge."[196]

Did this foray into Shakespeare divert Graham toward a pantomimic approach? *Eye of Anguish* prompted Winthrop Palmer to liken Graham to Noverre. Like the eighteenth-century ballet reformer she replaced "over-complicated steps" with "a flow of action" and "unconventionalized gesture."[197] *Eye of Anguish* seems nevertheless to have been uncompromising in terms of its abbreviation of plot, which Graham served up in impressionistic fragments. Persichetti scored sections such as "Cordelia's Dance," "the Curse Dance," "Lear's Dance of Grief," and "the Madness Dance." Helen McGehee, who played Goneril, thought it worked once Graham redesigned the costumes in the style of Hieronymus Bosch for the Paris premiere. Persichetti describes aspects of the dance he remembers:

> a fool and philosopher dance which is very painfully light-hearted . . . It seemed to me less typical Martha Graham dancing. In a good way, some fresh dancing, light . . . Almost jagged jigs in places. There is some irony in there because you just can't have a light-hearted dance, I mean, in Lear. And they crown the king with weeds. You feel Jesus in there.[198]

The cold critical reception may also have been a symptom of bad feeling hovering over Hawkins in the Graham milieu, which Helen McGehee thinks seeped down to the press.[199]

Eye of Anguish was one of the tipping points of their relationship. When Hawkins made the final break from Graham he found himself, as he put it, friendless. It is possible that Graham, with her eye for casting, had purposely miscast him. Prior to the New York premiere, on a tour that lasted from January until April 1949, Hawkins had his own billing, and got very good press in Dallas. On March 11, 1949, John Rosenfield wrote in *The Dallas Morning News* of Hawkins as Lear: "The fine power of Erick Hawkins, which has both dynamo smoothness and Herculean violence, focused the effects sought."[200] In the same review, the critic had some disparaging things to say of Graham in *Cave of the Heart*: "A little but not much edge has been lost to Miss Graham's own dancing which on the whole, commanded a fabulous range . . . Miss Graham's faults remain Miss Graham's faults. She is an abstractionist, bypassing the mind and addressing the emotions directly."[201] According to Hawkins, Graham flew into a rage about this review, which credited him at Graham's expense. The gendered rhetoric of the review is, of course, unmistakable, but Graham's work could still seem obscure outside of the sophisticated urban centers. Hawkins felt she should have more generously acknowledged that his performance was appreciated. He may have begun to suspect she did not want him to succeed.

Graham and Hawkins were married in July 1948, after the New York premiere of *Night Journey*, by a Presbyterian minister in Santa Fe.[202] This was apparently Hawkins's idea. In fact, Graham's disinterest in marriage may have been at least in part the cause of his earlier decision to separate from her in 1946. In what appear to be notes to himself dated March 1946 Hawkins writes: "My divagations came only when I felt left out of a joint life which is rightly that of the partnership of marriage."[203] Hawkins managed the Company's tour to Paris and London in 1950 with the Consolidated Concerts Corporation. *Eye of Anguish* was featured along with his own *Stephen Acrobat*. Not only did Graham give Hawkins unprecedented privileges on this tour but they were apparently functioning as a couple.[204] An internal tour sheet lists "European Room Reservations as of April 25, 1950," assigning "1 double bed for Mr. And Mrs. Erick Hawkins."[205] The tour was interrupted, however, due to an incapacitating knee injury Graham sustained in Paris, compounding an earlier injury. According to Bertram Ross, Graham initially injured herself—"I use that expression meaningfully—for she did indeed injure herself"—while rehearsing *Appalachian Spring* in New York.[206] This initial injury was then aggravated during a performance in Paris. "Doctors told her," said Robert Cohan, "if she danced she would never dance again. She could hardly walk after the first Paris performance. Her cartilage was torn."[207] Graham was in denial, and insisted on dancing. De Mille tells the story of Hawkins abandoning Graham and the Company in London out of sheer irresponsibility.[208] According to Hawkins, however, he walked out because she violently attacked him in a taxi on the way to a press conference where he announced the cancellation of the London season, perhaps recognizing more than she the reality of her injury. Her violent rejection of his entreaties to cancel the tour catalyzed the final breaking point of their relationship. They did hold a press conference in the lobby of the theater at which Hawkins announced the cancellation of the season. "For her not to imagine that I was doing it out of concern for her I guess was the saddest thing, one of the great wounds of my life."[209] These events have been interpreted predominantly in the opposite manner: Hawkins irresponsibly jilted Graham, and deserted her, leaving her in the lurch. Having listened carefully to the interviews Hawkins accorded Sears and McDonagh on this topic, I find his account convincing. It is, of course, difficult to fully judge the dynamics of any relationship. The predominance of the anti-Hawkins commentary, however, produces this: "When Graham injured herself in Paris at the start of her tour, and Hawkins suggested the tour continue nonetheless, their marriage was effectively over."[210]

With Hawkins withdrawn in frustration the tour fell apart, and Graham flew back to the United States. The hegemonic account of de Mille demonizes Hawkins as the guilty party who deserted Graham out of pure self-interest. Graham's letters to Hawkins in the summer of 1950 belie that account. Bethsabee de Rothschild wrote Hawkins on November 3, 1950: "I myself suggested you should not work together. But I admit I was astonished at the manner and timing of your departure."[211] In a letter to Katharine Cornell of September 8, 1950, from Santa Fe, where she was convalescing at the home of Cady Wells, Graham discussed her experience of shock, which was both physical and emotional. Because she did not perform in London, however, Graham managed to recover in six months without an operation to dance her 25-minute solo, *Judith*, at the New York premiere on December 29, 1950 to great acclaim.[212] Hawkins's departure had, in essence, saved her dancing career. "*Judith* was a magnificent work," Hawkins remarked in 1972.[213] A transitional work between *Night Journey* and *Voyage*, *Judith* was the first choreography in which Graham began to retreat from myth: "I am sorry to appear fuzzy," she wrote Schuman on June 24, 1949, "but in this I have no line of action to follow as story. I hope it means more. I do not want to make this in any way inhuman or goddess-like."[214]

It was at this point that Graham and Hawkins began to sift through the meaning of their relationship in letters to each other. On August 21, 1950, Hawkins sent Graham a letter typewritten up to the edges of the margin on 27 double-sided pages that attempted to explain his reasons for the second separation.[215] He isolates the issue of the age difference as being a motivating factor for her, although not for him. It led to insecurity and needless jealousy. Hawkins says his efforts to further Graham's career, while proof of his "productive" love, were misinterpreted as personal ambition. ". . . I mistakenly believed that in all this construction for your work I would realize my own potentialities too—that there was some process working whereby in working for a good outside myself I would cover the ground I needed for my own career." He calls their relationship at its best, in Fromm's terms, a productive relationship. "Genuine love," wrote Fromm, "is rooted in productiveness and may properly be called, therefore, 'productive love.'"[216] But, Hawkins found himself thwarted in his own productive impulse by Graham's distrust. Although he did not assume responsibility for her distrust the competition between them was undeniable.

Quoting in this letter from Fromm's *Man for Himself* (1947) Hawkins thinks in terms of Fromm's ethics of life as an art of living. When Hawkins used Graham as a yardstick for his own artistic development, she clearly surpassed him. Although she had found the truth of her work as an established artist, when he examined her as a productive *human being*—in Fromm's sense—he found she was very far from the truth.

> But I think a curious thing has happened in the last few years. In your work you have been pretty clear and sure and you have found a process of looking the truth in the face and working toward a result. In my work, I have kidded myself up to this day. But in terms of relationships and certain areas of faith, I feel you have not learned to face facts, while I have come to a certain point of conviction and insight.[217]

Hawkins disparaged his own artistic achievement at the aesthetic level, but still believed his own personal honesty and clarity were superior to hers. His art of life, in other terms, was superior to Graham's; his artistic competition with her became transferred to an ethical and moral level.[218] As David Sears pointed out later: "For Erick dance is a moral thing."[219] He disagreed with her training system and the way she failed to take care of her own body as instrument. He claimed that by the later 1940s she was no longer able to get off the ground. However, he continued to uphold certain of her works of the 1930s—notably *Primitive Mysteries* and *Frontier*—as major achievements of aesthetic modernism. He undervalued the period in which he himself was the most active.

At the moment of their decisive separation in 1950 he viewed the challenge as one of translating his own discerning human qualities into artistic attributes of a superior nature than Graham's. Once he began to work independently of Graham, he developed the idea of a very ethical relationship of the choreographer to his audience; this led him to disapprove of the torment in Graham's work of the 1940s, which he considered neurotic.[220] She, on the other hand, had theorized the life of the artist as an existence of essential aloneness. As much as she may have wanted to foster Hawkins as his own person, to foster him as an artist was not her role. Her struggle as a woman artist doubly precluded yielding the limelight to Hawkins. To do so would have disenfranchised her as an artist and limited her to being a "woman" in the most disempowering sense of that term for the period in which she lived. Yet, in the long letter she wrote Hawkins of September 3, 1950, which is her detailed response to his long letter, she recognizes the connection between their personal relationship and his artistic difficulties.

The fact that I seemed to reject all you did and to even reject your integrity as a man and as a husband may have caused you such inner disturbance that it took from your work. It is late to try to make amends but I tell you in case it might help.[221]

Graham herself in an earlier letter confirmed Hawkins's account of his departure in London:

I am more grateful to you than I can ever say for the consideration and care you gave me in Paris and London. You made things so much easier at a hard time. I only wish I could have so behaved that you might know how much I mean that. I made a mess of things again and it is done. I realize I am ill and I have to find the way out of this primeval forest of evasions.[222]

This letter confirms what I believe to be the more credible interpretation of Hawkins's actions, which contradicts the hegemonic account.

Graham expressed her intention to begin analysis with Frances Wickes in a letter to Hawkins on September 3, 1950. According to de Mille: "Martha was never psychoanalyzed. She merely talked conversationally to Mrs. Frances Wickes."[223] Given that Wickes was a Jungian analyst, however, and that analysis is known to be a talking cure, it seems undeniable that Graham *was* in analysis. Graham herself writes Hawkins about the insights she may gain into herself through analysis. In her remarks at Wickes's memorial service in 1964, Graham clearly indicated she was in analysis: "She knew when I was evading her and she would zoom in for the kill. . . . She wanted you to just get it over with, say it straight out, because somehow or other she was going to get it out of you anyway and she did."[224] De Mille did not have access to the Hawkins-Graham correspondence when she wrote her biography but she did most likely read Graham's correspondence with Wickes. De Mille does not, however, relate the correspondence to Graham's work. The audiotapes deposited at the Dance Collection of the New York Public Library, which contain the interviews she conducted, make it clear that de Mille never saw *Voyage*, and was relatively unfamiliar with Graham's work of the early 1950s. Her description of that period is murky although she does connect it to the beginning of Graham's alcoholism.[225]

Graham's engagement with myth is frequently linked to the chronology that would have her in analysis with Wickes as early as 1946. There is, however, no evidence that Graham consulted with Wickes in 1946 when she and Hawkins were first estranged. The evidence points clearly to a later date. Frequent art historical references to the unofficial connection between Graham and Abstract Expressionism locate Graham's analysis nevertheless in the mid-1940s presumably to bring it closer in time to Pollock's.[226] "Like most Abstract Expressionists," writes Steven Polcari, "Graham approached myth through Jungian psychology, and in the mid 1940s she underwent Jungian analysis. Her development thus paralleled that of Pollock, who had undergone Jungian analysis from 1938 to 1941."[227] Graham and Pollock had in common the milieu of New York Jungianism. Pollock's analyst was Joseph L. Henderson who, like Wickes, was a prominent figure in the Analytical Psychology Club of New York City, which still exists today as the C.G. Jung Center.[228] Graham and Pollock had a number of traits in common: the sense that art making was inseparable from biography, a connection to psychoanalysis, an interest in mythmaking (both personal and artistic), a deep connection to Native American culture, and the assimilation of art making to action (dance, action painting). Graham's analysis, however, occurred a full 10 years after Pollock's. This means Graham's Jungianism, evident in *Dark Meadow* in 1946, preceded her properly Jungian analysis. The original influence of Jung on her work came from her readings in analytic psychology. Jungian analysis did *not* underwrite Graham's interest in myth. To the contrary, her analysis coincided with her rejection of myth. Only one work—*Voyage*—was directly informed by Jungian analysis and this work, as we shall see in the next chapter, was antimythical.

Graham's move to abjure myth in *Voyage* was the artistic outcome of the loss of her relationship with Hawkins. To abjure myth meant to abandon the complex temporalities that had given formal coherency and theatricality to her works of the late 1940s. The change in her artistic direction of the early to mid-1950s is often associated with the creation of works for her Company, initiated with *Imagined Wing, Diversion of Angels* and *Eye of Anguish*, and continuing with *Ardent Song, Canticle for Innocent Comedians, Seraphic Dialogue*, and *Embattled Garden*. After their separation, Graham did not create a ballet with a central focus on herself for another eight years, and at that point she was ready to divorce Hawkins. The loss of Hawkins was a momentous event that Graham in most likelihood never fully recovered from; it drove her to alcoholism, but it also occasioned an immensely courageous will to radically alter her concept of choreography, if not her technique properly speaking. Through this seismic and completely misunderstood change in her work, Graham attempted to change herself.

"A Possible Somewhere (an impossible scene setting)"[1]

"Poetry, like a voyage, is an effort to renew life"
—Martha Graham, *Notebooks* (128)

Voyage went into rehearsals in the fall of 1951 as Graham started her analysis with Jungian psychotherapist Frances Gillespy Wickes. Both the analysis and the dance were motivated by Graham's state of mind in the immediate aftermath of her separation from Hawkins. Graham extended the analysis into choreography. "I am not a very satisfactory patient," she wrote to Wickes. "I have done only one outgoing thing. I had an idea for a dance."[2] *Voyage* is unique in the annals of twentieth-century choreography because it was conceived in analysis, and developed in a correspondence (and probably also in conversation) with the choreographer's analyst.[3] The choreographic process was not only co-synchronous, but also co-substantial, with Graham's analysis. It differed significantly from what we know of Jackson Pollock's analysis in which the artist's drawings were used for the purposes of analysis.[4] Graham did not subject her dances to analysis: she proposed to choreograph as an analytic activity.

Voyage is also of special interest to us today because Graham departed with this work from the productive myth formula of the mid- to late 1940s, which presupposed the reliving of experience of an earlier time through heroic personification. Instead, the unique connection between choreography and psychoanalysis in *Voyage* reorganized the synergy in Graham's work between choreography, psychoanalytic theory, and myth. Graham adopted a psychodramatic approach in which she sought to free herself from the demons of the present to face an uncertain future, free from what Harding called "asocial compulsions."[5] Graham was on a voyage whose destination was decidedly unclear. Her role as a glamorous middle-aged woman in *Voyage* was both contemporary and vulnerable. Donya Feuer, then an apprentice in the Graham Company, was captivated by *Voyage* but was personally attacked by Graham for defending the work to other company members in the studio. She and Paul Sanasardo later analyzed Graham as a vulnerable celebrity figure in their *Excursion for Miracles* (1957) and in *Laughter After All* (1964).[6] In this way, Pina Bausch must have heard about *Voyage* since she worked with Sanasardo-Feuer several years later, and it prefigured some aspects of *Tanztheater.*

Those who knew Graham intimately deemed the connection of *Voyage* to her personal history dangerous. It was crucial to conceal her emotional devastation from the public eye.[7] Her image as a powerful and commanding figure could be diluted by the need to use choreography for the working out of personal issues. She ran the risk of self-exposure, which, while potentially narcissistic, could also be considered courageous when it is occasioned by the need for self-examination. That Graham's turn from myth risked self-exposure seemed indubitable. "There is nothing so personal," said Robert Cohan of Graham in *Voyage*, "as being on stage without a named character to hang yourself on."[8]

On the verso of Graham's first letter to Wickes, the analyst wrote by hand: "to be sealed until after Martha Graham's death." "I know," wrote Graham to Wickes in that very letter, "I run great danger in this subject." The abjuration of myth in *Voyage* went hand in hand with her abjuration of mythological roles. "I did not want to fit myself into another woman's life again at this point." [9] Graham said of *Voyage*. "It is a new way of working and it is a new area and there is no story as such to shield me."[10] Myth was no longer a placeholder for an introspective mood rendered in symbolic and universal terms. The personal ritual stood revealed. But, part of the drama of *Voyage* was that it was not a success with the critics and the public. William Schuman was extremely sympathetic to the project, but recognized its difficulties. In his estimation: "[I]t was too abstract a work."[11] *Voyage* seemed too autobiographical to some, too abstract to others. In my opinion *Voyage* was a work of substantial value that deserves serious study.

Graham did not commission the musical score for *Voyage* but happened upon it through her acquaintance with William Schuman, who had written a piano work for a University of Chicago musical fraternity: "I said to myself, it's not a sonata, it's cyclical in a way, it's obviously some kind of program music but I had no program in mind."[12] Graham listened to the work at his request, and suggested he call it *Voyage*. She also asked him to orchestrate it for her new piece of the same name. Schuman did manage to obtain permission to preempt the Chicago concert premiere set for August 18, 1953, with the May 17, 1953, New York premiere of Graham's *Voyage*.[13] Unlike Graham's earlier collaborations with Schuman—*Night Journey* and *Judith*—she wrote no libretto for *Voyage*, but she did author copious notes, notebook entries, and letters.[14] In her analysis she was processing the separation with Hawkins as death and rebirth. On April 17, 1951, Graham reminded Wickes that it was nine months since Hawkins had left her in London.[15] She thought of *Voyage* as the offspring of their separation. But, rebirth could in this instance have no connotation of immortality. Graham remembers Wickes telling her: "You are not a goddess. You must admit your mortality."[16]

After the second and definitive separation in 1950 Hawkins and Graham maintained a circumscribed form of professional association. He continued to teach in her studio through 1952 although precautions were taken that their paths not cross.[17] Their letters indicate, however, that they did have long conversations in person, sometimes about finances, and especially about the financial crisis of unpaid taxes over the last two years. In a letter of March 10, 1952, Graham asked Hawkins not to teach anymore at the school. She acknowledged his request for a divorce in 1954, but they did not actually divorce until 1959.[18] Far from disappearing from her life, in 1950 Hawkins remained present professionally and financially, and was a cause of emotional preoccupation for Graham for another ten years.

As Graham set to work on *Voyage*, Hawkins was developing *The Minotaur Discovered*, one of a suite of five ten-minute solos making up *The opening of the (eye)* (1952). [Figure 5.1] Given that a Minotaur ballet was originally his idea, it is not surprising that Hawkins reappropriated this role for a suite of solos in which he would assert his unique choreographic and personal identity. He was looking at himself in the mirror image of a role he had conceived, but never embodied. But, this new identity was also an image, one originally meant to be symbolic of fascism, and which Graham had seized upon during their first separation to create *Errand into the Maze*. He was also exploring the conundrum of his own vilification, and hence discovering himself as a person whose identity was no longer enmeshed with that of Graham. And he was attempting to recognize himself in her distortions of his image—hence, the title: *opening of the (eye)*. Hawkins described *The Minotaur Discovered* solo as the long postponed descent into himself. Hawkins's Minotaur, very unlike Graham's Creature of Fear, was an unmelodramatic although quite mysterious apparition: in it Hawkins embodied the figure one might prefer to deny confronting, and transformed this encounter into a personal and subjective discovery of selfhood.

Voyage is the least known of the four works to which I devote a whole chapter in this book.[19] I discuss it not as the critics saw it—which they barely did, and did quite inadequately—but as Graham conceived it in her writing, and as she and her dancers (Bertram Ross, Robert Cohan, and Stuart Hodes) developed it in the studio over two years, and later remembered it in interviews.[20] There is no surviving work against which to measure my interpretation, and the matrix of oneiric and poetic images from which Graham developed *Voyage* is challenging from a production standpoint.

In her writing Graham speaks of the image, but her use of this term does not refer to her own image as constructed by the media. Instead, the image in *Voyage* is a potentially harmful delusion. *Voyage* is about the effort to shed delusions.

Figure 5.1   Erick Hawkins in his *The Minotaur Discovered* (1952). Courtesy of the Erick Hawkins Dance Foundation and the Music Division, Library of Congress

There are several layers of specular projection woven into this piece that are completely appropriate to its subject, which I understand to be the relation of love to delusion, the latter being conveyed as the contemplation of images. These images are reminiscent of Jung's "primordial images," which Bachelard described as "images that bring out the primitiveness in us."[21] In this sense, Jung's Wotan archetype was (according to Jung) a primal image able to move an entire people toward Fascism. But, for Graham, gender identity was also the stuff of the archetype's illusory, and hence primal, image qualities. Graham noted of her own role: "She is the feminine aspect of herself from which he [that is, her male interlocutor] can never escape."[22] Each character is the victim of the imago of the other and of the imago of the self as seen by the other. "She endures the aspects of herself as in a dream/she sees herself thru the eyes of 3 men."[23] Each character exists only as an image for the other, an image that also functions as a kind of distorting mirror determining the beholder's own personality. Hence, the reversal of the phrase in Graham's *Notebooks*, "To love is to contemplate the Images," which she reconsidered and corrected: "no—to contemplate the images is to love."[24] Love is the phenomenon of seeing oneself in the distorted mirror of the eyes of the other. There is almost a Platonic sense in which we are captive in a world of shadowy representations, but the reversal of the proposition just cited (unpublished in the *Notebooks*) indicates one can choose *not* to love.

In *Voyage*, Graham subjects love to extreme skepticism. Love as an activity of specular and psychic delusion must, at the very least, be subject to choice, or as Wickes would have said, to decision. Wickes's unpublished notes indicate her interest in the difference between choice and decision.

> The more clearly he can discern the essential meaning of the archetype appearing in relation to time and place where he stands, the more the individual can be said to choose his own way ... Through many choices we reach the place of decision where, almost instinctively, choice becomes part of that inner structure where the "other," the one who loves within, chooses for us ... Decision has taken over choice.[25]

Throughout *Voyage*, as her writing attests, Graham worked with the concept of the *imago*, a term Jung used in *Wandlungen und Symbole der Libido* (1911) translated in English as *Psychology of the Unconscious* (1916). Jean Laplanche and J.B. Pontalis attribute this term to Jung, and we know that Graham read *Psychology of the Unconscious*. Laplanche and Pontalis define the imago as an "[U]nconscious prototypical figure which orients the subject's way of apprehending others."[26] They further stipulate: "It should be looked upon ... as an acquired imaginary set rather than as an image: as a stereotype through which, as it were, the subject views the other person."[27] If the imago is an archetype that is also a stereotype, then it can be destructive. Graham seems to conceive of the imago in her preparatory notes for *Voyage* as deluded inter-subjectivity. But, the projection phenomenon, as Erich Neumann called it in 1955, is necessarily complex in the Jungian context because it does combine "interpretation both of woman's experience of herself and of man's experience of woman."[28]

The imago is an archetype with the negative effects of "repetitive psychological fixation" that could only be counteracted with a contemporary cynicism.[29] Hence, each character behaves like a figment of the imagination of the other. There is, it would seem—both for us and for these characters—nothing possible *but* interpretation. This makes the work difficult to get hold of, a difficulty that is compounded by the fact that, unlike the other works discussed in this book, there is no critical documentation with or against which to speak. *Voyage* is virtually unknown today. Yet, while all the ideas that went into making this piece may not have been realized choreographically in any one performance, it seems they were all present theoretically in the movements and relationships seen on stage when it was performed. I say this because the ideas are clearly conceptualized in the notes, notebooks, and letters. Although carefully worked out, these ideas must nevertheless have been difficult to get across to an audience as they depended on the stage depiction of image projection, which cannot take a clear-cut theatrical form as it occurs more in the minds of the characters than in their actions.

My reading shadows the work in several senses. Like the work, it is a process of *decrypting* that reverses the negative effects of the archetype both as content and as methodology because instead of reducing images and/or ideas to a lowest common denominator as a symbol they are unpacked as interlocking and proliferating options within the "spectacle." They are not delivered to the audience as a myth, and they are all the more difficult to convey to an audience as seen *by* the protagonist in visions. "Besieged by strange and terrifying powers & visions," the Woman was prey to her own memories.[30]

> She stands on the edge of a desert at sunset—
> alone and bereft or unfulfilled—
> As the night fades all of the present fades & she enters the violences of memory
> violent halls of memory—
> She steps across an invisible barrier & enters the Past . . .[31]

After the first performance Graham wrote Wickes:

> Voyage was a shock and a terror for me and I had to go into the dark a little to see it. I do not yet but even though I have been rehearsing it and have torn it to pieces I do not know yet but I shall. Now I know that I can speak of it. It had all the strangeness of handling something that was part of me and yet I had never seen it before and did not fancy it at all.[32]

Even as it was about terrifying visions, *Voyage* in itself became a terrifying and uncertain vision for Graham. She wrote Wickes of opening night: "It is a curious piece and in some ways it has tapped an area I seem a little afraid of. But I know it can come through. It was not right at all as it was at first. I missed by a wide mark."[33] Schuman wrote to Graham after the opening: "You were disturbed, I know, last night because 'Voyage' did not live up to your hopes for it. This is to say that my confidence in what you are doing with the work is unshaken and that I know you will find a way to solve its problems to your own satisfaction."[34] Robert Sabin saw every performance of *Voyage* and noted Graham's efforts to improve the work during its first run.

> At the first performance *Voyage* had some thin passages. By May 21 Miss Graham had tightened her own role and brought the rest of the work into focus. And on May 23 when she closed the season with another repetition of Voyage she had added a red scarf to her costume and changed the climax of this work by making an effective exit and adding other touches.[35]

Sabin was the only critic to recognize the uniqueness of *Voyage* in 1953: "*Voyage*," he wrote in *Musical America*, "reveals the vast range and daring of Miss Graham's imagination. It is different from anything that she or anyone else has ever done before and it is marvelously inventive in movement, gesture, and atmosphere."[36] He also commented: "the emotional tension becomes almost unbearable."[37] Pressure was nevertheless exerted on Graham by her own management between 1953 and 1955 to withdraw *Voyage* from the repertory.

Despite the attempt to engender skepticism, Graham was in thrall to her own images. Her struggle to create the dance was mirrored in a parallel struggle to come to terms with the separation. *Voyage* was an exercise in survival. Darkness and night—the time and space of the appearance of images—are much in evidence in Graham's initial ideas. "This is one night," she wrote about the project in 1951 with perhaps implicit reference to the endless journey the night had signified to her in 1947. "It is dark," she wrote Hawkins on December 30, 1950. "But it can be endured as it has been and it can be changed into light on some instant of time and it can be soon."[38] Rather than a mythic nocturnal journey ending in Jocasta's death this voyage traversed *one* dark night, but ended by leaving darkness behind and entering a new dawn. The return to light marks the end of the reign of images. The movement into the dawn could not, however, be taken for granted with the passage of time, but required a supreme effort: "Time seems only to serve as a crucible wherein fire intensifies the contents to its essence and the result is a quick and earnest poison utterly pure and incorrupt in its action."[39]

The time between darkness and dawn was the initial temporal setting of the piece. She listed the sequence as: "Storm at dark, moon-rise and moon set, deep dark and dawn." She would later use this sequence explicitly for *Ardent Song* (1954). Graham's notes evoke darkness as isolation and loss of direction.[40] One month later she reported to Wickes she had imagined herself lost in the dark, and flinging her arms out in the darkness she found herself uttering the words: "I salute my love." In the *Notebooks*, *I Salute My Love* is discussed under the rubric of an unchoreographed work, but it is a variant of *Voyage*. The letters to Wickes permit one to perceive this connection. At the end of this night, Graham envisages a green dawn (green was the color of Wickes's window shades, which were drawn during the session).[41] Graham charts the sequence as follows:

Twilight . . . which is like a sarabande of recognition
Moon-rise
Moon-full
Moon-set
Which is the evocation of memory deliberately and precisely done with no sense of tragedy
Deep Dark
Which is like a dark miracle where all is excluded except the absolute of the struggle
Dawn[42]

Of this temporal sequencing Graham wrote to Wickes on July 16, 1951:

> With my mind I add the dawn. I know there must be a dawn but as yet I have no sensation or knowledge of it. But it is logical that dawn comes. There is a luminous bathed essence of new day. Perhaps if I live through the progression up to that instant I shall capture some of the lovely instant of pervasive green which marks the return to color and life which is dawn. Perhaps I have not yet reached the instant of deep dark which precedes the dawn. I may be still living with the curious strange fantasies of the moon world, the images beautiful and terrifying but less so than the reality of the actual which would release me into the lovely anonymity which is dawn.[43]

The temporality of this scene was as important to Graham as it was demanding: "How can I objectify sunset or end of day?" she jotted down.[44] The challenge to objectify a passage of time choreographically corresponded to the challenge to overcome the experience of time as a slow burning from within, "to feel so possessed by flame as to be infinitely hot and about to disintegrate into an ash at any instant."[45] Although Graham avoids mythical narrative she retains the cycles of the moon, which Harding thought symbolized feminine nature. But, Graham also superimposes on the moon a temporal process whereby its presumed essence should ultimately be replaced by dawn. Dawn is, as she notes, anonymous actuality, a new beginning divested of symbolic iconography: a true unknown that is sought.

The working title for *Voyage* was *Point of the Wolves* or *Promontory of the Wolves*, suggested by the shapes of the twisted trees she had seen at Point Lobos on the coast of Northern California. "[I]t is essentially about one woman and her tide-pool at night where driftwood and dead things float after the surge up of the sea."[46] In a program for *Theatre for a Voyage* (1954) in the Netherlands Saint-John Perse's "Winds" is quoted: "O thou, desire, who are about to sing . . ."[47] In this poem, also reproduced in the *Notebooks* (127), we note a scene similar to that of the letters:

> Like a great tree shuddering in its rattles of dead wood, &
> its corollas of baked clay—
> Very great mendicant tree, its patrimony squandered, its
> Countenance seared by love and violence whereon desire
> Will sing again
> O thou, desire, who are about to sing . . .

Ravaged like Saint-John Perse's tree after a storm a woman contemplates the aftermath of catastrophe. Graham added to this the threatening presence of wolves: "hungry ones who tear at the heart with that cruel hunger that only wolves have."[48] The tide pool and the Point Lobos landscape are related to the changing stations of the night the work would chart. Graham also alludes to the three men of the cast as wolves when she calls them "desired guests" who are also "dreaded—but . . . invited, nonetheless."[49] As the Unidentified Guest of T.S. Eliot's play *The Cocktail Party* (1947) (also called the uninvited guest) remarks:

> [T]o approach the stranger
> Is to invite the unexpected, release a new force,
> Or let the genie out of the bottle.
> It is to start a train of events
> Beyond your control.[50]

In Eliot's metaphysical drawing room comedy, the unidentified guest is the psychoanalyst who intervenes in the lives of his acquaintances once they become his patients. In *Voyage*, the men, the wolves, and the psychoanalyst are collapsed into one another through the memory of a scene as correlated with the description of a landscape, and through the contrast of the natural devastation found in the Point Lobos tide pool with an elegant cocktail party: the height of well-bred artificiality. These two antitheses set up a tension between high society and bestiality that Graham would flesh out in the staging. At the beginning," noted Sabin, "all of the characters are formal and self-contained. But as the woman stirs the three men and becomes engaged in an emotional conflict with them, she begins to lose her self-command and her civilized restraints or inhibitions, if you will."[51] There was contradictoriness to the generative images of the tide pool and the cocktail party that conveyed the idea of the spectral quality of love.

Between the sense of solitary desolation and the façade of polite society lurked the danger of madness and self-abandon.

Voyage begins in the *Notebooks* with Graham, wearing an elegant evening gown, and three men, in tuxedos, at a dinner party in a house surrounded by a desert, or possibly on an ocean:

> There is a supper scene—in a courtyard or on a balcony or in some cool remote room of a tropical house in an imagined country—There are 3 men who speak—& one woman who is silent—The men speak—the lines are few but they are philosophizing about the great images by which we live—. A sentence—a word—releases the silent woman into the dark of the night.[52]

On stage there was no speaking although Graham initially imagined it that way, and it may have been done in rehearsal. "[S]he didn't want anybody to talk; we didn't talk to each other, and each person, when they would open their mouth, it would look as though they were talking, but they each were doing a soliloquy to himself."[53] We can also read in the *Notebooks*: "the setting should be reminiscent of a balcony on a patio or a large room in an aridity like Spain."[54] The Spanish or Moorish aspects of the scene with the matadors as well as the supercilious social atmosphere masking passion and unrest suggest a later work—*Embattled Garden*—which Graham choreographed in 1958 to a score by Carlos Surinach, who called the later work "a sort of spoof of hispanity."[55] The house and the location may have suggested themselves to Graham because of Cady Wells's adobe houses outside Santa Fe where she convalesced from her knee injury in September 1950. In a letter of September 8, 1950, to Katharine Cornell from that location Graham called the house she was staying in after the European debacle "a little oasis in the desert," and she mentions attending "little parties in the evening."[56] These elements suggest that *Voyage* is reconstructing a state of mind in the immediate aftermath of the separation when Graham was in the desert. The images themselves are like the wolves that hound her. And to relinquish myth is to relinquish the image of herself that had hounded others. As she confessed to Hawkins in 1950: "I had built and fostered an image . . . The saying thou shalt have no other gods before me had constant meaning in daily life."[57]

Voyage reminds me of *The Cocktail Party* also because it starts somewhat like a play. Ross thought of the initial movements of the foursome in *Voyage* as a sort of estranged dialogue: "They were all talking, but they were all soliloquies—they weren't talking to each other in any way." Following the initial dialogue, Ross explains, "[S]omeone got up and went out onto the veranda, out of the house, out of the living room where the party was taking place. And there was this vast, vast, like . . . desert. Then the other two went out. And then somehow there was a connection. And we flipped her over—the whole world changed."[58] In performance the flip was followed by the removal of her hair clips, and the letting down of her hair signaling the entrance into a different realm or a second level of reality.

> She was on her knees and we danced around and turned her and turned her after that cartwheel to change the whole world, and I took one of these things out of her hair. I think they were to be knives. I took one out, and then the other man took one out, and the other man took one out and all her hair fell down.[59]

Unlike earlier works where one of two scenes was invariably encrypted to create an apparently smooth surface, the transition between worlds exists in a parallel potential space only differentiated by light and dark, civilized conversation and desert-like emptiness. In the Notebooks Graham sketched the action of the wolves as a play within a play where the woman confronts the three men as a bull in a ring would confront three matadors. The very absence of this action on stage is revealing. In the Notebooks the table and chairs were upstage and the bull arena center stage. Although Graham first considered dividing the stage in half to represent these spaces, she decided ultimately against this idea. "The action takes place on two levels of experience," she specified in the Notebooks. The second level to which she refers is "the phantom arena of a woman's being" that she also calls "an arena reminiscent of the bull ring—circular with barrier."[60] In that arena, according to the Notebooks, the men become "matadors"—variants of the wolves. What remained were the personae of the matadors, which Graham brought back later in Embattled Garden, a work that gives us a stylistic glimpse into Voyage from the perspective of the male performers.

   Although one might be tempted to assume that the antinomy of elegance/ savagery was meant to configure absolute space in Voyage—it does typify (particularly Jungian) clichés of the conscious and the unconscious for the period as savagery beneath the civilized veneer—it actually displaces absolute space with the spectral play of images. And, in this sense, the coexistence of a visible and an invisible world is no longer properly mythical in Voyage: instead, it is more strictly analytical. Rather than surface opposed to but also contiguous with depth, both illusion and reality are to be found in Voyage in effects of light and darkness at the surface. Voyage avoids the category of the monomyth that Eliot and Campbell claimed for Joyce. Campbell explained myth in 1946 as "a source of this undifferentiated yet everywhere particularized substratum of being."[61] The substratum was no longer contained underground, as it were, but exposed in visible space precisely because it was inviting differentiation. In an early draft of *I Salute My Love* Graham imagines the "outline of figures hovering on the edge of the stage—If possible these should be like tall elongated *wire* figures—suspended—almost transparent, strange and enormous—."[62] *Voyage* offered the superimposition of dichotomies without encryption—ambiguities, that is, which lay open to inspection at the surface, and divisions, which constitute psychic uncertainty represented in visual terms.

This is where the idea of theater itself becomes relevant, and is probably why Graham opted for the word "theater" in the title of the second version. Despite the lack of a mythic role she was not playing herself in *Voyage*—as Helen McGehee said to me: "Never herself; always an idea of herself."[63] Perhaps the most accurate role attribution is that of "The Actress." As she put in the *Notebooks*: "The actress/The one who plays a part."[64] The role was that of herself as a producer of images. By the same token, she also placed the three men in a theatrical realm when she called them clowns. With this idea, the men became less a projection of her fears and attractions and more themselves subjects of doubt. This prefigures Graham's interest in giving the men in the cast autonomy in the creation of the piece while placing them at its center, and her later decision to change the title to *Theater for (a) Voyage*, and also foreshadows her interest in the actor as "comedian" in her *Canticle for Innocent Comedians* (1952). In *Canticle* Graham even further deconstructed a mythical belief in absolute space by having the dancers take apart and reassemble the set in different pieces "to create each time a new aspect of the world."[65] The world itself is made of pieces that can be taken apart and put together again at will. The dancers were "innocent" and hence childlike. But, "play," Graham reminds us, "is deadly and implacable in the true sense because it is done innocently, for itself."[66]

The meaning of the theater conceit for *Voyage* returns us again to the image or imago. Everything that transpired on stage had a specular quality, which is proper to theater, but also what theater has in common with psychic projections. Graham's focus on the image per se may also have been a commentary on her own mythical celebrity and the hubris it entailed for which she held the loss of the relationship with Hawkins in part responsible. Graham was reading Robert Payne's *The Wanton Nymph. A Study of Pride*, which she quoted in a scenario she wrote for *I Salute my Love*. "An image grows," wrote Payne, "acquires accretions from foreign sources, twists and turns within the changing contours of the times, and by acquiring so many accretions and so many changes becomes another image entirely."[67] The image could not be controlled any more than could the persona. This is the strongest rationale for creating a work without a mythical backdrop. Myth was the packaging of the archetype as a misleading and hence potentially harmful image.

Ross felt Graham took another risk in allowing the men to be the dominant characters:

> [S]he thought she would direct the piece through the three men, so that instead of a main protagonist, as you have in drama, it would be three. Then she said it was impossible, the piece would have to go through her, and back again to the three men, and there was that confusion.[68]

This decision may have resulted in the de-theatricalization of Graham's performance style such that she appeared at certain moments to be an actress focusing on small, naturalistic detail.[69] "She was passive," adds Ross, "acted upon, and that's not Martha's role, and has never been her role on the stage."[70] "[S]he wanted," said Ross, "to make the point of view the three men . . . the reason it was not successful and that she was not successful was that it was making her passive and the men active."[71] This approach to performance demagnified Graham's persona, and thus came dangerously close to contradicting the image of Martha Graham as a larger than life personage. "She was trying to work outside of what had been her main interest in creating theater," remembers Helen McGehee.[72] This other kind of theater, or this "outside" of theater, was something akin to psychodrama, although critics did not use this term. If myth is the reliving of another's experience through identification and/or heroic personification, psychodrama is the attempt to free oneself from the demons of the present by rejecting dominant images from the past. In the *Notebooks* Graham writes: "This is a woman's experience as a woman not as a symbol as in Voyage."[73] With "This" at the beginning of the sentence Graham refers back to "the passage from sunset into night," which she also calls "self-examination" in the same passage. Despite the tortured syntax, I take the meaning of this sentence to be that woman's experience as *a* woman is depicted in *Voyage* whereas the symbol (archetype of the Feminine) belongs to her earlier mythographic thinking.

In addition to the relationship of *Voyage* to psychoanalysis there was also the specter of its possible relationship to a sort of psychodrama. In *Psychodrama*, first published in English translation in 1946, Jacob Moreno describes the emergence of psychodramatic therapy in the Viennese analytic context of the 1920s, as a challenge to psychoanalysis. We don't know if Graham read Moreno's seminal study but she may well have come across it by 1950 once she started analysis and imagined *Voyage*. The idea of psychodrama would likely have appealed to Graham as a form of alternative psychoanalytic theory. Whether or not she read Moreno, however, she did use psychodramatic techniques in the early rehearsals for *Voyage*. The reticent critical reaction to *Voyage* inadvertently mirrored the analytic community's earlier resistance to psycho-drama, which arose, for Moreno, "because private problems are treated in public."[74]

Voyage was not only important for Graham herself; it seemed to have great personal meaning to the dancers. "Here's a flop dance," remembers Hodes. "The critics didn't like it; the audience didn't like it. It was the most important dance I ever did." Of the first rehearsals for *Voyage* Bertram Ross said: "I used to be in tears all the time . . . [E]ach person I think was responding to the strangest im-provisation; we didn't know what was happening, and the piece began to build itself. It was my favorite piece of all time."[75] Robert Cohan said: "Martha and we men were good at getting together and making up, improvising, little choreo-graphic dramas. Like 'If I do this what would you do' or 'if I do this does it mean this, or that,' and then 'would you do this, or that?'" Hodes remarked: "[S]he tried to build the character and the dance based on what we were discovering about ourselves in that context."[76] "Each rehearsal was singularity," also com-mented Hodes. "Performance itself was easier in a way."[77] *Voyage* had a psycho-dramatic effect not only on Graham, but also on her dancers. Bertram Ross in his ability to follow Graham's creative process and participate tirelessly in problem solving seems to have taken the *Voyage* process in a psychodramatic direction as well. The choreographic act became social in the sense of being shared through discussion, and open to spontaneity. Ross adds: "I felt that it was the most per-sonal piece for me. I think it was a personal piece for everybody."[78] By saying it was personal for everyone, Ross also meant it was a shared social experience, in the sense of psychodrama.

His account of a nocturnal rehearsal gives us a glimpse of what might have been psychodramatic in the rehearsal process. Ceramics left over from an exhi-bition of the Baroness Bethsabee de Rothschild's mother filled the studio. Although quite different from its ultimate decor, the studio at the time of the first rehearsals at 36 East 67th Street was clearly influential on the work:

> They brought all these cases in with all these ceramics, and they had trellis screens with plants as décor, and chairs or benches . . . When we first started to choreograph they had not removed them yet from the studio. . . . We turned out all the lights and put one lamp on. It was very, very dark . . . and each dancer improvised something. We were given numbers. She was first. Stuart [Hodes] was second, Bob Cohan was third, I was last. And I was behind not the mesh screen that the plants hang on, the florist screen. I was behind one of the screens that was solid. And so she went, she did something. Stuart did something. Bob did something. And I slid out on the floor. I'll never forget that: I sud-denly appeared. And then we repeated that again. As if hearing

something, somebody went and opened the door, and Martha got up and went out. And then I went out. And then we all made this . . . design where everyone was like connected.[79]

The choreographic events seem to have been constructed through improvisation and a vivid sense of the unspoken as well as the spoken. Ross progresses from describing movements ("I slid on the floor") to describing actions ("Martha got up and went out"). In contrast to her contemplation of imagery in the letters Graham collaborated intuitively with the young dancers in the studio encouraging them to enter into this intuitive rapport. At this stage, choreographic control was not being exerted so much as shared. From the therapeutic perspective, psychodrama makes the analytic process less of a private, introspective effort and more of a socially oriented experiment. Rebirth demanded dynamic interaction with others, and this appears to have happened in rehearsal. In psychodrama, Moreno noted, "[T]he individual is urged to face the truth that these experiences are not really 'his,' but public psychological property."[80] By "a connection" Ross explains that something happened between the four dancers that was unnerving, but essential to developing the work: "It was a kind of mystical connection. We didn't touch hands. An electricity ran through the five of us."[81] Graham sought spontaneous action with this method and experimented during the rehearsal process with relinquishing choreographic control by becoming part of a shared psychodramatic improvisation. Of course, she was not always successful. Ross relates this moment in the creation of their final duet:

I stood behind her, and I put my arms around her, and I put my head on top of her head, and I made her lift her arms—the simplest thing in the world, and open them, and lift the arms up through center, and open them, and go from side to side, to bring her assertiveness and her peace back again. She said to the pianist, "Isn't that terrible? I cannot submit to his doing that to me." I could feel her tension, and I said "Relax," and I made her move with me as one person, and she could not, she fought it. She said, "Isn't it terrible? I just cannot give in to that and let him do that."[82]

There were clearly limits to how far Graham was willing to go with relinquishing control. On the other hand, she probably collaborated to a greater degree with Ross than with anyone else. At the same time, working so patiently and improvisationally with each other was a model for a healthy relationship. Ross remembers Graham saying: "Don't tell me that people's marriages and relationships, if people worked at them, with as much care as we took to be that patient—."[83] Although Ross's paraphrase of Graham cuts her sentence off, the implication is that Graham meant if people lived the way we rehearse they would be able to solve the problems of their relationships. The rehearsal process itself became a model for a more viable relationship than had been possible with Hawkins. The choreographic act was reconfigured as therapeutic.

Despite its limited exposure and uneven critical reception *Voyage* holds a unique if unrecognized place in Graham's creative output. She believed strongly in the work. "After the premiere," remembers Hodes, "we were right back in the studio."[84] Terry noted later in that season: "Miss Graham apparently has been working on "Voyage" and it is now considerably more effective than it was, both choreographically and with respect to performance."[85] Although it was reworked, its performance history was nonetheless limited. It was presented again as *Theater for a Voyage* on a tour of the Netherlands in eight cities between March 25 and April 5, 1954. A revised version, *Theater for Voyage*, was subsequently presented at the Anta Theater in New York City on May 5, 1955. *The Dance Observer* called it "a completely new version" although we don't know what changes were made beyond new costumes. *The Dance Observer* gave the 1955 remake a positive review:

> It is a tremendously courageous composition, as merciless in its exposed clarity as a line drawing . . . It combines an incredibly bold, almost clinical study of animal passions with the most clear-headed knowledge of the fact that no human being can use another as a drug or as an aphrodisiac and achieve happiness in the process.[86]

"*Voyage* . . . had three different versions," said Bertram Ross in a 1976 interview, "the last of which was never performed, and which was the best, I thought; the most mysterious."[87] Graham intended to bring *Voyage* on the State Department tour in 1955 through 1956, but problems with transportation of the set from the United States eliminated it from the repertory as well as *Dark Meadow* and *Canticle for Innocent Comedians*. The third version Ross refers to was presumably rehearsed for the Asian tour, but never performed. *Voyage* was subsequently withdrawn from the repertory. The set was reused in 1963 for *Circe*, a Company work made as a vehicle for Mary Hinkson.

The basic line of the action is retrievable from reviews and oral histories. Douglas Watt, a music critic, thought *Voyage* was about "a rather complicated shipboard romance that came up like a squall and disappeared as rapidly."[88] "Miss Graham," continued Watt, "stunningly gowned, had no sooner come out on deck, probably to admire the stars, than she was braced by three tall and handsome young men." Hodes remembers that Graham entered from the wings.[89] The three men followed her out onto the stage as the curtain opened. Graham wore an off-the-shoulder evening gown of black and brown satin designed by Hattie Carnegie.[90] The men wore "cotton evening clothes that looked like silk—satin—very shiny," remembers Hodes, "not bright, but smoky . . . with the latest cummerbunds and shoes."[91] Ross remembers that Arthur Todd, "a dance critic that worked for *Vogue*, managed to get the latest in evening clothes— before they were introduced. The tuxedos were made of a polished cotton that looked like silk . . . The colors were very unusual as was the silky sheen."[92] "She had this idea," related Ross, "that we would be dressed in the latest fashion. It had to be the ultimate in elegance."[93]

The elegant attire might have suggested to Watt the idea that *Voyage* takes place on board a ship. Like Bette Davis aboard a cruise ship in *Now, Voyager*, Graham, enabled by her psychoanalyst, was rewriting her life and identity. Hodes had a slightly different memory: "She finds the desert, not arid but a potential in which anything could be realized."[94] The ambiguity between sea and desert as vast expanse was rendered by Isamu Noguchi's set into the image of an oceanic expanse at the middle of which stood an archway and a boat. [Figure 5.2] "Center stage is a high arch," notes Hodes, "a portal of the house, perhaps. But the other is unmistakably a ship!" Noguchi originally designed the archway as a threshold through which the characters would enter, but Graham

Figure 5.2 Isamu Noguchi's set for Martha Graham's *Voyage* (1953). Courtesy of the Music Division, Library of Congress

wanted transformation to be conveyed differently. "So then the archway became a cloud, which was much more spiritual; it was like thought, and then this boat."[95] In other terms, the desert resolved itself into the expanse of sky, which suggests *Wilderness Stair* (1948) in which the desert was also rendered as a sky inhabited by angels in flight.

"This dance," read the program note for *Voyage*, "is a theatre for four characters voyaging on the strange seas of intimacy, caught in the ebb and flow, the tragic and the comic cross-currents of relationships." The term voyage was used metaphorically. Walter Terry understood the work as "the emotional voyage of a woman in quest of romance, a perfect romance." John Martin, who took the title to mean both symbolically and literally "a kind of luxury cruise," resumed the plot in schematic terms:

> A woman in a dinner gown invites involvement with three men in dinner jackets, to the extent of letting her hair down, again both literally and figuratively. As the adventure progresses, they strip off their formal restraints, typified by their costume, and in the most exciting passage of the work, have her isolated on the top of Noguchi's fantastic portal while they dance a kind of war dance about her. Eventually, she is saved from the situation by the return of one of the men to normal social behavior and the entire affair is dissipated.[96]

"These evening clothes," relates Ross, "the height of sophistication, were stripped off, and you came to the barbaric, down to the skin, with savage hieroglyphics on our bodies."[97] A shoe, a jacket, a shirt disappear as they fall to the floor and roll, after a jump, or in the wake of episodic exits and reentrances. "The men," wrote Sabin, "take off their coats in an ingenious passage of circling jumps and eventually emerge naked to the waist and barefoot."[98] Graham had originally wanted the men's skin to be "all tattooed and painted until we got more and more savage," but they ultimately used what Hodes called "Texas dirt," a body paint that gave a tawny sheen and "glistened like silver under light." It was an "artificial copper: a reddish-copper."[99] Graham describes the men's dancing as "commanding, brilliant, relentless" and a "reminder that we're at times the victim of our images."[100] There is not only an irony in the sophisticated atmosphere of the opening scene juxtaposed with the subsequent degeneration into savagery, but also in the worldly and sophisticated context of the cocktail party juxtaposed to the disparate broken fragments of wood and shell washed up by the tide at night.

Walter Terry wrote: "Revisions, I think, are in order for a new work not yet worthy of the masterpieces which surround it in one of the most distinguished dance repertories of our age."[101] Graham wrote Wickes: "I think certain of the critics were shocked. I have not read them yet but I have been told certain things." Audience shock may have derived from the scene of the three men disrobing:

> Suddenly as he [Cohan] was dancing, we were all jumping, and he fell to the ground and he got up and his coat was off. And he jumped off stage holding the coat. And when he came back he had no shirt, the shoes and stockings were gone, the pants were slightly rolled up. People said it was very shocking. It was like seeing somebody dressed . . . and then suddenly . . . It was like thinking the bathroom was empty and walking in finding someone half-clothed in the bath-room . . . Until finally all three men were like that and we did this very savagely until Martha became like some bird of prey and we picked her off that Circe cloud and zoomed her all over the stage and put her on top of Stuart. She was like a bird of prey that knocked him down.[102]

The duets that followed showed Graham in a different relationship with each man. According to the *Notebooks* she thought of Cohan as The Poet, Hodes as The Warrior, and Ross as "The clown lover."[103] In her dance with Cohan she played the role of a lyre that he strummed. Cohan said: "I remember my move-ment was as if I was singing poetry. My arms were often overhead held in the shape of a Greek lyre. I was often on my own as though distant and thinking."[104] Ross said:

> He had the poetic lyre, but it was her body . . . You really didn't see her as a woman . . . It was like the depths of degradation. It was as if her body was made into a lyre and he was Orpheus, and he was using her to make poetry, or to make songs, because I remember her saying, 'But what happens to me as a woman?' She was only an image, or something being used.[105]

Cohan also remembers: "Stuart's dance with Martha was very macho and strongly male. She told him to move like a peacock spreading its tail or like a cock crowing; Bert I remember hiding a lot and suddenly appearing."[106]

> They both got into a cape that she wore, together, and you just saw the two heads sticking out on top and it was like being in a tent with the most horrible obscenities going on. It went down and down and got very debauched, and then Bob Cohan came in and joined her at the height of her depravity.[107]

Observing this scene, Ross put his clothes back on and approached Graham.

> They had her knotted up in this cape, and she was doing like a shimmy
> dance and they were lowering her to the floor and raising her inside of
> it, by holding onto the cape, not her, and swinging her around, and get-
> ting wilder and wilder . . . I stood by that sail or cloud and I watched
> this, and finally I came over and broke the cape; sent the other two men
> out, and I led her back to the sail with me, and I gave her three flowers,
> actually, carved out of teak.[108]

[Figure 5.3] Watt relates: "He [Ross] handed her her ornaments, which she took
one by one, and put her hair back up with them. Boy and girl seemed to have
found each other, or now, arm in arm, they moved proudly and sedately about."[109]
In the rehearsal of this scene Ross remembers Graham said:

> Doesn't that make you too passive to see me in the arms of other men,
> carrying on this way. Wouldn't you get angry?' And I said: 'No. I know
> this is something you have to go through. And I'll wait. Because I know

Figure 5.3 Bertram Ross and Martha Graham in *Voyage* (1953). Courtesy of the Music
Division, Library of Congress

that you'll need me. This is just some compulsive behavior that you have to go through.[110]

The final duet with Ross was the most tender ("I knew she didn't want romantic . . . but it was creeping in"). "We called it the Voyage lift . . . I was on my hands and feet, making a bridge, and she sat; my body was like a hammock, and she lay there . . . The man's body was cradling her."[111]

The critical reproach that the action was quickly dissipated, as Martin put it, or of the sudden disappearance of a squall at sea, as Watt put it, were at one level accurate, but still misconceived perceptions. Ross called *Voyage* "a sophisticated party where you do and you don't relate; you may have an intense moment together, and then suddenly it's very "cut" and you're off doing your independent thing. There is a certain alienation, an urban alienation."[112] Watt said: "the two other men, also fully dressed again, reappeared, and after some more mixing, all four got in a line, circled around the stage, and floated off."[113] *Voyage* exposed a contemporary and disabused sense of the nature of relationships out of tune with the conventionalism of the early 1950s.[114] Ross sums up: "There was no happy ending; everybody was an individual at the end. We didn't pay any attention to each other."[115] Graham had created an unrecognizably contemporary work that demystified relationships. This is another way of saying that *Voyage* was ahead of its time. From the analytic standpoint, it was about the "fate" of relationships that were no longer fated, about the realization that intimacy would henceforth lack the imprint of Moira, which Graham defined as "[T]he whole content of the notion of Destiny."[116] She had suddenly and unexpectedly done away not only with the mythical format of her past triumphs, but with the very underpinning of destiny that had determined the shape of her work at least since *Deaths and Entrances* (1942).[117]

Despite the generally negative critical reaction, *The Dance Observer* provided the most trenchant overview:

> *Voyage* is a work of contrasts, of formality and unconventionality, of calm and violence, of tenderness and ruthlessness. Like many of the great dramas it conveys a sense of bringing the spectator in to witness a moment of action, which he may or may not understand, but with which he cannot escape being intrigued or excited.[118]

This critic also noted that *Voyage* was unlike any of Graham's preceding 125 works. But, another critic found *Voyage* "inconstant and disappointing, lacking point of view, its impulse erratic, its achievements fugitive."[119] The latter opinion seems to have prevailed.

In some important sense, Graham's attempt to individuate herself involved her liberation from mythographic thinking as well as from myth as a theatrical vehicle. Was she successful, and to what extent did her success rely upon the success of the work itself? One danger was to depend on critical reaction for the completion of one's self-analysis. There was also a danger in the analytic process becoming confused with the choreographic process. As an example of this, consider a letter to Wickes that Graham wrote on June 25, 1953: "I have been going through a strange time with my new work . . . Voyage . . . I wish you had seen it."[120] There was a possibly confusing circularity between the work and its personal meanings for Graham herself. That is, *Voyage* seems to have contained the elusive secret of what she wished to understand analytically, in the same way her analysis seems to have contained the elusive secret of what she wished to achieve choreographically. Just as the figure of the labyrinth or maze reformulated encryption as a dramatic element at the surface in *Errand into the Maze*, so the necessity to undergo analysis to construct a dance, and by the same token to construct a dance as a way to undergo analysis, had the disabling effect of turning introspective and aesthetic procedures inside out.

The contemporary qualities of *Voyage* were not in themselves entirely novel for Graham. In the solo *Gospel of Eve* (1951) she had satirized a vain contemporary woman. Graham subtitled it in notes "a dream confessional" and "a woman's tragicomic destiny."[121] This work was not successful.[122] Her 1960 self-portrait in *Acrobats of God* may have begun as self-examination, but it concerned her role as teacher and choreographer and resolved itself, unexpectedly for the cast, into a predominantly humorous mode in performance. While these were also self-portraits, they were in no way compromising either personally or professionally. *Voyage*, however, was not pitched at the comic or satirical level and it lacked the familiar references to myth, dream, and the unconscious that critics and audience had come to expect from Graham's postwar work. Part of what made *Voyage* unacceptable to Graham's Manager Craig Barton and to the critical establishment was precisely this contemporary quality. That Graham was going for this rather original look for modern dance in the 1950s is underlined by the costume changes she made to the second version of *Voyage* in 1955:

> Martha broke away from her traditional costume for herself and designed a red, backless halter dress that was knee length. Mesh stockings and heeled shoes completed the outfit. . . . The men wore black lace tee-shirts, red pants and regular rope soled espadrils . . . After the first performance of the second version, Matt Turney came back and was ecstatic about the way we all looked. She said that when the curtain went up and we were all on that boat it was breathtaking and that "Martha looked ravishing . . . unbelievably gorgeous." But Craig Barton came back. He

did not like the new image. . . . The next night she appeared in a long
sleeved black top and red dress.[123]

This costume change was obviously a bold one in the context of Graham's
previous works. It put *Voyage* in a contemporary theatrical context, closer to
Tennessee Williams' *Cat on a Hot Tin Roof* than to *Night Journey*. But, as a
choreographer Graham had been typecast, and such a bold move was almost
impossible to pull off.

Voyage had no temporal montage and no tragic heroism. Instead, Graham
attempted to lay the past to rest, to come to terms with personal emptiness in a
less-than-perfect future. Rather than a mythic nocturnal voyage-journey, this
voyage was itself a "theater" of the delusional present. The voyage, as Graham
conceived of it, was to wean herself from her attachment to Hawkins through
the development of a concept of relationships in flux: relationships would
henceforth be sophisticated, jaded, and aleatory. "The whole idea of a voyage,"
explained Ross, "is that you go out and there are going to be new relationships,
new combinations."[124] The psychoanalytic purpose of *Voyage* was to come to
terms with the separation from Hawkins by arriving at a different emotional
life and a substantially new personal identity.[125] If *Night Journey* was an anticipatory ritual of separation, *Voyage* was a post-ritual of becoming separate—individuation, in Jungian terms. Esther M. Harding explained that individuation
"affects the very character of the basic instincts, which instead of remaining
bound to their biological goals in a compulsive way, are transformed for the
service of the psyche."[126] Graham wrote Wickes: "I suppose the individuation
has to do with the displacement or sacrifice or re-slanting of the thing called
personality."[127] It seems clear that Wickes introduced Graham in treatment to
the Jungian concept of individuation. As Jung explained it, individuation
involves becoming oneself and overcoming what he calls "the primordial images" that are also associated in his writing with archetypes. As often with Jung,
the terms are difficult to differentiate. But, he does make the important distinction between individualism and individuation that was likely at the heart of
Wickes's therapeutic practice:

> We do not sufficiently distinguish between individualism and individu-
> ation. Individualism means deliberately stressing and giving promi-
> nence to some supposed peculiarity rather than to collective
> considerations and obligations . . . Individuation, therefore, can only
> mean a process of psychological development that fulfils the individual
> qualities given; in other words, it's a process by which a man becomes
> the definite, unique being he in fact is. In so doing he does not become
> "selfish" in the ordinary sense of the word, but is merely fulfilling the

particularity of his nature, and this, as we have said, is vastly different from egotism or individualism.[128]

Although some idea of the collective lies at the root of many Jungian concepts, and the "primordial image" is equated with the archetype, the therapeutic goal of individuation is to free the individual from the tyranny of the image, thereby allowing him or her to function productively as a social being. In this connection, the persona "implies only a mask of the collective psyche, a mask that *feigns individuality*, making others and oneself believe that one is individual whereas one is simply acting a role."[129] Given that Graham cast herself as the Actress in *Voyage*, she positioned individuation as the polar opposite of the persona. "The dissolution of the persona," added Jung to the appendices of "The Structure of the Unconscious," "is therefore absolutely necessary for individuation."[130] In sum, wrote Jung in "The Function of the Unconscious," "the aim of individuation is nothing less than to divest the self of the false wrappings of the persona on the one hand, and the suggestive power of primordial images on the other."[131] Graham cast herself as an Actress—the character who knows personae intimately—in order to signify her "voyage" toward individuation, her divestment of this very role in her life. It may have been too much to expect any choreography to render this analytic trajectory legible to an audience, and to contribute to a successful analysis.

Since Graham had been cultivating her interest in myth together with Hawkins since 1938 her choice in *Voyage* to jettison myth was understandable. Her separation from Hawkins had shaken Graham's faith in the mythic structure of life so that, by the early 1950s, mythic narrative in the interest of encryption no longer suited either her political or personal agenda. With *Voyage*, the consulting room reveals not a tired theatricality doomed to heavy-handed psychological motivation, but a postmodern aesthetic that Graham's detractors of the 1960s, focused as they were by 1958 on *Clytemnestra*, had not remembered or seen. *Voyage* does not represent the case of the reinterpretation of a work become overly familiar, but in need of rescue from the oblivion to which it was consigned by a legend of fame—the mythic image of the great artistic personality—that as Rank had warned in 1932 could spell the downfall of the modern artist. *Voyage* suggested an untried choreographic direction for Graham, which, had it been better received in New York might have opened up new and different directions for her late work.[132]

This is not to deny *Voyage* did also have an affirmative context through the idea of rebirth. Jung postulated many sorts of rebirth, but the kind Graham seems to have been concerned with in *Voyage* was what Jung called "rebirth within the span of an individual life," with a transformative aspect: "total rebirth of the individual."[133] Jung also calls this transmutation, and he relates it to "the transformation of a mortal into an immortal being" although Graham's cynical approach seems to preclude immortality, and the work is an attempt to evade such beliefs in immortality.[134]

The spiritual connotations of self-transformation were certainly present in later works, especially in *Seraphic Dialogue* (1955), which ends with the beatification of Saint Joan. Graham manipulated ideas to ring every possible viable theatrical realization out of them. She wrote Schuman on June 14, 1949, of her plans for *Judith*:

> This is what I call a legend of re-birth. It may take place in us at any time, as . . . when we write something after the time of fear and insecurity and driving hunger that makes us do it. *I say write because that means dance, too . . . a different kind of writing than music but still the writing of a soul's journey.*[135]

In this letter Graham linked choreography to the act of writing, which indicates how intermeshed writing and choreography had become for her. But, the fact that Graham equated dance with writing—I believe this is the only time she actually did this—also points to a changing relationship of dance to text in her choreographic practice of the early 1950s. Rather than compose scenarios whose deleted sections would subsist as repressed material within a finished dance— what I have called *encryption*—Graham's notes, notebooks, and letters of the early 1950s generated a sprawling matrix of images that she experimented with and reworked in a number of interrelated pieces.

Her association with poet Ben Belitt may have facilitated this new sense of expansion and amplification of stage images from a textual matrix. *Voyage, Ardent Song, Canticle for Innocent Comedians,* and *Embattled Garden* all emerged from a related matrix of images concerning innocence and experience.[136] *Diversion of Angels* also belongs to this cycle. Belitt's significance to Graham was not just through his poetic thought and suggestive verbal phrasing, although these indeed counted for much, but in what I should like to call a matrixial thinking. Because these pieces were an attempt to work through different ways of considering innocence and experience through one fund of images, they are variants of one another. Although she continued to read and quote other writers extensively, Graham's choreography of the early to mid-1950s was developed from a poetic and philosophical web of reflections that kept bifurcating and ramifying.

Although Belitt did not make a connection between *Canticle* and *Voyage,* his understanding of *Canticle* shows it to be an alternative reading of the dancer as actor-clown in Graham's notes for *Voyage.* The skepticism about relationships, which Graham wished to convince herself of in *Voyage,* took a new turn in *Canticle.* As Belitt remarked: "There is something comical about innocence.

To be skeptical about skepticism is to fall back into innocence . . . The last of all things you have to cancel out with skepticism is skepticism itself."[137] [Figure 5.4] The tongue-in-cheek archetypal characters of *Canticle* design a new space of innocence in the wake of skepticism. The dancers—For Sun, For Earth, For Fire, For Moon, and so on—become stand-ins for mythical or elemental forces whose archetypal import remains unknown to them. "The dancers," wrote Graham, "will not portray these powers in a symbolic sense."[138] As in *Voyage*, the idea of theater as a playing out of roles and positions allowed Graham to appear to return to mythical subject matter while treating it self-consciously as a theatrical exercise.

Figure 5.4 Mary Hinkson as For Earth in Martha Graham's *Canticle for Innocent Comedians* (1952). Courtesy of the Music Division, Library of Congress

Belitt thought Graham developed *Errand into the Maze* from one word. What he gave less emphasis to in looking back on their interchange was Graham's transference of words into spatial configurations. In the wake of *Night Journey*, Graham abandoned the idea of the labyrinth or maze for the wilderness or open sky in *Wilderness Stair*, renamed *Diversion of Angels*. She seems to have sought an alternative to the labyrinth: a space through which one could fall, but also a space through which one could fly. [Figure 5.5] Belitt, with whom she consulted and who gave her the title, understood this wilderness as a kind of desert. *Wilderness Stair*, in fact, although about the sky, was also a desert piece. Graham had sentimental associations with that landscape because she associated it both

Figure 5.5 Robert Cohan and Pearl Lang in Martha Graham's *Wilderness Stair* (1948).
Courtesy of the Music Division, Library of Congress

with Hawkins in 1939 and with their trip to Santa Fe where they were married in 1948. Belitt remembered: "The dance had some relation to her previous return to Santa Fe. It was a desert dance. People don't know that. They don't view it as such."[139] Myth in Graham's work, which had induced a certain way to see a dance while obscuring its personal ritual meaning, was exchanged for spatial conceits that collapse myth and ritual into spatial contradictions. Although there was no set, Noguchi originally "devised a full burlap backdrop, stretched along all its edges by ropes through grommets. From behind, here and there, long rods were pushed to modulate the cloth into undulating clouds of breasts and valleys."[140] Bertram Ross remembers that these undulating clouds also resembled mounds of sand, creating the desert atmosphere. But the desert landscape was also a metaphor for the celestial space of the heavens. In a similar manner, *Voyage* suggested a contradictory location: a desert that was also an ocean. *Voyage* was not an antidote to *Wilderness Stair*, but its disabused aftermath.

Voyage is thus an unrecognized turning point in Graham's work for more reasons than one. It reveals that her methodology in the 1950s was to choreograph from a matrix of images without erasing the work's genesis through encryption. Each work in this cycle contained genetic elements proper to the others. *Voyage* placed the conscious and the unconscious forces on an equal plane of visibility, and it is perhaps for this reason that all of these works were related to ideas of space as expanse: desert, ocean, sky. Expanse suggests visibility and militates against the secretive enclosures of the maze, the cave, or the underground meadow. One can observe this shift in approach not only in the dances themselves but in the notes that led up to them where dreams, fragments of quotes from reading, and associations noted down from daily life also furnished compositional ideas directly from poetic language.

Many works of the early 1950s were also connected by similar settings. For example, the ambiance of *Embattled Garden*, a retelling of *Adam and Eve* recalls Graham's notes for *Voyage*: a hot climate or southern locale associated with Spain. [Figure 5.6] As composer Carlos Surinach put it, "The serpent shows Eve how to make love to Adam; Lilith teaches Adam how to make love to Eve. And, then, the thing ends exactly as it began, but no one is pure anymore."[141] This analysis seems to correspond point for point to Lefebvre's characterization of abstract space as a "whole set of locations where contradictions are generated." Lefebvre describes the space of these contradictions as the medium "in which [they] evolve and which they tear apart, and lastly the means whereby they are smothered and replaced by an appearance of consistency."[142] If the crypt belongs to absolute space, abstract space by contrast seals off the subterranean dimension and replaces it with the extended surfaces of desert, ocean, and sky. Abstract space is made up of conflicting energies expended in the exploration of alternatives or in the exercise of contradictions—for example, the contradiction

Figure 5.6 Martha Graham's *Embattled Garden* (1958). Courtesy of the Dance Collection,
New York Public Library for the Performing Arts

between ocean and desert in *Voyage,* or between desert and sky in *Diversion of
Angels.* In *Embattled Garden,* innocence and experience are apparently opposed
yet finally become collapsed into one another in an overly charged dramatic
framework where nothing further can happen, but in which the end resembles
the beginning. The end of *Embattled Garden* is the dead end of bourgeois con-
ventionality, just as the end of *Voyage* carried the promise of a future for antiso-
cial perversity. Thus, Graham's endings in these works are tantamount to the
working out of dilemmas. The spatial antitheses of abstract space in these works
reflected the contradictions, mendacity, and conformism of Cold War culture.
But, the unpacking of antithetical alternatives also indicates a kind of trap or
stasis. The works of the early 1950s are not spin-offs of the great myth works of
the late 1940s, but a marked change of direction. While archetypes and mythical
references are not entirely absent in the 10 years between *Diversion of Angels*
and *Embattled Garden,* they appear to be uprooted from the alternative psychoanalytic theory that had informed them in the 1940s, and retheatricalized as
anti-tragedies.

Given that the early 1950s was the era of McCarthyism in the United States
and a time of consensus thinking and conformity, Graham's gesture in *Voyage*
could be considered either oblivious to her social and political surroundings
because obsessed with her personal problems or, in fact, highly perspicacious, if
still ever cautious, in offering the most cleverly oblique of antidotes to the reality

that all social life was now encrypted. It was time to *decrypt* the contradictions and impasses of political and sexual life, which she had until now *encrypted* in mythic terms. Contradictions were now situated in abstract rather than absolute space where they were not only visible, but were also rendered in contemporary terms. Although the theme of rebirth could imply a mystical context, the works in which rebirth was stymied were the most contemporary. The biblical *Embattled Garden* was as contemporary as *Voyage* in that the critics perceived the theme of suburban wife swapping, and Noguchi's décor suggested modern furniture in the Garden of Eden. *Embattled Garden* suggested that experience is the simulacrum of innocence. In the early 1950s Graham undertook a critique of experience, which she had earlier set up as the strongest rationale for dancing. All acts and thoughts could now stand exposed and be analyzed, albeit with the admission of their intense artificiality, their commoditization—in sum, their fully theatricalized nature.

Conclusion

Martha Graham's political and sexual self-consciousness were forged in the crucible of the prewar and war periods that corresponded to a period of intense creative activity linked to her relationship with Erick Hawkins. Despite the fact that Graham's choreographic reputation is most firmly based on her myth works, she rejected myth at the beginning and the end of this period. In 1938 her rejection of myth was due to its Fascist implications in the tradition of Sorel. *American Document* was a pro-democracy work with a popular front politics that deftly substituted utopia for myth. Through the association of patriarchy with authoritarianism Graham also shunned the National Socialist position on women as begetters of male children for the fatherland. With *American Document*, however, her work became more accessible to a general public as she began to choreograph roles for men and women. Rejecting biological motherhood and defending her autonomy as a woman artist, Graham nevertheless served as an icon of productive femininity for the Allies during the war, which helped to advance her career despite her deep ideological resistance to this role. During the war Graham continued her Americana-themed work, but encrypted her left-oriented politics to make them appear centrist.

In the postwar period she turned to myth in order to explore a pre-patriarchal concept of womanhood that, while inspired by Bachofen and Harrison, was so ahead of its time that it risked appearing politically retrogressive in the immediate postwar context. In the consumerist and conformist society of the late 1940s, Graham's use of myth set her apart from the norms and values of the society that, in wartime, had fostered her image as role model for the average American woman. By the end of the decade, with many women leaving the workplace and returning to the domestic sphere, Graham was herself established as a mythical subject, a sacred monster of dance modernism, and a public figure whose insight was oracular and prophetic, but also perverse. Although the mainstream media had promoted her career before and during the war, it could only grasp her myth works as the production of a new "intellectual" priesthood of dance, while the general public received these works as an anthropological and psychoanalytic exploration of the unconscious, helping them to confront the unacknowledged darkness of their own lives. In fact, the myth works were engaged with post-Freudian theory thanks to which the primacy of the Oedipus complex was questioned and a reexamination of the neglected role of the mother in psychoanalytic theory took place. These works had a depth and complexity unfamiliar to most other dance of the period, but they were also accessible to the average contemporary theatergoer. The performance of myths masked the personal rituals embedded in them, thanks to which Graham sought to work through her foundering relationship with Hawkins. In this way, she developed a multichanneled psychoanalytic relationship to her work and to her audience. The sites of this relationship were all Jungian-based images of the feminine: the labyrinth, the cave, the tomb, the ship.

Graham rejected myth a second time in *Voyage* (1953) in an attempt to undo the impasse mythmaking had created in her relationship with Hawkins. Graham had become defined by myth both personally and professionally. Mythical thinking became intertwined, in particular, with her understanding of interpersonal dynamics and permeated her psychoanalytic experience with Jungian analyst Frances Wickes. Her transformation in *Voyage* from a tragic actress of mythical roles to a contemporary woman in a cocktail dress was difficult for the public and the critics to fathom and accept. Graham, it turned out, was trapped in a formula, condemned to relive myth repeatedly in her future work, and unable to transform the social and personal terms of her engagement with Hawkins, even as a retrospective gesture. The tyranny of myth was at once Graham's greatest choreographic invention and her most tragic personal ordeal.

The purpose of Graham's myth choreographies of the late 1940s and of her psychodramatic experiments of the early 1950s was to dramatize her own quest for individuation both personally and artistically, a quest that had psychoanalytic connotations in the Jungian milieu of Graham's analysis but also political connotations in the context of her own life. Graham was a marriage-resister throughout her career. As Adrienne Rich has noted:

> The twentieth-century, educated young woman, looking perhaps at her mother's life, or trying to create an autonomous self in a society which insists that she is destined primarily for reproduction, has with good reason felt that the choice was an inescapable either/or: motherhood or individuation, motherhood or creativity, motherhood or freedom.[1]

It follows that Graham did not so much reject the mother role on stage as embody mother and daughter as two codependent figures independent of men. The layered quality of many of her roles harks back to the Demeter-Kore (Persephone) pair that she first found in Jane Harrison. She encountered it again in 1953 in "The Psychological Aspects of the Kore" where Jung identifies the double figure as an archetype of the dancer.[2] Jung remarks that a "frequent modulation" of the mother-maiden figure "is the *dancer*, who is often formed by borrowings from classical knowledge, in which case the 'maiden' appears as the *corybant, maenad,* or *nymph*."[3] In *Prolegomena to Greek Religion* Jane Harrison sees the binary as facets of one identity: "It is important to note that primarily the two forms of the Earth or Corn-Goddess are not Mother and Daughter, but Mother and Maiden, Demeter and Kore. They are, in fact, merely the older and younger form of the same person."[4] Opposed qualities in related feminine figures or opposed identities within one feminine figure point to a mythical synthesis in many Graham characters. The Demeter/Kore dyad was Graham's first and most significant character compression. Esther Harding wrote: "the mother or the old woman is a universal figure in nearly all mythologies. This woman has a child but no husband."[5] Kerényi quoted Jung as saying: "Demeter-Kore exists on the plane of mother-daughter experience, which is alien to the man and shuts him out. In fact, the Demeter cult has all the features of a matriarchal order of society, where the man is an indispensable but on the whole disturbing factor."[6] Although Graham envisaged motherhood as a symbol of rebirth (being one's own mother), or through mythologically inflected aspects of mother and daughter in danced characters, she never took on the theme of biological motherhood per se. She was herself both old and young—prolonging her dancing career miraculously into her 60s. Until the mid-1950s her age was difficult to determine on stage: she embodied concurrently what for most people are distinct phases of life.

By 1962 the effects of aging and alcoholism on Graham's choreography and dancing were inescapable. With *Phaedra* we had the first look at a different Graham who was well past her prime and no longer entirely in control of her image. Ross cites one spectator's reaction to *Phaedra* in Holland: "This proves Martha's humanness. At last a bad Graham work."[7] Her company, although maturing in age, never looked better: Ethel Winter, Yuriko, Helen McGehee, Mary Hinkson, Matt Turney, and Ross himself understood the theatricality of her work and how to perform it to maximum effect. However, Graham's new work appeared highly decadent in several senses, and she could no longer dominate the dance scene as she had done in the 1940s and to a great degree even across the 1950s. Throughout the 1960s she continued to create large-scale dramas with herself at the center of the action. Graham had become a caricature of herself: a psychoanalytic monster. As Jill Johnston wrote in 1968: "[T]he way she's been depicting herself in her works all these years is clearly as an inverted homo hetero sado masochistic sodomist. Why not? It doesn't matter."[8] In 1969, however, LeRoy Leatherman, executive director of the Company, wrote to board member Jeannette Roosevelt of "a case of incurable alcoholism" and of the Company as a "sunken ship."[9] While I do not intend to analyze the last 30 years of Graham's career I would like to reflect on the significance of her work for American culture beyond the 1940s. Graham's afterlife should, in my view, not be assessed in terms of the publicity coups and celebrity turns of her survival during the last 30 years of her life, nor in the works she created in those years.

Many pages of this book have been devoted to the influence on Graham of Anglo-American modernism. Although that influence is rooted in the beginning of the twentieth century I also want to indicate how Graham's work looked ahead. The true afterlife of Graham's mythic status as the mother of modern dance is neither her self-parody in the 1960s nor her failure to outlive herself, but her prefiguration of the analysis of patriarchy that followed the reevaluation of motherhood in the late 1960s leading up to the publication of Kate Millett's *Sexual Politics* (1970).[10] Some day it will have to be told how Jungianism, which started out in US art more or less as anti-Fascist psychoanalytic modernism, turned into the analysis of patriarchy and thereby cleared the way heroically, for what was to come. The relays in Graham's work between the political and the personal at mid-century performed both retrospective and prophetic gestures.

Throughout the 1940s Graham both fashioned and resisted images of herself and her art in the guise of publicity, myth, archetype, persona, and fame. In developing a subject position as a major woman artist at mid-century, her image was at once a necessity, a brilliant accomplishment, and a double-edged sword. Her work is interlaced with a questioning of the image that counsels caution when confronted by discourses that position dance as emblem and symbol. Historian Warren I. Susman discussed Graham's *Appalachian Spring* as an emblem of the 1940s, which he dubbed "the age of Jung."[11] "[T]he new lyric theater . . . strove to provide a new sense of common belief, common ritual observance, common emotional sharing that the psychological conditions of the era seemed to demand. Heroes, symbols, myths, and rituals: A Jungian age in America."[12] While Susman's characterization is not misplaced, it occludes the political and personal complexity out of which *Appalachian Spring* emerged, and does not acknowledge the very different contribution *Night Journey* made to the "psychoanalytic conditions of the era." I have tried to fill in the gaps and missing pieces here to show that, in the final analysis, the history of dance is not "dance history," but, in fact, *history*.

ENDNOTES

Introduction

1. Amanda Porterfield, "Modern Grace" in *Feminine Spirituality in America. From Sarah Edwards to Martha Graham* (Philadelphia: Temple University Press, 1980), 189–201. For a study of Graham in the context of religious studies, see Kimerer L. LaMothe, *Nietzsche's Dancers. Isadora Duncan, Martha Graham, and the Revaluation of Christian Values* (London: Palgrave Macmillan, 2006). LaMothe sees Graham's work as a "theopraxis": "Her dances present 'dancing' in contested interdependence with textual practices as a complementary medium for interpreting symbols, themes, and texts from western, mostly Christian, religions" (154). While I understand the relation Graham practiced between choreography and text to be essential to her productivity, I do not understand Graham's relation to texts as religious exegesis.
2. Howard Gardner, *Creating Minds. An Anatomy of Creativity Seen Through the Lives of Freud, Einstein, Picasso, Stravinsky, Eliot, Graham, and Gandhi* (New York: Basic Books, 1993), 265–309.
3. There is a trend among dance scholars to see the authorship of Graham's autobiography *Blood Memory* as questionable. See Victoria Geduld, "Martha Graham's Gilded Cage: *Blood Memory: An Autobiography* (1991)" in *Dance Research Journal* (2012).
4. A similar point has been made recently by Joellen A. Meglin and Lynn Matluck Brooks: "We dare say that much less has been written about Graham than anyone else on Gardner's list (or even some lesser or less radical artists)." "Why a Special Issue on Martha Graham?" in *Dance Chronicle* 33/1 (2010), 1.
5. This perspective is made also possible by the opening of the archives of both Martha Graham and Erick Hawkins at the Music Division of the Library of Congress in Washington, D.C., and of the Bertram Ross Papers at the Dance Collection of the New York Public Library for the Performing Arts, in conjunction with access to interviews McDonagh and de Mille recorded with Graham's associates in preparation for their biographies. Interviews concerning Graham recorded since the 1970s, and housed at the Dance Collection and at Library of Congress, further supplement these materials. These resources are also supplemented in turn by author interviews of key informants over the last two years.
6. According to Bertram Ross, Graham's last appearances on stage were in *Time of Snow* and *Lady of the House of Sleep* in 1968. Bertram Ross Papers, Jerome Robbins Dance Collection, New York Public Library for the Performing Arts, box 24, folder 14.
7. Selby Wynn Schwartz, "Martha@Martha: a Seance with Richard Move," in *Women & Performance* Vol. 20, No. 1 (March 2010), 61–87.
8. This is not to deny that there have been remarkable interpreters of Graham's repertory, particularly in the 1980s, notably Christine Dakin and Teresa Capucilli.

9. Emiko Tokunaga notes: "Martha offered little help in the reconstruction of her dances which were not currently being performed in the company repertoire." *Yuriko: An American Japanese Dancer: to Wash in the Rain and Polish with the Wind* (n.p.: Tolunaga Dance Ko., 2008), 105. One notable exception was Graham's investment in coaching Mary Hinkson in a revival of *Deaths and Entrances* and *Cave of the Heart*. Graham seems to have had a particular identification with Hinkson on stage. I am grateful to Mary Hinkson for discussing this with me on September 15, 2011, in New York City. Helen McGehee wrote that Graham offered no help in the original reconstruction of *Cave of the Heart* in 1965 when McGehee performed Medea. However, Graham did generously coach her in *Errand into the Maze* when it was revived in 1959. Helen McGehee, *To Be a Dancer* (Lynchburg, Virginia: Editions Heraclita, 1989), n.p.

10. It should be noted, however, that Graham had no interest in commercializing her work through contact with either Hollywood or Broadway. On January 16, 1944, she wrote to David Zellmer: "I had the experience of saying no to an offer from one of the biggest agents in the country, a man who owns 20% of RKO films. He wanted to sign me up to sell to Hollywood and a Broadway show ... It is not that I feel superior but that I feel it is not my area ..." Martha Graham letters to David Zellmer, Dance Collection, New York Public Library for the Performing Arts at Lincoln Center, (S)*MGZMD 117.

11. Amy Koritz, *Culture Makers. Urban Performance and Literature in the 1920s* (Urbana & Chicago: University of Illinois Press, 2009), 168, note 3.

12. Edwin Denby, *Dance Writings*, edited by Robert Cornfield and William Mackay (New York: Knopf, 1986), 42.

13. Alma Lubin, "New Dance Ideas Offered In Latest Graham Creations" in *Cincinnati Enquirer* (January 9, 1944), Martha Graham Collection, Music Division, Library of Congress, Scrapbooks.

14. My personal history of watching Graham's work on stage goes back to 1962.

15. Eric Gould, *Mythical Intentions in Modern Literature* (Princeton: Princeton University Press, 1981), 6.

16. This corresponds in visual art to the transition between Regionalism as typified by Thomas Hart Benton and Abstract Expressionism as typified by Jackson Pollack. See Erika Lee Doss, *Benton, Pollock and the Politics of Modernism: from Regionalism to Abstract Expressionism* (Chicago: University of Chicago Press, 1991).

17. Reminiscences of Ben Belitt (February 17, 1979), Bennington Summer School of the Dance Project, page 36 in the Columbia University Center for Oral History Research Office, Columbia University, 36.

18. For an important discussion of the invisible and the absent in contemporary dance, see Gerald Siegmund, *Abwesenheit: eine performative Ästhetik des Tanzes; William Forsythe, Jérôme Bel, Xavier Le Roy, Meg Stuart* (Bielefeld: Transcript Verlag, 2006)

19. Of course, another major influence on Graham was nineteenth-century American literature—particularly Nathaniel Hawthorne—and Emily Dickinson. Graham's connection to the American Transcendentalist School was particular to the early 1940s.

20. Susan Jones, "'At the Still Point.' T.S. Eliot, Dance, and Modernism," in *Dance Research Journal* 41/2 (Winter 2009), 44.

21. Martha Graham letter to William Schuman, June 24, 1949, William Schuman Records and Papers, Music Division, New York Public Library for the Performing Arts, JPB 87-33, box 18, folder 10.

22. Ibidem.

23. See Mary Carruthers, "Rhetorical *Ductus*, or, Moving through a Composition" in *Acting on the Past: Historical Performance Across the Disciplines* edited by Mark Franko and Annette Richards (Middletown: Wesleyan University Press, 2000), 99–117.

24. Wassily Kandinsky, *Concerning the Spiritual in Art*, translated by M.T.H Sadler (New York: Dover Books, 1977), 32.

25. Martha Graham letter to William Schuman, June 14, 1949, William Schuman Records and Papers, Music Division, New York Public Library for the Performing Arts, box 18, folder 10.

26. Reminiscences of Abram Kardiner (June 1965), The Psychoanalytic Movement Project: oral history (1965–1982), Oral History Research Office, Columbia University, 456. I wish to thank Mary Marshall Clark for her generous help in introducing me to this material.

27. Adrienne Rich, *Of Woman Born: Motherhood as Experience and Institution* (New York & London: W.W. Norton & Co., 1995), 72.

28. David Sears published "Martha Graham: The Golden Thread" in *Ballet Review* 14/3 (Fall 1986): 44–64. He calls this "the labyrinth article"; also, "Graham Masterworks in Revival," *Ballet Review* 11/12 (1982): 25–34. Sears's critical methodology was very influenced by Joseph Campbell. Sears's thesis of the golden thread through Graham's work transforms the idea of the labyrinth into a category of thematic criticism applicable to all of her work. The influence of Campbell was ultimately an obstacle to the development of his critical insights.

29. David Sears interview with Lesley Farlow, March 27, 1992, Jerome Robbins Dance Collection, New York Public Library of the Performing Arts: (*MGZMT 3–1657), 16.

30. David Sears Papers, Jerome Robbins Dance Division, New York Public Library for the Performing Arts: (S)*MGZMD 184.

Chapter 1

1. For a discussion of Graham's politics and aesthetics from the early to mid-1930s, see my *Dancing Modernism/Performing Politics* (Bloomington: Indiana University Press, 1995) and *The Work of Dance: Labor, Movement, and Identity in the 1930s* (Middletown: Wesleyan University Press, 2002).

2. Martha Graham, Letter to Rudolf von Laban, March 14, 1936. Scrapbooks, Martha Graham Archive, Library of Congress. Those who would not be welcome in Germany were the Jewish members of Graham's company.

3. Leonore Latimer, "Dance Activities of Martha Graham Outside the Concert Field" (prepared in the class of Martha Hill, Juilliard School of Music), Typescript in Martha Graham Clippings File, Jerome Robbins Dance Collection. New York Public Library for the Performing Arts: *MGZR Res-17.

4. Cecile Whiting, *Antifascism in American Art* (New Haven & London: Yale University Press, 1989), 41.

5. Morgan contributed to a discussion about the inclusion of photography in the American Artists' Congress. See her "Photography and the Plastic Arts," in *The American Artist. News Bulletin of the American Artists' Congress* vol. 1/no. 2 (Summer 1937).

6. *3rd Annual Membership Exhibition. American Artists' Congress* (February 5–26, 1939). Archives of American Art, Smithsonian Museum, Washington, D.C. The John Reed clubs charter contained a platform against imperialist war and Fascism since 1932. See also Matthew Baigell and Julia Williams, editors, *Artists against War and Fascism: Papers of the First American Artists' Congress* (Rutgers: Rutgers University Press, 1986). I have been unable to locate the text of Graham's talk, "The Dance: An Allied Art." The theme was "the artist in relation to peace," according to "The Open Session at Carnegie Hall," *American Artist. News Bulletin of the American Artists' Congress* Vol. I, no. 3 (Winter 1937), 1.

7. "A Call to a Congress of American Artists in Defense of Culture," June 6–8, 1941, New York City. Archives of American Arts, Smithsonian Museum, Washington, D.C. Barbara Morgan lobbied for the inclusion of photography in the membership of the American Artists' Congress: "To incorporate this group of workers in the body of the Congress would be a great stimulation," she wrote in "Photography and the Plastic Arts," in *The American Artist. New Bulletin of the American Artists' Congress*, vol. I, no. 2 (Winter 1937), 1.

8. E. J. Hobsbawm, *Nations and Nationalism since 1780: Programme, Myth, Reality* (Cambridge: Cambridge University Press, 1990), 147.

9. See "The American Artists' Congress: Its Context and History," in *Artists Against War and Fascism*, 2–44.

10. Graham cited in Marcia Minor, "Graham Interprets Democracy" in *The Daily Worker*.

11. Lewis Mumford, *Men Must Act* (New York: Harcourt, Brace and Company, 1939).

12. Lewis Mumford, "A Call to Arms," in *New Republic* 95/1124 (May 18, 1938), 39–42.

13. R. Alan Lawson, *The Failure of Independent Liberalism (1930–1941)* (New York: G.P. Putnam's Sons, 1971).

14. "A Dancer and an Educator on Fascism," *Dance Observer* (March 1937). See also, Lilian Karina, "Laban's Downfall and Post-Labanism," in Lilian Karina and Marion Kant, *Hitler's*

Dancers. German Modern Dance and the Third Reich, translated by Jonathan Steinberg (New York and Oxford: Berghahn Books, 2003), 57–61.

15. Susan Manning, *Ecstasy and the Demon: Feminism and Nationalism in the Dances of Mary Wigman* (Berkeley: University of California Press, 1993), 194. "Although her leadership of German dance was undermined," notes Manning, "her status as the figurehead of the movement was never challenged. More important, neither her life nor her livelihood was ever endangered" (*Ecstasy and the Demon*, 207). "Wigman did contribute however to Nazi spectacle," adds Manning, "as part of a team that staged the opening-night festival for the 1936 Berlin Olympic Games." (275–278). Unlike Laban, Wigman did not fall from favor with the Culture Ministry until 1941–42.

16. Martha Graham, "A Dancer Speaks," a talk delivered at the Professional Conference against Nazi Persecution, published in *TAC* (January 1939).

17. Lincoln Kirstein published an article on Nazi painting, sculpture and architecture in 1945, but never wrote about Nazi dance. See his "Art in the Third Reich—Survey, 1945," in *Magazine of Art* 35/6 (October 1945), 223–238; 240–242. Strangely, as regards dance, we had to wait almost 50 years for information. See Lilian Karina and Marion Kant, *Hitler's Dancers* and Laure Guilbert, *Danser avec le IIIe Reich. Les danseurs modernes sous le nazisme* (Brussels: Editions Complexe, 2000).

18. Mark Rothko and Adolph Gottlieb, precursors of the abstract expressionists, were the first to introduce non-narrative, mythical subjects in their painting between 1938 and 1941. Both rejected, however, nationalist engagement in art. See Whiting, "Antinationalist Myth," in *Antifascism in American Art*, 170–196.

19. Adolf Hitler quoted in Alex Scobie, *Hitler's State Architecture. The Impact of Classical Antiquity* (University Park & London: The Pennsylvania State University Press, 1990), 16.

20. Erin Manning analyzes Riefenstahl's techniques of rendering movement in the cinematographic image in her *Relationscapes: Movement, Art, Philosophy* (Cambridge, Mass.: MIT, 2009). See also, Anson Rabinbach, "The Body without Fatigue: A Nineteenth-Century Utopia," in *Political Symbolism in Modern Europe. Essays in Honor of George L. Mosse*, edited by Seymour Drescher, David Sabean, and Allan Sharlin (New Brunswick & London: Transaction Books, 1982), 42–62.

21. "In 1938, Martha Graham made a totally unexpected overture in my direction. She asked me to work with her in her new production for Bennington. She needed a leading man." José Limón, *An Unfinished Memoir* edited by Lynn Garafola (Hanover & London: University Press of New England, 1999), 87.

22. Walter Benjamin, "The Work of Art in the Age of Mechanical Reproduction" in *Illuminations* edited by Hannah Arendt (New York: Schocken Books, 1969).

23. See David Smith, *Medals for Dishonor* (New York: Independent Curators Incorporated, 1996). I thank Candida Smith for introducing me to the connections between Smith and Graham.

24. "Graham's view of the American past reflected contemporary racial segregation and appropriation." Julia Foulkes, *Modern Bodies. Dance and American Modernism from Martha Graham to Alvin Ailey* (Chapel Hill & London: University of North Carolina Press, 2002), 151. Manning claims Graham's work became "revolutionary" in 1944 when she cast the Japanese dancer Yuriko in *Appalachian Spring*. (Manning, *Modern Dance/Negro Dance*, 141).

25. Reminiscences of Francis Fergusson, February 12, 1979, Bennington Summer School of Dance Project, Oral History Research Office, Columbia University, 54.

26. Bertram Ross Papers, Dance Collection, New York Public Library for the Performing Arts at Lincoln Center, box 10, folder 25, p. 2.

27. Emiko Tokunaga, *Yuriko. An American Japanese Dancer: To Wash In the Rain and Polish With the Wind (N.p.: Tokunaga Dance Ko, 2008), 63.*

28. Merle Armitage interview with Don McDonagh, 1972, Dance Collection, New York Public Library for the Performing Arts at Lincoln Center, *MGZTL 4–2524.

29. In this letter Graham was trying to dissuade Zellmer from his romantic interest in Lang. There is much evidence in Graham's correspondence with Zellmer, in which she only mentions Hawkins once, of her own attraction to him. Graham also predicts that Lang would not marry a non-Jew.

30. Martha Graham letter to David Zellmer, June 5, 1945, Dance Collection, New York Public Library for the Performing Arts at Lincoln Center.

31. Pearl Lang interview with Agnes de Mille, November 29, 1982, Dance Collection, New York Public Library for the Performing Arts, *MGZTC 3–1627.

32. Pearl Lang interviewed by Don McDonagh, October 1, 1977, Dance Collection, New York Public Library for the Performing Arts at Lincoln Center, *MGZTL 4–2484.

33. Ellen Graff, *Stepping Left. Dance and Politics in New York City, 1928–1942* (Durham & London: Duke University Press, 1997), 127.

34. Peter Viereck, *Metapolitics. From the Romantics to Hitler* (New York: Alfred A. Knopf, 1941), 230.

35. "Dance Libretto: *American Document*, by Martha Graham," in *Theatre Arts* 26/9 (September 1942), 566. It is hereafter referred to in notes as "Dance Libretto." Francis Fergusson relates that while he was at Bennington he wrote "a little scenario for Martha Graham, which she used, but I think she never acknowledged it." Later in the same interview Fergusson modifies this claim: "I didn't really give her a whole scenario; just a dab that she needed some assistance with—you know, a minute and-a-half, two minutes." However the collaboration occurred, the fact remains that all Graham's other scenarios were single authored. Francis Fergusson interview with Theresa Bowers, February 12, 1979, Bennington Summer School of Dance Project, Oral History Research Office, Columbia University, 30; 32–33.

36. "Dance Libretto," 566.

37. André Jolles, *Einfache Formen* (Tübingen: Max Niemeyer Verlag, 1958).

38. Roland Barthes, *Mythologies* translated by Annette Lavers (New York: Hill & Wang, 1982), 147.

39. William Carlos Williams, *The Autobiography of William Carlos Williams* (New York: Random House, 1948), 178. Williams relates that Graham wrote to him about *In the American Grain*, "saying she could not have gone on with her choreographic projects without it" (237). Although he attempted to meet with her in Bennington he was not able to gain an audience.

40. "Dance Libretto," 565.

41. "Dance Libretto," 565.

42. Alice Yaeger Kaplan, *Reproductions of Banality: Fascism, Literature, and French Intellectual Life* (Minneapolis: University of Minnesota Press, 1986), 125.

43. Inge Baxmann, *Mythos Gemeinschaft: Körper und Tanzkulturen in der Moderne* (Munich: Wilhelm Fink, 2000), esp. 179–252.

44. Georges Sorel, *Reflections on Violence*, translation by T. E. Hulme & J. Roth (Glencoe, IL: the Free Press, 1950), 58.

45. Sorel, *Reflections on Violence*, 55–56.

46. Erin Manning, *Relationscapes*, 121.

47. Sorel, *Reflections on Violence*, 56.

48. Sorel, *Reflections on Violence*, 57.

49. Philippe Lacoue-Labarthe and Jean-Luc Nancy, "The Nazi Myth" translated by Brian Holmes in *Critical Inquiry* 16 (Winter 1990), 304.

50. Sorel, *Reflections on Violence*, 57.

51. Willy Gianinazzi, *Naissance du mythe moderne. Georges Sorel et la crise de la pensée savante (1889–1914)* (Paris: Editions de la Maison des Sciences de l'Homme, 2006), 85.

52. David Gross, "Myth and Symbol in Georges Sorel," in *Political Symbolism in Modern Europe. Essays in Honor of George L. Mosse*, edited by Seymour Drescher, David Sabean, and Allan Sharlin (New Brunswick & London: Transaction Books, 1982), 105.

53. Martha Graham quoted in Merle Armitage, *Martha Graham* 1937; rpt. New York: Dance Horizons, 1966), 103; Lewis Mumford, "Call to Arms," *New Republic* 95/1224 (May 18, 1938), 39–42.

54. "Dance Libretto," p. 568.

55. Erick Hawkins interview with Don McDonagh, November 17, 1972. Jerome Robbins Dance Collection, New York Public Library for the Performing Arts: *MGZTL 4–2556.

56. Ray Green interview with Theresa Bowers, March 11, 1979, Bennington Summer School of Dance Project, Oral History Research Office, Columbia University, 21.

57. "Dance Libretto," 567.
58. Langston Hughes, "Let America Be America Again," in *The Collected Poems of Langston Hughes*, edited by Arnold Rampersad (New York: Alfred A. Knopf, 2001), 189–191.
59. George W. Beiswanger, "The New Theatre Dance," in *Theatre Arts Monthly* 23/1 (January 1939), 54. As Susan Manning points out, these "reformist" tendencies disappeared by the early 1940s. I think the term "anti-Fascism" is more historically revealing and pertinent to the analysis than "reformism." Susan Manning, "American Document and American Minstrelsy," in *Moving Words, re-writing dance*, edited by Gay Morris (London: Routledge, 1996), 183–202.
60. Erick Hawkins interviewed by Don McDonagh, November 17, 1972, Jerome Robbins Dance Collection, New York Public Library for the Performing Arts: *MGZTL 4–2556.
61. William Carlos Williams, *In the American Grain*, ix.
62. Martha Graham interviewed by Leah Plotkin on The Works Progress Administration Federal Radio Theatre program: Exploring the Seven Arts, June 23, 1937. Typescript of interview in Martha Graham, Clippings File, Jerome Robbins Dance Collection, New York Public Library for the Performing Arts: *MGZR Res.-box 17.
63. Erdman specialized in the speaking role of *Letter to the World* and later experimented with the text of James Joyce's *Finnegan's Wake* in her *The Coach with the Six Insides* (1966). Jane Dudley relates that Graham set the group sections of *American Document* in New York in the late spring. Graham spent her rehearsal time at Bennington making the duets and solos for herself and Hawkins, which left the female members of her company to rehearse on their own. "It was a drag," stated Dudley. Jane Dudley interview with Theresa Bowers, December 20, 1978, Bennington Summer School of the Dance Project, Oral Research History Office, Columbia University, 34.
64. Erdman and Campbell were married on May 5, 1938. Erdman was also in Bennington as a student in the summer of 1937. See Jean Erdman interview with Theresa Bowers (Theatre of the Open Eye, NYC, 16, July 1979), Bennington Summer School of the Dance Project, Oral Research History Office, Columbia University, 18 & 43.
65. Erdman states that de Mille was wrong about Graham meeting Campbell at Sarah Lawrence College, where he was teaching. Erdman, however, did meet Graham there.
66. "[T[here can be little doubt, either that myths are of the nature of the dream, or that dreams are symptomatic of the dynamics of the psyche." Joseph Campbell, *The Hero With a Thousand Faces* (Princeton: Princeton University Press, 1949), 255.
67. Jean Erdman interview with Don McDonagh, October 4, 1993. Jerome Robbins Dance Collection, New York Public Library for the Performing Arts: *MGZTL 4–2567.
68. Joseph Campbell interviewed by Agnes de Mille, Jerome Robbins Dance Collection, New York Public Library for the Performing Arts, MGZTC 3–1612.
69. Joseph Campbell interviewed by Agnes de Mille, Dance Collection, New York Public Library for the Performing Arts, MGZTC 3–1612. *Immediate Tragedy* premiered in July 1937 at Bennington. The second anti-Fascist solo, *Deep Song*, was premiered in December 1937 in New York.
70. Robert Ellwood, *The Politics of Myth. A Study of C.G. Jung, Mircea Eliade, and Joseph Campbell* (Albany: State University of New York Press, 1999), 138–140. According to Robert Ellwood "... [A]ll three mythologists [Jung, Eliade, and Campbell] have at times been associated with the politics of the extreme right, even, according to some charges, with sympathy for fascism and anti-Semitism." (p. vii).
71. M. Esther Harding, Eleanor Bertine, and Kristine Mann founded the Analytical Psychology Club of New York. See Maggy Anthony, *The Valkyries. The Women Around Jung* (Longmead, Shaftesbury and Dorset: Element Books, 1990), 45. I thank Ann Foley for calling my attention to this book. Graham read Harding in the late 1940s.
72. Otto Rank letter to Jessie Taft quoted in E. James Lieberman, *Acts of Will. The Life and Work of Otto Rank* (New York: The Free Press, 1985), 379. Jung's "Wotan" article was originally published in Zurich in 1936, and appeared in *The Saturday Review of Literature* on October 16, 1937. A longer version in a different translation is in the *Collected Works*, volume 10 (179–193). The ambiguities of Jung's statements between 1936 and 1939 about the Third Reich did not register with the American public during the war although they were

discussed in intellectual circles. According to William Graebner, Jungianism was part and parcel of 1940s Americanism: "Americans of the forties also explored Jung's interest in a collective unconscious by fusing the Jungian emphasis on the collective with certain early-1940s ideas of nationalism and the 'people' to locate, assert, and celebrate a deep interest in 'folk identity.'" William Graebner, *The Age of Doubt. American Thought and Culture in the 1940s* (Boston: Twayne Publishers, 1991), 75. On Jung's role in German psychotherapy under the Nazis, see Andrew Samuels, *The Political Psyche* (London & New York: Routledge, 1993), 287–316. Questions were raised about Jung's politics in the United States after the war. The *Bulletin of the Analytical Psychology Club of New York City* 8/1 (1946) contained an unsigned article "Dr. C.G. Jung and National Socialism" (9–11). The views expressed in the *Bulletin* seem to reflect a leisured, white, upper-class milieu. One would not expect such a milieu—the one Graham also frequented socially with upper-class non-dancer friends such as Merle Armitage—to be free of casual anti-Semitism and racial prejudice at that time. Symptomatic of a phlegmatic approach to racism is another article by Cary Jones, "The Negro Problem" in the *Bulletin* 9/1 (January 1947), 5–9. Bertram Ross relates there was uncertainty about Jung after the war, and by extension, about Graham's interest in Jung.

After seeing Martha for the first time in New York I went to a bookstore in the Village to buy all that was printed about Martha. I guess it was a left wing book store for in talking to me they discussed Martha in political terms. . . . 'Look at the titles of the sections of *Dark Meadow* . . . She believes that things can be passed in the blood.' This was a period right after the war.—There was confusion about Jung in left wing circles.—Hadn't Hitler used some of Jung's writing to fortify his beliefs?

Bertram Ross Papers, Jerome Robbins Dance Collection, New York Public Library for the Performing Arts, box 10, folder 20, p.7. The first article on Graham by Jessie E. Fraser appeared in 1950: "Martha Graham: Modern Artist" in *Bulletin* 12/1 (January 1950), 11–14. Two other pieces related to Graham subsequently appeared in the Bulletin: Robert S. McCully, "A Bit of History and Martha Graham" in *Bulletin* 53/6 (October 1991), 4, was a tribute to Graham upon her death. Following that, Mary Virginia Stieb-Hayes offered reminiscences of Graham's tribute to Wickes at the 1964 memorial service: "Jungiana" in *Bulletin* 53/7 (November 1991), 4.

73. Jung, *Collected Works*, 10, p. 181. His ideas were echoed by his disciple Esther M. Harding in *Psychic Energy*: "Deep within the Germanic unconscious, forces that were not contained or held in check by the archetypal symbols of the Christian religion, but had slowed back into pagan forms, notably Wotanism, were galvanized into life by the Nazi call" (6).

74. Gladys Taylor & Josephine Jenks Warren, "The Artist and the Life About Him," in *Bulletin of the Analytical Psychology Club of New York City* 1/2 (March 1939), 1–2.

75. The phrase is from Martha C. Carpentier, *Ritual, Myth, and the Modernist Text. The Influence of Jane Ellen Harrison on Joyce, Eliot, and Woolf* (Amsterdam: Gordon & Breach Publishers, 1998), 26. See also, Ellwood, *The Politics of Myth*, 138–140. Campbell and Erdman only met with Jung personally after the war at his retreat in Bollingen in 1953 (Ibid., 142).

76. I have used the term "dramaturgical" to characterize the second phase of Graham's work (*Dancing Modernism/Performing Politics*, 51). Graham's press representative Isadora Bennett identified "a new cycle" starting in 1939 with *Every Soul is a Circus*, but she adds of *American Document*: "some might consider this, because of size and form, as the precursor of the new phase." Martha Graham Center of Dance Records (1944–45), Dance Collection, NYPL, (S)*MGZMD 152 (folder 4). Graham knew she needed a male dancer for this work, and approached José Limón before Hawkins appeared on the scene. See José Limón, *An Unfinished Memoir* (Hanover & London: University Press of New England, 1999), 87.

77. McDonagh, *Martha Graham*, 135.

78. Erick Hawkins quoted in David Sears, "Total Theatre Hawkins-Style," unpublished typescript (no date), David Sears Collection, New York Public Library for the Performing Arts, folder 8.

79. Hawkins sailed for Europe on June 22, 1933, and returned on August 5th.

80. Lincoln Kirstein led Ballet Caravan from 1936 to 1940. It was part of his stated project to Americanize ballet of which he wrote a great deal in the 1930s. He chronicled its rise and fall in "Our Ballet and Our Audience" (1938) and "Transcontinental Caravan" (1939) both collected in *Ballet: Bias and Belief. Three Pamphlets Collected and Other Dance Writings of Lincoln Kirstein* (New York: Dance Horizons, 1983), 53–67.

81. See Martin Duberman, *The Worlds of Lincoln Kirstein* (New York: Knopf, 2007), 315–316 & 318–320. Duberman makes *Show Piece* Hawkins's third ballet, implies the Minotaur piece actually reached the stage, and calls his first work a failure without naming it. David Sears dates the debut of *Show Piece* in Saybrook, Long Island, on July 15, 1937.

82. The translation dated November 27, 1927, and signed Frederick Hawkins mentions "a feast to the Minotaur selected youths and the glory of unmarried maidens." Erick Hawkins Collection, Library of Congress, "School and College Essays," box 5, folder 10.

83. See Gertje R. Utley, *Picasso: the Communist Years* (New Haven & London: Yale University Press, 2000), 15. See also: Sidra Stich, "Picasso's Art and Politics in 1936," *Arts Magazine*, October 1983, vol. 58, 113–118.

84. Erick Hawkins interviewed by David Sears, 6/9/85 "Erick Hawkins 6/9/85 on the Maze— in his studio on 5th Avenue," unpublished typescript. David Sears Papers, Jerome Robbins Dance Collection, New York Public Library for the Performing Arts, box 22, folder 9. Stapp was later to design décor for Graham's *Letter to the World*.

85. Ibid., p. 6.

86. Graham held yearly summer residencies at Bennington College from 1934 until 1942. See Sali Ann Kriegsman, *Modern Dance in America—the Bennington Years* (Boston, Mass.: G.K. Hall, 1981).

87. Hawkins was listed as guest artist in Graham's programs until 1939.

88. It premiered March 26, 1947, at the Central High School of Needle Trades in New York City. See Lincoln Kirstein, *Program Notes 1934–1991*, edited by Randall Bourscheidt (New York: Eakins Press Foundation Alliance for the Arts, 2009), 83–84.

89. "Try to get formality—a new form of ballet rather than like Pocahontas or Fire Bird in which the dancing of group tried to fit story but lost in importance per se. Like a play of Sophocles. Like Shankar's Mime. Completely held in, but always flowing movement." Erick Hawkins Collection, box 50, folder 1. Some of Hawkins's notes play with the idea of modern costume: "Minotaur with dictator costume. Military tunic . . . Theseus in workman's street clothes." Choreographic Notebooks, Erick Hawkins Collection, Library of Congress, box 50, folder 2.

90. Martha Graham letter to Erick Hawkins, Erick Hawkins Collection, Library of Congress, box 55, folder 1.

91. Agnes de Mille notes that during the making of *American Document* "Martha had fallen profoundly in love." Agnes de Mille, *Martha: The Life and Works of Martha Graham* (New York: Random House, 1991), 233. De Mille has Hawkins and Graham first meeting at Bennington in the summer of 1936 (224); Janet Soares has Graham present at a performance of *Show Piece* at Bennington in 1937 (139) as does Kriegsman, who adds that they met for the first time earlier in the winter of 1937. Don McDonagh places their first meeting on July 17, 1936, when Ballet Caravan performed at Bennington; David Sears has their first meeting on January 28, 1938, at the New York Hippodrome in a "Dance for Spain Benefit" where Graham performed *Deep Song* and Ballet Caravan performed Hawkins's *Show Piece*. (David Sears, "Martha Graham: The Golden Thread" in *Ballet Review* 14/3 (Fall 1986), 51. Before Hawkins came to Bennington in the summer of 1938 he took the June course at the Graham studio in New York.

92. Erick Hawkins Collection, Library of Congress, undated letters from Santa Barbara, 1939–1940.

93. Erick Hawkins, "Diaries," Erick Hawkins Collection, Library of Congress, box 77, folder 6.

94. Erick Hawkins interviewed by Don McDonagh, July 19, 1971, Jerome Robbins Dance Collection, New York Public Library for the Performing Arts: *MGZTL 4–2551.

95. "Dance libretto," 86.

96. See Chapter Two.

97. George J. Zytaruk & James T. Boulton, editors, *The Letters of D.H. Lawrence* (Cambridge: Cambridge University Press, 1981), volume 2: 470.

98. Lawrence took these ideas from Frazer. See Phillip L. Marcus, "'A Healed Whole Man': Frazer, Lawrence and Blood Consciousness," in *Sir James Frazer and the Literary Imagination. Essays in Affinity and Influence*, edited by Robert Fraser: London: Macmillan Press, 1990: 232–252.

99. *The Letters of D.H. Lawrence*, 470.

100. Graham cited in Wayne D. Shirley, *Ballet for Martha and Ballets for Martha* (Washington: Library of Congress, 1997), 14.

101. "The novel is then not so much an organic unity as a symbolic act that must reunite or harmonize heterogeneous narrative paradigms which have their own specific and contradictory ideological meaning." Fredric Jameson, *The Political Unconscious: Narrative as a Socially Symbolic Act* (Ithaca: Cornell University Press, 1981), 144.

102. See Franko, *The Work of Dance*, 22–23.

103. Even as she was just training Hawkins she also made him her dance partner and allowed him to run rehearsals, which led to conflict between him and the other dancers.

104. David Diamond, "With the Dancers," in *Modern Music* XVII/2 (January–February 1940), 118.

105. "Dance Libretto," 573.

106. "Dance Libretto," 574.

107. I am grateful to Arnold Rampersad for his advice on the possible relation between Hughes and Graham.

108. Langston Hughes, "Democracy" in *The Collected Works of Langston Hughes*, edited by Arnold Rampersad (Columbia & London: University of Missouri Press, 2001), vol. 2, 77.

109. Langston Hughes, *The Collected Poems of Langston Hughes*, edited by Arnold Rampersad (New York: Alfred A. Knopf, 2001), 191.

110. "Dance Libretto," 574.

111. "Hughes's consistent stress on 'Hitlerism at home' seems to be intended to remind U.S. leftists that the international fight against fascism was structurally linked to the endurance of white racial oppression." Jonathan Scott, *Socialist Joy in the Writing of Langston Hughes* (Columbia & London: University of Missouri Press, 2006), 83.

112. "Dance Libretto," 566. Manning softens her position on *American Document* in *Modern Dance/Negro Dance*, 252, note 54.

113. George W. Beiswanger, "The New Theatre Dance," in *Theatre Arts Monthly* 23/1 (January 1939), 53.

114. Owen Burke, "An American Document," in *New Masses* 24/4 (October 18, 1938), 29.

115. "If the Indians had not been perceived as vanishing, they could not have become the exemplary instance of what it meant to have a culture." Walter Benn Michaels, *Our America. Nativism, Modernism, and Pluralism* (Durham & London: Duke University Press, 1995), 38.

116. Program note transcribed by David Sears, David Sears Papers, Jerome Robbins Dance Collection, New York Public Library for the Performing Arts, box 20, folder 3.

117. "Dance Libretto," 570.

118. Arnold Kaye cited in Kriegsman, *Modern Dance in America*, 197.

119. A film shot by Ann Barzel of Graham's performances in 1938–1941 is held at the Dance Collection of the Lincoln Center Library for the Performing Arts, New York City.

120. Jeffrey Schnapp, *Staging Fascism: 18BL and the Theater of Masses for Masses* (Stanford: Stanford University Press, 1996), xv.

121. The original score by Ray Green is preserved in the Music Division of the Library of Congress. Green was married to Graham dancer May O'Donnell.

122. See Lincoln Kirstein, "Dance: Martha Graham at Bennington," in *The Nation* (September 3, 1938), *American Document* clippings file, Dance Collection, New York Public Library for the Performing Arts at Lincoln Center. Owen Burke's review in *New Masses* was highly favorable.

123. *Memphis Commercial Appeal* (March 2, 1939) quoted from a 1940 flyer of "Martha Graham and Dance Group," Martha Graham archive, Library of Congress, Washington, D.C.

124. Marcia Minor, "Graham Interprets Democracy. Uses Militant Theme as Climax of Dance Presented in the Form of a Documentary Play," in *the Daily Worker* (October 4, 1938).

Statements that reveal Graham's political intent were confided only to the *Daily Worker* or in personal correspondence.

125. Review dated March 11, 1939, quoted from a 1940 flyer of "Martha Graham and Dance Group," Martha Graham archive, Library of Congress, Washington, D.C.

126. See Catherine Vickery, "'American Document' Tours America," in *Dance Observer* 6/4 (April 1939), 205–206. This article weighs the size of turnout in different geographical locales and the level of audience enthusiasm. In 1936 Graham herself embarked on a transcontinental solo tour that took her to Detroit, Seattle, Portland, Tacoma, Oakland, San Francisco, San Jose, Stanford, San Mateo, Santa Barbara, Colorado Springs, Chicago, Baltimore, and Washington D.C.

127. Reminiscences of Jean Erdman (1979), Bennington Summer School of Dance Project, page 60 in the Columbia University Center for Oral History Research Office, Columbia University, 60.

128. Marcia Minor, "Graham Interprets Democracy. Uses Militant Theme as Climax of Dance Presented in the Form of a Documentary Play," in *the Daily Worker* (October 4, 1938).

129. For a fuller discussion of Graham's politics in relation to her stage persona see my *The Work of Dance: Labor, Movement and Identity in the 1930s* (Middletown: Wesleyan University Press, 2003) 63–71.

130. Barbara Morgan, "Modern Dance," in *Popular Photography* 16/16 (June 1945), 68.

131. Morgan specifies: "Today great latitude of speed has become a commonplace by virtue of fast pan film emulsions, fast corrected lenses, synchroflas, speedlamps, moviefloods, and photofloods. Action has free rein!" The place of action in Morgan's aesthetics of dance photography deserves further analysis. Barbara Morgan, "Dance Photography," in *The Complete Photographer* 18/3 (New York: National Educational Alliance, 1942), 1133.

132. Barbara Morgan, "Dance Into Photography," in *Martha Graham: Sixteen Dances in Photographs* (Hastings-on-Hudson: Morgan & Morgan, 1941), 149.

133. Morgan, "Dance Photography," 1134.

134. Morgan, "Modern Dance," 68.

135. Morgan, "Dance Photography," 1136.

136. Morgan, "Modern Dance," 68.

137. "Communities are to be distinguished, not by their falsity/genuineness, but by the style in which they are imagined." Benedict Anderson, *Imagined Communities*, 6.

138. Phillip E. Wegner, *Imaginary Communities: Utopia, the Nation, and the Spatial Histories of Modernity* (Berkeley & Los Angeles: University of California Press, 2002).

139. "Dance Libretto," 573.

140. *You Have Seen Their Faces* was first published in 1937. It also forecasts Graham's interest in myth and archetype, which continued to emerge throughout the 1940s.

141. Natlee Posert, "Martha Graham Dances Ideas and Interprets Our America," in *The Memphis Commercial Appeal* (March 2, 1939), n.p. Martha Graham Clipping File, Jerome Robbins Dance Collection, New York Public Library for the Performing Arts: *MGZR—Res. Box 14.

142. Sophie Maslow remembers: "Each of us had a different movement to do." Legacy of Martha Graham Transcripts (April 2001), 202. Martha Graham Collection, Library of Congress.

143. Mark Franko, *The Work of Dance: Labor, Movement, and Identity in the 1930s* (Middletown: Wesleyan University Press, 2002), 38–58.

144. "Dance Libretto," 573–574.

145. "Dance Libretto," 574.

146. Ellen Graff, *Stepping Left. Dance and Politics in New York City, 1928–1942* (Durham: Duke University Press, 1997), 125–26.

147. Charles A. Beard and Mary R. Beard, *America in Midpassage*, volume 2 (New York: Macmillan Company, 1939), 925.

148. Ibid., 814.

149. Lincoln Kirstein, "Dance: Martha Graham at Bennington," in *The Nation* (September 3, 1938), *American Document* clippings file, Dance Collection, New York Public Library for the Performing Arts at Lincoln Center. This review was reprinted in *Ballet: Bias and Belief.*

Three Pamphlets Collected and Other Dance Writings of Lincoln Kirstein (New York: Dance Horizons, 1983), 69–71.

150. See F.R. Ankersmit, *Aesthetic Politics: Political Philosophy Beyond Fact and Value* (Stanford: Stanford University Press, 1996), especially Chapter One: "Political Representation: the Aesthetic State," 21–63.

151. Isabel Morse Jones, "American Dance Play Impressive" in *Los Angeles Times* (March 11, 1939), n.p. Martha Graham Clippings File, Jerome Robbins Dance Collection, New York Public Library for the Performing Arts: *MGZR-Res. Box 14 (unnumbered folder).

152. See Kirstein, "Martha Graham at Bennington."

153. Betty Bandel, "Graham's Art Pleases Here" in *Arizona Daily Star* (March 7, 1939). Erick Hawkins Collection, Library of Congress, box 78, folder 1.

154. Manning hypothesizes that the following politically critical text was cut from the published version in 1942, but printed in *TAC* (December 1938): "We are not all good—but the Land is good—The Rights are good. We forget too much. I want to remember. I do remember—Things I am ashamed of: Indian affairs; slaves; Sacco and Vanzetti; sharecroppers; the Scottsboro boys." (Manning, *Modern Dance*, 133). If these words did make up part of the original scenario, Graham repeated them almost verbatim in her interview with the *Daily Worker* (see note 124, above). Graham was nevertheless cautious not to associate herself with the Communist party. In a letter to Hawkins of September 16, 1941, she wrote:

> I have to be a little careful at this time with both the China Relief and the Soviet as the C's are hard at work. I have accepted Katherine Cornell's invitation to serve on her Committee for China because I am pretty sure that it has been checked. These other requests come from too far east in the 19th and 23rd St. districts to trust. But that is for us to know and not the public.

Erick Hawkins Collection, Library of Congress, box 55, folder one. As Ray Green noted: "Martha's company became known as being practically a Left-Wing dance company. Well, of course, she was also playing along, Martha; she played along with the currents." Reminiscences of Ray Green (1979), Bennington Summer School Project, pages 47–48 in Oral History Research Office, Columbia University.

155. See her "American Document and American Minstrelsy," in *Moving Words, re-writing dance*, edited by Gay Morris (London: Routledge, 1996), 183–202.

156. Denby, *Dance Writings*, 230.

157. *The American Dancer* (April 1942), Martha Graham Collection, Music Division, Library of Congress, Scrapbooks.

158. Maureen Needham Costonis was the first to cite *American Document* for Graham's demonstrated ability to mix politics with art. See her "*American Document*: A Neglected Graham Work," in *Proceedings Society of Dance History Scholars*, Twelfth Annual Conference, Arizona State University, February 17–19, 1989, 72–81.

159. See Victoria Geduld, "Dancing Diplomacy: Martha Graham and the Strange Commodity of Cold-War Cultural Exchange in Asia, 1955 and 1974," in *Dance Chronicle* 33 (2010), 44–81.

Chapter 2

1. Hayden White, "Bodies and Their Plots," in *Choreographing History*, edited by Susan Leigh Foster (Bloomington: Indiana University Press, 1995), 233. A 1935 program note reads: "In every country there are basic themes of thought and action. These themes are part of national consciousness and form an inheritance that contributes to the present." Particularly relevant to *Appalachian Spring* is the theme of Dedication. "This theme is based on that early intensity of fanaticism with which our Puritan fathers sang their hymn of dedication of a new nation." David Sears transcription, David Sears Papers, Jerome Robbins Dance Collection, New York Public Library for the Performing Arts, box 20, folder 1.

2. Graham was experimenting with Americana as early as 1935 with *Panorama*.

3. See my analysis of the solo *Frontier* in *The Work of Dance: Labor, Movement and Identity in the 1930s* (Middletown: Wesleyan University Press, 2002), 68–70. Evoking comparisons

of Graham's performance style in *Frontier* and *Appalachian Spring*, Marcia B. Siegel observed that in the latter work "Graham lost some of her firmness and independence." Marcia B. Siegel, "*Frontier* to *Appalachian Spring* (Martha Graham)," in *The Shapes of Change. Images of American Dance* (Boston: Houghton Mifflin, 1979), 140–152.

4. Aaron Copland and Vivian Perlis, *Copland since 1943* (New York: Saint Martin's Press, 1989), 51.
5. Graham cited in Wayne D. Shirley, *Ballet for Martha and Ballets for Martha* (Washington: Library of Congress, 1997), 14.
6. Mark Franko, *Dancing Modernism/Performing Politics* (Bloomington: Indiana University Press, 1995), 51.
7. Edward D. Andrews, *The Gift to be Simple. Songs, Dances and Rituals of the American Shakers* (New York: Dover Publications, Inc., 1940), 7.
8. Ibidem.
9. William Graebner, *the Age of Doubt. American Thought and Culture in the 1940s* (Boston: Twayne Publishers, 1991), 59.
10. Grant Wood (1940) cited in Cécile Whiting, *Antifascism in American Art* (New Haven & London: Yale University Press, 1989), 100.
11. The *Atlantic Monthly* article is cited in Gail Levin and Judith Tick, *Aaron Copland's America. A Cultural Perspective* (New York: Watson-Guptill Publications, 2000), 99–100.
12. Cecile Whiting, *Antifascism in American Art*, 77. In the debate that raged between Stuart Davis and William Hart Benton most of the accusations of Benton's Fascist sympathies were focused on his caricatured depictions of blacks and Jews. On this debate, see Erika Doss, *Benton, Pollock, and the Politics of Modernism: from Regionalism to Abstract Expressionism* (Chicago & London: University of Chicago Press, 1991), 275–281.
13. H. W. Janson, "Benton and Wood, Champions of Regionalism," in *Magazine of Art* 39/5 (May 1946), 184–186; 198–200.
14. "NAME?," Aaron Copland Collection, Music Division, Library of Congress, 5.
15. Ibidem.
16. "House of Victory," Aaron Copland Collection, Music Division, Library of Congress, 1.
17. All of these phrases are taken from the first page of "House of Victory."
18. "NAME?," Aaron Copland Collection, Music Division, Library of Congress, 1.
19. "NAME?," Aaron Copland Collection, Music Division, Library of Congress, 2.
20. "NAME?," Aaron Copland Collection, Music Division, Library of Congress, 2.
21. "NAME?," Aaron Copland Collection, Music Division, Library of Congress, 2.
22. See *House Reports. 68th Congress, 2nd Session* (December 1, 1924–March 4, 1925) (Washington: Government Printing Office, 1925), vol. 1.
23. See Robert Sabin, "Dance at the Coolidge Festival," in *Dance Observer* 11/10 (December 1944), 20.
24. Erick Hawkins Diaries, August 21, 1946, Erick Hawkins Collection, Music Division, Library of Congress, box 77, folder 6.
25. "Writings on Martha Graham," Erick Hawkins Collection, Library of Congress, box 5, folder 13. And: Box 53, personal correspondence: Letter of Douglas Hudelson to a Mr. Wells resumes the production and fundraising history of the 1940s (folder 3).
26. Agnes de Mille in interview with Gertrude Macy, March 10, 1983, Jerome Robbins Dance Collection, New York Public Library for the Performing Arts: *MGZTC3-1630. According to Macy, Graham met Katherine Cornell through Mrs. Wallach Morgenthau and Laura Elliot, who taught voice to Marion Seldes, among others. Macy first met Cornell in 1928.
27. Erick Hawkins letter to Elizabeth Sprague Coolidge, Erick Hawkins Collection, Music Division, Library of Congress, box 56, folder 4.
28. Ibidem.
29. Erick Hawkins Collection, Music Division, Library of Congress, box 56, folder 5.
30. Aaron Copland letter to Erick Hawkins, May 19, 1948, Erick Hawkins Collection, Music Division, Library of Congress, box 56, folder 5. Hawkins also approached William Schuman with this idea, and in 1976 he tried again to interest Schuman in composing *Moby Dick*. "The Ahab idea is my life's blood. I will put everything into it." Erick Hawkins letter to William Schuman, December 20, 1976, William Schuman Papers

(JPB 87–33), Music Collection, New York Public Library for the Performing Arts, box 101, folder 1.

31. See Marta Elaine Robertson, "'A Gift to be Simple': the collaboration of Aaron Copland and Martha Graham in the genesis of *Appalachian Spring*" (Dissertation, University of Michigan, 1992), and Howard Pollack, *Aaron Copland. The Life and Work of an Uncommon Man* (New York: Henry Holt & Co., 1999), 393–406.

32. Jacqueline Shea-Murphy, *The People Have Never Stopped Dancing: Native American Modern Dance Histories* (Minneapolis: University of Minnesota Press, 2007).

33. Ibid., 166.

34. Langston Hughes, *The Langston Hughes Reader* (New York: George Brazillier, Inc., 1958), 134. John Brown figured in Hughes's poetry as early as 1932.

35. She discusses this in her letters to Copland. See Martha Graham, "House of Victory," manuscript, Aaron Copland Collection, Music Division, Library of Congress, box 255, folder 22.

36. "NAME?," Aaron Copland Collection, Music Division, Library of Congress, 1.

37. Hayden White, "The Value of Narrativity in the Representation of Reality" in *The Content of the Form. Narrative Discourse and Historical Representation* (Baltimore and London: The Johns Hopkins University Press, 1987), 14.

38. The original principles in addition to Graham were Erick Hawkins, Merce Cunningham, and May O'Donnell.

39. Anonymous, "Purely Symbolic," *Time* (May 28, 1945).

40. Program, Bennington College, June 23–24, 1945. Martha Graham Archive, Library of Congress, Washington, D.C.

41. Martha Graham, "House of Victory," Aaron Copland Collection, Music Division, Library of Congress, 8–9.

42. In a letter of Graham to Copland dated November 7, 1942, she mentions revising the libretto to be "less severe" with more of the flavor of Thornton Wilder's *Our Town*. In a letter Copland wrote Harold Spivacke, Chief of the Music Division at the Library of Congress, on June 8, 1943: "I've written to her, suggesting a few changes." The letter is produced in facsimile in Shirley, *Ballet for Martha*, 20.

43. Martha Graham, letter to Aaron Copland (July 10, 1943), Aaron Copland Collection, Library of Congress.

44. "House of Victory," Aaron Copland Collection, Library of Congress, 4.

45. "NAME?," Aaron Copland Collection, Library of Congress, 4.

46. "House of Victory," Aaron Copland Collection, Library of Congress, 3.

47. Oliver Wendell Holmes wrote: "The abolitionists had a stock phrase that man was either a knave or a fool who did not act as they (the abolitionists). . . . When you know that you know persecution comes easy. It is as well that some of us don't know that we know anything." Letter to Frederick Pollock (August 30, 1929) in Richard A. Posner, editor, *The Essential Holmes. Selections from the Letters, Speeches, Juridical Opinions, and other writings of Oliver Wendell Holmes, Jr.* (Chicago & London: University of Chicago Press, 1992), 108–109.

48. W.E.B. Du Bois, *John Brown*, 211.

49. "NAME?," Aaron Copland Collection, Library of Congress, 4.

50. "NAME?," Aaron Copland Collection, Library of Congress, 9.

51. "NAME?," Aaron Copland Collection, Library of Congress, 9.

52. "NAME?," Aaron Copland Collection, Library of Congress, 10.

53. Howard Pollack, *Aaron Copland. The Life and Work of an Uncommon Man* (New York: Henry Holt & Co., 1999), 393. Pollack outlines all the switches Graham made between score and action (396–399).

54. Robertson, "A Gift to be Simple" 222.

55. Robertson charts these "derivations" in "A Gift to be Simple," 178.

56. Ibid., 181.

57. W.E.B. Du Bois, "The Call of Kansas" in *W.E.B. Du Bois. A Reader*, edited by David Levering Lewis (New York: Henry Holt & Co., 1995), 173.

58. *John Brown* was the only work Hawkins created in the forties that he chose to revive for his own Company. *God's Angry Man: A Passion Play of John Brown* was presented at the Joyce Theater in New York in 1984.

59. Stark Young, "Martha Graham," in *New Republic* 112/23 (June 4, 1945), 790.
60. *New York Herald Tribune* (May 17, 1945).
61. Jacqueline Shea-Murphy, "Her Point of View: Martha Graham and Absent Indians," in *The People Have Never Stopped Dancing. Native American Modern Dance Histories* (Minneapolis & London: University of Minnesota Press, 2007), 157.
62. Elizabeth B. Crist, *Music for the Common Man. Aaron Copland During the Depression and the War* (Oxford & New York: Oxford University Press, 2005), 172.
63. Helen Thomas explains the variations possible in the role of the Bride in "Appalachian Spring" in her *Dance, Modernity and Culture. Explorations in the Sociology of Dance* (London & New York: Routledge, 1995), 150–151.
64. Program note transcribed by David Sears, David Sears Papers, Jerome Robbins Dance Collection, New York Public Library for the Performing Arts, box 20, folder 1.
65. Harry S. Stout, "Edwards as Revivalist," in *The Cambridge Companion to Jonathan Edwards*, edited by Stephen J. Stein (Cambridge: Cambridge University Press, 2007), 139.
66. Ibid., 153.
67. "NAME?," Aaron Copland Collection, Music Division, Library of Congress, 9.
68. Marta Elaine Robertson, "The Gift to Be Simple," 222–223.
69. J. Laplanche and J.B. Pontalis, *The Language of Psychoanalysis*, translated by Donald Nicholson-Smith (New York: Norton & Co., 1973), 82.
70. Ibid., 83.
71. "NAME?," Aaron Copland Collection, Music Division, Library of Congress, 2.
72. May O'Donnell, Legacy of Martha Graham Transcripts (November 1999), 53. Martha Graham Collection, Library of Congress.
73. Robertson, "A Gift to Be Simple," 198.
74. Robertson, "A Gift to Be Simple," 199–200.
75. "House of Victory," Aaron Copland Collection, Library of Congress,
76. Helen Thomas, "Appalachian Spring," 150–151.
77. See Howard Pollack, *Aaron Copland. The Life and Work of an Uncommon Man* (New York: Henry Holt & Co., 1999), 400.
78. W.E.B. Du Bois, *John Brown* (New York: the Modern Library, 2001), 120.
79. Du Bois, *John Brown*, 117.
80. These terms are adapted from Julia Kristeva, "L'Engendrement de la formule," *Semiotike. Recherches pour une sémanalyse* (Paris: Seuil, 1969), 278–371.
81. Robertson, "A Gift to be Simple," 175.
82. Ibid., 31–32.
83. Michael Denning, *The Cultural Front. The Laboring of American Culture in the Twentieth Century* (London & New York: Verso, 1996), 26.
84. John Martin, "The Dance: Annual Award" in *The New York Times* (August 1945). Emotional continuity had clearly been provided until now by Graham's own performance.
85. Rebekah J. Kowal, *How to Do Things With Dance. Performing Change in Postwar America* (Middletown: Wesleyan University Press, 2010), 65.
86. Erick Hawkins diary entry, Erick Hawkins Collection, Music Division, Library of Congress, box 53, folder 11.
87. Kowal, *How to Do Things With Dance*, 24.
88. Barbara Melosh, *Engendering Culture: Manhood and Womanhood in New Deal Public Art and Theater* (Washington, D.C.: Smithsonian Institution Press, 1991), 53.
89. See Barbara Melosh, "The Domesticated Frontier," in *Engendering Culture*, esp. 43–51.
90. Pearl Lang cited in Aaron Copland and Vivian Perlis, *Copland in 1943* (New York: St. Martin's Press, 1989), 42–43.
91. Martha Graham notebook, Martha Graham Collection, Music Division, Library of Congress, box 275, folder 1.
92. Ibidem.
93. "The new piece" Graham writes of is *Deaths and Entrances*.
94. Ramsay Burt, "Memory, Repetition and Critical Intervention. The Politics of Historical Reference in Recent European Dance Performance," in *Performance Research* 8/2 (2003), 41.

95. Virgil Thompson, "Two Ballets," in *New York Herald Tribune* (May 20, 1945) cited in *The Art of Judging Music* (New York: Knopf, 1948), 161–164.
96. Not coincidentally, it was around the same time that Graham began experimenting with character splitting. In *Letter to the World* the Emily Dickinson role was split into two roles: She Who Speaks and She Who Dances. This splitting, which was also a pairing or creation of twins, seems to stage the pheno-geno distinction overtly, although it is justified formally by the differences between speech and movement.

Chapter 3

1. Ramsay Burt, "Dance, Gender & Psychoanalysis," in *Dance Research Journal* 30/1 (Spring 1998), 48.
2. Edwin Cox, "Private Lives," in *Seattle Washington Times* (August 16, 1942). In a letter Graham writes of a locket with a piece of cloth from a saint's robe given her by Stark Young. The saint is a woman. In the cartoons, Mussolini poses for photographers standing on a table to increase his stature and Hitler submits to nose surgery.
3. Toril Moi, *Feminist Theory and Simone de Beauvoir* (Oxford: Blackwell, 1990), 27.
4. "Transcript of Talk" June 5, 1941, NBC Shortwave Monitoring Service. Scrapbooks, Martha Graham Collection, Music Division, Library of Congress.
5. Bertram Ross interview with Agnes de Mille, November 21, 1983, Dance Collection, New York Public Library for the Performing Arts at Lincoln Center, *MGZTC 3–1635.
6. "New York Daily Doings," December 13–14, 1935, Martha Graham Collection, Music Division, Library of Congress, Scrapbooks.
7. Shirley Spencer, "Your Handwriting: Martha Graham," in *New York News* (January 16, 1942). Scrapbooks, Martha Graham Collection, Music Division, Library of Congress, Washington, D.C.
8. "Lights of New York," in *Charlottesville, Va. Progress* (March 20, 1942). Scrapbooks, Martha Graham archive, Library of Congress. Sol Hurok played no role in Graham publicity in the early 1940s as he only represented her between 1946 and 1947. "It was most likely the critical and popular success of *Appalachian Spring* . . . that gave Hurok the idea of presenting Graham in a Broadway theater and on tour." Harlow Robinson, *The Last Impresario. The Life, Times, and Legacy of Sol Hurok* (New York: Viking, 1994), 296.
9. T.J. Jackson Lears, "From Salvation to Self-Realization. Advertising and the Therapeutic Roots of the Consumer Culture, 1880–1930," in *The Culture of Consumption: Critical Essays in American History, 1880–1980*, edited by Richard Wightman Fox and T.J. Jackson Lears (New York: Pantheon Books, 1983), 22. Lears's essay helps us to understand that Graham was not only attractive to the advertising industry as a prominent public figure, but also as a modernist: "As the advertising executive Ernest Elmo Calkins recalled, 'Modernism offered the opportunity of expressing the inexpressible, of suggesting not so much a motor car as speed, not so much a gown as style, not so much a compact as beauty.' It offered, in other words, not information but feeling." (Ibidem). Graham's attractiveness to advertising executives was over-determined by her artistic innovation, her political prominence, and her gender.
10. Otto Rank, *Art and Artist. Creative Urge and Personality Development* translated by Charles Frances Atkinson (New York & London: W.W. Norton & Company, 1932), 407.
11. *New York Post*, January 5, 1939. Martha Graham Clippings File, Jerome Robbins Dance Collection, New York Public Library for the Performing Arts: *MGZR-Res., box 14.
12. Martha Graham, letter to David Zellmer, August 25, 1943, Jerome Robbins Dance Collection, New York Public Library for the Performing Arts.
13. Bertram Ross Papers, Dance Collection, New York Public Library for the Performing Arts at Lincoln Center, box 10, folder 20.

14. Pearl Lang interview with Agnes de Mille, November 29, 1982, Dance Collection, New York Public Library for the Performing Arts at Lincoln Center: *MGZTC 3–1627.
15. William H. Chafe, *The Paradox of Change. American Women in the Twentieth Century* (New York & Oxford: Oxford University Press, 1991), 154.
16. Martin Graebner coined this phrase: "The first half of the forties was a culture of war: public, nationalistic, pragmatic, and realistic; championing the group and its political equivalent, democracy; committed to production and to new roles for women it required." Martin Graebner, *The Age of Doubt. American Thought and Culture in the 1940s* (Boston: Twayne Publishers, 1991), 1.
17. Unidentified Clipping, Martha Graham Collection, Music Division, Library of Congress, Scrapbooks.
18. Franko, *Dancing Modernism*, 56.
19. Mary Ann Doane, *The Desire to Desire. The Woman's Film of the 1940s* (Bloomington & Indianapolis: Indiana University Press, 1987), 28.
20. Jacqueline Hunt, "Dance for Poise, Grace, Martha Graham Urges," in the Tulane, Calif. *Advance Register* (August 21, 1942). Scrapbooks, Martha Graham archive, Library of Congress.
21. Martha Graham, "As You Control Your Body So You Shape Your Life," in *Glamour* (April 1943). Scrapbooks, Martha Graham archive, Library of Congress.
22. Ida Jean Kain, "Martha Graham, Dancer, Coaches Women Workers," in Louisville Ky. *Courier-Journal* (April 9, 1943). This article was syndicated across the country as noted next to the scrapbook clipping, probably by Louis Horst. Scrapbooks, Martha Graham archive, Library of Congress.
23. "New Graham Work," in *Christian Science Monitor* (Boston, Mass: March 20, 1942). Scrapbooks, Martha Graham archive, Library of Congress.
24. Scrapbooks, Martha Graham archive, Library of Congress.
25. Walter Terry, "Martha Graham—1942," in the *New York Herald-Tribune* (March 1, 1942). Scrapbooks, Martha Graham Collection, Music Division, Library of Congress.
26. Eric Bentley, "Martha Graham's Journey," in *What is Dance? Readings in Theory and Criticism*, edited by Roger Copland & Marshall Cohen (New York: Oxford University Press, 1983), 200.
27. John Dunning, *On the Air. The Encyclopedia of Old Time Radio* (New York: Oxford University Press, 1998), 684.
28. Consolidated Concert Corp press release, "A Statement by Martha Graham Concerning Her Experience as 'Miss Hush,'" also called: "'Miss Hush' Story." Bertram Ross Papers, Jerome Robbins Dance Collection, New York Public Library for the Performing Arts: box 10, folder 20.
29. "'Hush' Hubbub," in *Life* 23/25 (December 22, 1947), 69–70.
30. "She is the Priestess of the Intellectual Ballet" in *Life* 17 (March 1947), 101–104.
31. Letter to Martha Graham from Isadora Bennett, Martha Graham Center of Dance Records (1944–45), Jerome Robbins Dance Collection, New York Public Library for the Performing Arts: (S)*MGZMD 152, folder 1.
32. Ben Belitt interview with David Sears, July 7, 1985, Jerome Robbins Dance Collection, New York Public Library for the Performing Arts: *MGZTL 4–1522. Belitt's phraseology recalls Harding's characterization of Jung's description of Picasso and Joyce as venturing "into the primordial slime from which life first emerged" (*Woman's Mysteries*, 222).
33. Bertram Ross Collection, Jerome Robbins Dance Collection, New York Public Library for the Performing Arts: box 10, folder 19.
34. Maria La Place, "Bette Davis and the Ideal of Consumption. A Look at Now Voyager," *Wide Angle* 6/4 (1985), 39.
35. Bette Davis, *The Lonely Life* (New York: G.P. Putnam's Sons, 1962), 67.
36. Richard Dyer, *Stars* (Middlesex: British Film Institute, 1979), 69.
37. Ibid., 70.
38. Erick Hawkins Collection, Library of Congress, folder 3.
39. See Henrietta Bannerman, "Martha Graham's House of the Pelvic Truth: the Figuration of Sexual Identities and Female Empowerment," in *Dance Research Journal* 42/1 (Summer 2010), 30–45.

40. Frances Wickes, Unpublished notes, Papers of Frances G. Wickes, Manuscript Division, Library of Congress, box 15, folder 12.
41. See T.S. Eliot, "Tradition and the Individual Talent," in *Selected Essays* (London: Faber & Faber, 1932), 13–23; and, Maud Ellman, *The Aesthetics of Impersonality: T.S. Eliot and Ezra Pound* (Sussex: the Harvester Press, 1987).
42. Frances Wickes, Unpublished notes, Papers of Frances G. Wickes, Manuscript Division, Library of Congress, box 15, folder 12. Wickes here transforms Harding's terminology for whom feminine nature is itself impersonal: "The nature of woman is non-personal and has nothing to do with her own wishes, it is something inherent in her as feminine being and must not be regarded as something personal." *Woman's Mysteries*, 233.
43. Ibidem.
44. Ibidem.
45. Esther Harding, *Woman's Mysteries, ancient and modern* (London: Longman's Green and company, 1935), 13.
46. Graham makes these remarks in the context of her developing role of Emily Bronte whom she also called "the moor creature" in *Deaths and Entrances*.
47. Harding, *Woman's Mysteries*, 15.
48. Erick Hawkins interview with David Sears, May 27, 1983, David Sears Papers, Jerome Robbins Dance Collection, New York Public Library for the Performing Arts, Box 21, folder 4.
49. Robert Briffault placed Demeter in this group as a non-Olympian deity in 1927: "This group is concerned with the very forces of life and death, and has a mystic character which is lacking among the sky-gods. But these deities, which are often called chthonic, or earthly, were not, in any sense, deities of the earth. They are deities of the underworld simply because, as heavenly bodies, in the course of their cycle they pass under the earth, and they appertain to the primitive lunar region." Robert Briffault, *The Mothers*, 374. Adrienne Rich comprehensively reviews this matrix of ideas in "The Primacy of Mother" in *Of Woman Born*, 84–109.
50. Karl Kerényi, *Eleusis: Archetypal Image of Mother and Daughter*, translated by Ralph Mannheim (New York: Bollingen Foundation, 1967), 34. Kerényi notes that he began publishing on Kore in German in 1941, but that these studies also appeared in 1950 in *Essays on a Science of Mythology. The Myth of the Divine Child and the Mysteries of Eleusis* in collaboration with Jung. Graham wrote to Wickes on August 4, 1953, that she was rereading this book. Frances Wickes Papers, Manuscript Division, Library of Congress, box 2, folder 8.
51. Harding, *Woman's Mysteries*, 218.
52. Carl Gustav Jung, "Conscious, Unconscious and Individuation," in *The Archetypes and the Collective Unconscious* translated by R.F.C. Hull (Princeton: Princeton University Press, 1959), 275. This essay was originally written in 1939 and appeared in English in *The Integration of the Personality* translated by Stanley Dell (London: Kegan Paul, 1940).
53. Frances Wickes Papers, Library of Congress, box 15, folder 12. This text is in quotation marks in Wickes's typescript and starred to the name: Louis Lavelle.
54. Jessie Weston, *From Ritual to Romance*, 44.
55. Adrienne Rich, *Of Woman Born*, 100.
56. The premiere was on May 10, 1946, as *Serpent Heart* at the MacMillan Academic Theater, Columbia University, New York City.
57. Martha Graham letter to Aaron Copland, Aaron Copland Collection, Music Division, Library of Congress. "Correspondence," box 255, folder 22.
58. "Daughter of Colchis" scenario, Aaron Copland Collection, Music Division, Library of Congress, box 255, folder 22.
59. Graham, *Notebooks*, 305. Her ballet *Punch and the Judy* can hence be tracked back to this "awakening."
60. Erick Hawkins interview with David Sears, April 24, 1982, David Sears Papers, Jerome Robbins Dance Collection, New York Public Library for the Performing Arts, box 21, folder 4.
61. Martha Graham letter to Aaron Copland, Aaron Copland Collection, Music Division, Library of Congress, box 255, folder 22.
62. Ibidem.

63. Erick Hawkins, Diary entry, August 21, 1946, Erick Hawkins Collection, Music Division, Library of Congress, box 77, folder 6.
64. Hawkins's lobbying to present his own work resulted in Cunningham presenting his "Mysterious Adventure" as well.
65. Martha Graham letter to Erick Hawkins, August 28, 1946, Erick Hawkins Collection, Music Division, Library of Congress, 55, folder 25.
66. Ethel Winter, interview with the author, July 27, 2010, New York City.
67. Diary entry, July 6, 1947, Erick Hawkins Collection, Music Division, Library of Congress, box 77, folder 6.
68. Erick Hawkins letter to Martha Graham, August 21, 1950, Martha Graham Collection, Music Division, Library of Congress, box 229, folder 3.
69. Ibidem.
70. Ibidem.
71. *Dark Meadow* had its premiere on January 23, 1946, with Erick Hawkins, May O'Donnell and Graham herself in the leading roles. The work remained in active repertory until 1953, not to be revived again until 1968.
72. Phone interview with the author, August 10, 2010.
73. Erick Hawkins interview with David Sears, April 24, 1982, David Sears Papers, Jerome Robbins Dance Collection, New York Public Library for the Performing Arts, box 21, folder 4.
74. Maud Ellman, *The Aesthetics of Impersonality*, 92.
75. David Sears interview with Lesley Farlow, March 27, 1992, Jerome Robbins Dance Collection, New York Public Library for the Performing Arts, Transcript: *MGZMT 3–1657t, 17.
76. For an analysis of Martin's encounter with *Dark Meadow*, see my "History/Theory—Criticism/Practice" in *Corporealities. Body, Knowledge, Culture, and Power*, Susan Foster, ed. (London: Routledge, 1995), 25–52.
77. Carl Gustav Jung, *Memories, Dreams, Reflections*, ed. Aniela Jaffe (New York: Vintage Books, 1963), p. 23. This material was presumably not available to Graham when she titled her work in 1946.
78. *Dark Meadow* is intended to provoke reflection on primary processes without visualizing or dramatizing the unconscious as such. For a discussion of Jung's influence on *Dark Meadow*, see Suzanne Shelton, "Jungian Roots of Martha Graham's Dance Imagery," in *Dance History Scholars Proceedings* (Riverside: Dance History Scholars, 1983).
79. The collective unconscious was "not individual but universal . . . It is, in other words, identical in all men and thus constitutes a common psychic substrate of a suprapersonal nature which is present in every one of us." Carl Gustav Jung, *The Archetypes and the Collective Unconscious*, trans. R. F. C. Hull (Princeton: Princeton University Press, 1980), 3–4.
80. I borrow this term from Teresa de Lauretis, *Alice Doesn't. Feminism, Semiotics, Cinema* (Bloomington: Indiana University Press, 1984), 141.
81. "[T]he passage through the film would simply instate or reconfirm male spectators in the position of the mythical subject, the human being; but it would only allow female spectators the position of the mythical obstacle, monster or landscape." Ibid., 141.
82. Erich Neumann, *The Great Mother. An Analysis of the Archetype* (Princeton: Princeton University Press, 1955), 28.
83. Bertram Ross Papers, Jerome Robbins Dance Collection, New York Public Library for the Performing Arts, box 10, folder 20.
84. Jessie Weston, *From Ritual to Romance* (1920; rpt. New York: Anchor Books, 1957), 13.
85. Erick Hawkins interview with David Sears, April 24, 1982, David Sears Papers, Jerome Robbins Dance Collection, New York Public Library for the Performing Arts, box 21, folder 4.
86. Adrienne Rich, *Of Woman Born. Motherhood as Experience and Institution* (New York & London: W.W. Norton, 1995), 99–100.
87. Gaston Bachelard, *The Poetics of Space* translated by Maria Jolas (Boston: Beacon Press, 1969), 53.
88. Ibidem.

89. Frances Steuben, (aka Edna Ocko), "Symbolism and Surrealism in the Dance" in *New Masses* April 2, 1946.

90. De Lauretis, *Alice Doesn't*, 144.

91. Program note transcribed by David Sears, David Sears Papers, Jerome Robbins Dance Collection, New York Public Library for the Performing Arts, box 20, folder 1. The program was from performances at the Maxine Elliott Theatre, February 19, 1948.

92. Ibidem. (identical with note 91)

93. David Sears transcribed portions of the text that has since disappeared. Some of his transcriptions may also be from Hawkins notes to the piece.

94. Ibidem.

95. Ibidem.

96. Ted Hughes cited in Janet Malcolm, *The Silent Woman: Sylvia Plath and Ted Hughes* (New York: Vintage, 1993), 3.

97. Erick Hawkins interview with David Sears, April 24, 1982, David Sears Papers, Jerome Robbins Dance Collection, New York Public Library for the Performing Arts, box 21, folder 4.

98. David Sears interview with Lesley Farlow, March 27, 1992, Jerome Robbins Dance Collection, New York Public Library for the Performing Arts: *MGZMT 3–1657), 17.

99. Erich Neumann, *The Origins and History of Consciousness* (London: Maresfield Library, 1989), 159–160.

100. "In the symbolic equations of a Feminine that nourishes, generates, and transforms, tree, djed pillar, tree of heaven, and cosmic tree belong together." Erich Neumann, *The Great Mother*, 243.

101. Martha Graham letter to Erick Hawkins, no date, Erick Hawkins Collection, Music Division, Library of Congress, box 55, folder 1.

102. Erick Hawkins Collection, Music Division, Library of Congress, box 53, folder 11.

103. Martha Graham, "Daughter of Colchis" scenario, Martha Graham Collection, Music Division, Library of Congress, 5. It is hereafter referred to in notes as "Daughter of Colchis" scenario.

104. David Sears transcription, David Sears Papers, Jerome Robbins Dance Collection, New York Public Library for the Performing Arts, box 20, folder one.

105. Martha Graham letter to Erick Hawkins, September 2, 1950, Erick Hawkins Collection, Music Division, Library of Congress, box 255, folder 22.

106. David Sears transcription, David Sears Papers, Jerome Robbins Dance Collection, New York Public Library for the Performing Arts, box 20, folder one.

107. Ethel Winter interview with the author, July 27, 2010, New York City.

108. Martha Graham letter to Erick Hawkins, October 19, 1946, Erick Hawkins Collection, Music Division, Library of Congress, box 55, folder 4.

109. Case studies from the year 1946 are missing from Fromm's case records at the Manuscript Division of the New York Public Library, Schwarzman Building. This possibility has been suggested to me by Fromm biographer and historian Lawrence Friedman.

110. Martha Graham letter to Erick Hawkins, October 14, 1946, Erick Hawkins Collection, Music Division, Library of Congress, box 53, folder 11.

111. Ben Belitt, "Dance Piece" from *Wilderness Stair* (New York: Grove Press, 1955).

112. Ben Belitt interview with David Sears, July 7, 1985, Jerome Robbins Dance Collection, New York Public Library for the Performing Arts: MGZTL-4-1522.

113. Ibidem.

114. Ibidem.

115. Ibidem.

116. Penelope Reed Doob, *The Idea of the Labyrinth from Classical Antiquity through the Middle Ages* (Ithaca & London: Cornell University Press, 1990), 66 & 72.

117. The first phrase is in a letter of October 18, 1946; the second phrase is found in a letter of October 27, 1946. Erick Hawkins Collection, Music Division, Library of Congress, box 55, folder 25.

118. Ibidem. Hawkins took notes for a ballet entitled *Primer for Action* (1/15/40), a title Graham took herself for an essay she wrote on modern dance. Among other Hawkins ideas that

Graham took much later is *Lucifer, a Dance of Satan* for which there are notes dated June 16, 1939, Erick Hawkins Collection, Library of Congress, box 50, folder 3.

119. Program note from the early 1950s transcribed by David Sears, David Sears Papers, Jerome Robbins Dance Collection, New York Public Library for the Performing Arts, box 20, folder one.

120. Erich Fromm, "Faith as a Character Trait," reprint from *Psychiatry: Journal of Biology and Pathology of Interpersonal Relations* vol. 5, number 3 (August 1942). Erich Fromm Papers, New York Public Library, box 7, folder 1.

121. Martha Graham letter to David Zellmer, July 28, 1943, Jerome Robbins Dance Collection, New York Public Library for the Performing Arts.

122. Esther M. Harding, *Psychic Energy. Its Source and its Transformation* (1947; rpt. Washington D.C.: Bollingen Foundation, 1963), ix. Harding was a student of Jung. Harding begins the book with these words: "Beneath the decent façade of consciousness with its disciplined moral order and its good intentions lurk the crude instinctive forces of life, like monsters of the deep—devouring, begetting, warring endlessly." Ibid., 3.

123. Ibid., 8.

124. Louis Mumford, *Faith for Living* (New York: Harcourt, Brace & Co., 1940), 3.

125. Franklin D. Roosevelt in Samuel Rosenman, editor, *The Public Papers of Franklin D. Roosevelt, Volume Two: The Year of Crisis, 1933* (New York: Random House, 1938), 11–16.

126. Archibald MacLeish, *Panic. A Play in Verse* (Boston & New York: Houghton Mifflin Company, 1935), 7. The performances took place on March 14–15, 1935, at the Imperial Theatre in New York City.

127. Louis Mumford, *Faith for Living* (New York: Harcourt, Brace & Co., 1940), 118.

128. Erich Fromm, "Faith as a Character Trait," reprint from *Psychiatry: Journal of Biology and Pathology of Interpersonal Relations* vol. 5, number 3 (August 1942). Erich Fromm Papers, New York Public Library, Steven A. Schwarzman Building, box 7, folder 1., 309. The offprint is written over with a correction in Fromm's hand.

129. Although the text of these comments does not survive, the paraphrase in "A Dancer and an Educator on Fascism" underlines Graham's psychological approach to Fascism as a problem within. The account also underlined: "America has its own enemies within." *The Dance Observer* (March 1937).

130. *Authority and the Family* translated by A. Lissance (New York: 1937), New York Public Library, Schwarzman Building: TDI.

131. Ibid., 3.

132. "[U]nder the Nazi regime women counted merely as mothers who should bear and rear as many children as possible, and . . . Nazi antifeminism tended to promote, protect, and even finance women as childbearers, housewives, and mothers." Gisela Bock, "Racism and Sexism in Nazi Germany: Motherhood, Compulsory Sterilization, and the State," in *When Biology Became Destiny. Women in Weimar and Nazi Germany* edited by Renate Bridenthal, Anita Grossman, and Marion Kaplan (New York: Monthly Review Press, 1984), 273.

133. Robert Sabin, "Martha Graham and Her Company Give Repertory Season," in *Dance Observer* 14/4 (April 1947), 43.

134. Martha Graham cited in Isamu Noguchi, *A Sculptor's World* (New York & Evanston: Harper & Row Publishers, 1968), 126.

135. For Harding, "The Moon Goddess [whom she also calls the Moon Mother] belongs to a matriarchal not to a patriarchal system. She is not related to any god as wife or 'counterpart.' She is her own mistress, virgin, 'one-in-herself.'" She adds: "She is represented as having no husband. She is goddess of sexual love but not of marriage. There is no male god who rules her conduct or determines her qualities." Harding also wrote that "the moon was the visible representation of womanhood. . . . the very essence of woman in its contrast to the essence of man." See "The Moon in Modern Life" in *Woman's Mysteries. Ancient and Modern* (London, New York, Toronto: Longman's, Green & Co., 1935), 82; 117; see also, Adrienne Rich, *Of Woman Born*, 107. Harding draws heavily on Robert Briffault, *The Mothers. The Matriarchal Theory of Social Origins* (1927; rpt. New York: Howard Fertig, 1993).

136. Rank, *The Trauma of Birth*, 17.

137. Ibid., 73.

138. Erick Hawkins interview with David Sears, June 9, 1985, Typescript: "Erick Hawkins 6/9/85 on the Maze—in his studio on 5th Avenue." David Sears Papers, Jerome Robbins Dance Collection, New York Public Library for the Performing Arts, box 22, folder 9. De Mille claims Hawkins danced the role opposite Graham in Paris, although this seems unlikely as Mark Ryder and Stuart Hodes normally performed it, and Hodes was on that tour. One reason Graham may never have asked him to do the role is that he was too close to being the fearful figure himself, and the piece was originally his idea.

139. For a discussion of the variety of sexual fantasies that revolve around Fascism, see Dagmar Herzog, *Sex after Fascism. Memory and Morality in Twentieth-Century Germany* (Princeton: Princeton University Press, 2005).

140. "Sword of Dictator Hangs Over Life of Dance, She Says," in *Milwaukee Journal* (March 21, 1939). Scrapbooks, Martha Graham archive, Library of Congress.

141. Marcia B. Siegel, *The Shapes of Change: Images of American Dance* (Boston: Houghton Mifflin, 1979), 199.

142. Martha Graham letter to David Zellmer, December 14, 1942 (my emphasis), Jerome Robbins Dance Collection, New York Public Library for the Performing Arts.

143. Herbert Marcuse, *Negations. Essays in Critical Theory* (London: Free Association Books, 1988), xviii. Philippe Lacoue-Labarthe and Jean-Luc Nancy, in "The Nazi Myth," in *Critical Inquiry*, 312, make a very similar point.

144. Erick Hawkins interview with David Sears, June 9, 1985, Typescript: "Erick Hawkins 6/9/85 on the Maze—in his studio on 5th Avenue." David Sears Papers, Jerome Robbins Dance Collection, New York Public Library for the Performing Arts, box 21, folder 4.

145. Carl G. Jung, *Man and His Symbols* (London: Aldus Books, 1964), 147.

146. Rank, *Art and Artist*, 215.

147. Rank, *Art and Artist*, 387.

148. Stephen Polcari, "Martha Graham and Abstract Expressionism," in *Smithsonian Studies in American Art* (Winter 1990), 3–27.

149. Reminiscences of Ben Belitt (1979), Bennington Summer School Project, Oral History Research Office, Columbia University: 34.

150. Ibid., 36.

Chapter 4

1. *Night Journey* was the last of Graham's Coolidge commissions for original scores. Its first performance took place at the Harvard University Symposium on Music Criticism with the Boston Symphony conducted by Louis Horst on May 3, 1947. The New York premiere took place on February 17, 1948.

2. However, Bertram Ross felt the film did not represent the dance as well as it could have because the sharp black and white contrasts were overly clinical. Also, Graham wore a dark dress from the ballet *Clytemnestra* whereas her costume for the role on stage was white and gold: "She was a victim and vulnerable." Bertram Ross Papers, Jerome Robbins Dance Collection, New York Public Library for the Performing Arts, box 24, folder 13.

3. The idea for *Voyage* is already implicit in her *Judith*—the second of four works Schuman composed for her—and her planning for *Voyage* began in 1951. The fourth and last work Schuman composed for Graham was *The Witch of Endor* (1965).

4. Graham referred to *Dark Meadow* as "a landscape of the journey of the Soul." Graham, *Notebooks*, 189. Her language, however, was deceptively religious. Like Harding, Graham used soul "not in the theological sense of an immortal part of man which shall replace him at death, but in the psychological sense of an unseen figure which represents the unconscious, or relatively unconscious part of the psyche." Elizabeth Harding, *Woman's Mysteries*, 217.

5. Martha Graham, letter to William Schuman, October 28, 1946. William Schuman Papers & Records, Music Collection, New York Public Library for the Performing Arts: JPB 87–33, box 18, folder 10.

6. As art critic Clement Greenberg noted in 1946: "The example of surrealism inspired them [Abstract Expressionist painters] to introduce into their pictures symbols and metaphors drawn from Freudian theory, archaeology, and anthropology." Clement Greenberg cited in translation from French by Michael Leja, *Reframing Abstract Expressionism: Subjectivity and Painting in the 1940s* (New Haven & London: Yale University Press, 1993), 33.

7. Leja, *Reframing Abstract Expressionism*, 8. Art historians frequently point out connections between Graham and the New York School. The only Abstract Expressionist that Graham is known to have had contact with, however, was David Smith. Smith arrived in New York in 1926, the year of Graham's first independent concert. Graham was Smith's elder by 12 years, and it would appear her work influenced his rather than the other way around. Although he sketched her, Smith did not collaborate, as did Isamu Noguchi, with Graham. Dorothy Dehner, a visual artist and Smith's first wife, studied with Graham, and Smith most probably came into contact with Graham through her.

8. Bertram Ross Papers, Jerome Robbins Dance Collection, New York Public Library for the Performing Arts, box 24, folder 2.

9. My focus in this book differs somewhat from that of Morris in that she is interested in the tension between embodiment and narrative accessibility whereas my focus is on how Graham weights the reciprocally determining subfields of dancing and choreography.

10. Gay Morris, *A Game for Dancers. Performing Modernism in the Postwar Years, 1945–1960* (Middletown, Connecticut: Wesleyan University Press, 2006), 24.

11. "Myth connects the self to society and world, unlike rationality, which depersonalizes and objectifies that which is other than the self." Robert Ellwood, *The Politics of Myth. A study of C. G. Jung, Mircea Eliade, and Joseph Campbell* (Albany: State University of New York Press, 1999), 28.

12. Graham adopted many aspects of ballet technique by the mid- to late 1940s, as Gay Morris has pointed out. Morris relates the balletic qualities that entered the Graham technique initially to Hawkins's teaching of ballet in the Graham school when he first joined the company. "Bourdieu, the Body, and Graham's Post-War Dance," in *Dance Research* 19/2 (Winter 2001), 61–62.

13. Bertram Ross Collection, Dance Collection, New York Public Library for the Performing Arts at Lincoln Center, box 10. These notes of Ross are dated 1991.

14. Joseph Campbell claimed *Deaths and Entrances* was Graham's first mythic work, although there were no references to Greek mythology.

15. Martha Graham letter to David Zellmer, December 28, 1943, Jerome Robbins Dance Collection, New York Public Library for the Performing Arts.

16. Ibidem.

17. Ibidem.

18. Martha Graham letter to David Zellmer, October 23, 1943, Jerome Robbins Dance Collection, New York Public Library for the Performing Arts.

19. Hawkins has referred to "suchness" as the primacy of the materials used over the appearance they are meant to project. This, of course, intersects with the modernist notion of the real thing. Erick Hawkins interviewed by Don McDonagh, November 17, 1972, Jerome Robbins Dance Collection, New York Public Library for the Performing Arts: *MGZTL 4–2556.

20. Martha Graham letter to David Zellmer, June 12, 1944, Dance Collection, New York Public Library for the Performing Arts at Lincoln Center.

21. Graham's booking agent Isadora Bennett wrote a synopsis of the development of the Company in which she noted of the season at the National Theatre from May 7–14, 1944: "One full week of repertory—the first on Broadway for an American dancer and the first for any dancer since Pavlova." Martha Graham Center of Dance Records, 1944–1955, box 1, folder 4 (Jerome Robbins Dance Collection, Lincoln Center Library for the Performing Arts: (S) *MGZMD 152.

22. "Important Memo" from Isadora Bennett announcing Sol Hurok's representation of Martha Graham. "Martha Graham Center" file, Jerome Robbins Dance Collection, New York Public Library for the Performing Arts, box 1, folder 9.

23. The original concept of raising $20,000 using the Katharine Cornell Foundation, and the idea of a "limited partnership" was the brainchild of Hawkins in 1943. Gertrude Macy, who

worked for Katharine Cornell and Guthrie McClintock, managed Graham nominally in connection with Cornell's fundraisers. Frances Hawkins, who also worked for Lincoln Kirstein, first officially represented Graham. When she left, Erick Hawkins filled in the void until Isadora Bennett took over Graham's representation.

24. While this may have been less true of *Letter to the World* and *Deaths and Entrances*, both of which were structured around her own solos, it began in earnest with *Appalachian Spring*.

25. William Schuman interviewed by John Gruen, May 7, 1975. Dance Collection, New York Public Library for the Performing Arts: *MGAMT 3–561.

26. Martha Graham letter to David Zellmer, January 30, 1944, Jerome Robbins Dance Collection, New York Public Library for the Performing Arts.

27. This struggle occurred particularly in making *Appalachian Spring*. Martha Graham letter to David Zellmer, July 9, 1944, Jerome Robbins Dance Collection, New York Public Library for the Performing Arts.

28. Bertram Ross, typescript dated February 1991 and titled "Personal" (page 3). Bertram Ross Papers, Dance Collection, New York Public Library for the Performing Arts, box 10, folder 23.

29. Martha Graham letter to Bertram Ross, August 30, 1953. Bertram Ross Papers, Jerome Robbins Dance Collection, New York Public Library for the Performing Arts, box 1, folder 19.

30. Ethel Winter interview with the author, July 27, 2010, New York City.

31. Program copy of the Erick Hawkins Dance Company, circa 1983, outlined his past collaboration with Graham as follows: "With Hawkins as her partner, Graham transformed her all-female company, creating dances to explore male-female relationships in dramatic and lyrical ways. The degree Hawkins played a part in this change cannot be underestimated, for he not only taught the company certain ballet principles, but also was involved in suggesting composers, orchestration, scenic and costume details, mythic themes, and patronage." David Sears Papers, Jerome Robbins Dance Collection, New York Public Library for the Performing Arts, box 21, folder 3.

32. Bertram Ross Papers, Jerome Robbins Dance Collection, New York Public Library for the Performing Arts, box 10, folder 13. This typescript gives a very complete view of the first version of *Clytemnestra*, and the subsequent changes Graham desired to make.

33. Ibid., box 10, folder 25.

34. Bertram Ross interview with Agnes de Mille, May 23, 1974, Jerome Robbins Dance Collection, New York Public Library for the Performing Arts: *MGZTC 3–1635. In notes for his memoir Ross attributes his downfall with Graham in the late sixties to his sexual distance from her.

35. Erick Hawkins, interview with David Sears, April 24, 1982, David Sears Papers, Jerome Robbins Dance Collection, New York Public Library for the Performing Arts, box 21, folder 4 (my emphasis).

36. For Kristeva, the semiotic erupts or transgresses an order, be it the order of language (the 'symbolic') or of narrative. Feeling is not the signified of narrative, but its byproduct. The analytic model for Kristeva's semiotic is psychosomatic.

37. My interpretation of *Night Journey* is at the opposite end of the spectrum from that of Marcia Siegel. It will become evident that this difference is probably due to the fact that Siegel sees only Freud, not post-Freudian theory, in Graham's treatment of the Oedipus legend.

38. A rundown of Graham's career by her press representatives Isadora Bennett and Richard Pleasant starts with "a new cycle" announced by *Every Soul is a Circus*. The press release adds of *American Document*: "some might consider this, because of size and form, as the precursor of the new phase." While one rarely seeks historical accuracy in press releases, this one seems to pinpoint accurately the beginning of the dramaturgical phase in her work of which I have spoken elsewhere. See Martha Graham Center of Dance Records (1944–45), Jerome Robbins Dance Collection, New York Public Library for the Performing Arts: (S)*MGZMD 152.

39. William Butler Yeats, "Introduction by William Butler Yeats to *Certain Noble Plays of Japan* by Pound and Fenollosa" in Pound and Fenollosa, *The Classic Noh Theatre of Japan* (Westport, Connecticut: Greenwood Press, 1977), 151.

40. "I first met Martha around 1926 with Michio Ito who was a dancer and who taught at the John Murray Anderson School, and there was Martha." Isamu Noguchi, "Tribute to Martha Graham," in *Isamu Noguchi. Essays and Conversations*, edited by Diane Apostolos-Cappadona & Bruce Altshuler (New York: Harry N. Abrams, Inc., 1994), 120. The editors place the first meeting of Noguchi and Graham in 1929 (122). According to Helen Caldwell, Ito presented *At the Hawk's Well* "twice in the United States, in New York in 1918 and in California in 1929." Helen Caldwell, *Michio Ito. The Dancer and his Dances* (Berkeley & Los Angeles: University of California Press, 1977), 54.

41. Janet Mansfield Soares, *Louis Horst. Musician in a Dancer's World* (Durham & London: Duke University Press, 1992), 60–61.

42. It was Ezra Pound, according to Helen Carr, who discovered Ito in London and introduced him to Yeats: "Ito was an intriguingly postmodern figure, who had arrived in England with almost no knowledge of Noh drama—he had last seen it performed when he was seven—but with an excellent training in European dance, having been inspired by Nijinsky and the Russian Ballet in Paris, and spending several years training in the Dalcroze Institute in Germany.... When he discovered that Pound wanted Noh, he read it up in books and obligingly reinvented himself as a traditional Noh dancer." *The Verse Revolutionaries*, 812.

43. Carr, *The Verse Revolutionaries . . . Ezra Pound, H.D. and the Imagists* (London: Jonathan Cape, 2009), 813.

44. Fenollosa died in 1908, and his widow Mary Fenollosa asked Pound to edit his unfinished manuscripts on Japanese Noh and Chinese poetry. See *The Translations of Ezra Pound* (London: Faber & Faber, 1970).

45. Martha Graham, letter to William Schuman, August 30, 1946, William Schuman Papers and Records, Music Division, New York Public Library for the Performing Arts: box 18, folder 10. Yeats wrote *Sophocles' King Oedipus. A Version for the Modern Stage* in 1928. "Graham's work owes as much to Yeats's Plays for Dancers," writes Fiona Macintosh, "as it does to psychoanalytic theory; and like Yeats's Noh-inspired plays, it hovers between the realms of life and death, reality and other layers of consciousness." Fiona Macintosh, *Sophocles: Oedipus Tyrannus* (Cambridge: Cambridge University Press, 2009), 183.

46. Soares, *Louis Horst*, 73–74. Graham also appeared on the same program with Kreutzberg on December 27, 1932 at Radio City Music Hall in New York City. She performed "Choric Dance—For an Antique Greek Tragedy" and he danced "The Angel of Fate."

47. Soares, *Louis Horst*, 74.

48. See Joellen Meglin "Blurring the Boundaries of Genre, Gender, and Geopolitics: Ruth Page and Harald Kreutzberg's Transatlantic Collaboration in the 1930s," in *Dance Research Journal* 41/2 (Winter 2009), 52–75; Yutian Wong, "Artistic Utopias: Michio Ito and the Trope of the International," in *Worlding Dance* edited by Susan Leigh, Foster (London: Palgrave Macmillan, 2009), 144–162.

49. Martha Graham Collection, Music Division, Library of Congress, box 218, folder 2. The review appeared in *The New York Times* on January 22, 1941. Of course, Graham used spoken text in both *American Document* and *Letter to the World*. Her use of the spoken word between 1938 and 1941 corresponds to her first use of male dancers.

50. Martha Graham, letter to Erick Hawkins, July 27, 1943, Erick Hawkins Collection, Music Division, Library of Congress, box 55, folder 1.

51. Frances Wickes, *The Inner World of Man* (London: Methuen, 1950), 252.

52. One can almost imagine the whole concept dawning on her with *Letter to the World* where Graham plays "One Who Dances" to Jean Erdman's "One Who Speaks." But, she quickly moves beyond the simplicity of this arrangement.

53. Martha Graham, letter to Erick Hawkins, undated but likely 1939–1940, Erick Hawkins Collection, Music Division, Library of Congress, box 55, folder 1.

54. Martha Graham, Notes for *Canticle for Innocent Comedians*, Martha Graham Collection, Music Division, Library of Congress, box 224, folder 4.

55. T.S. Eliot cited in Susan Jones, "At the Still Point: T.S. Eliot, Dance and Modernism," in *Dance Research Journal* 41/2 (Winter 2009), 38.

56. See Graham, *Notebooks*, 305–306.

57. On the close connections between choral dancing and acting in Greek tragedy, see Herbert Golder, "Making a Scene: Gesture, Tableau, and the Tragic Chorus," in *Arion* 2 (Spring 1996), 1–19.

58. See William Chase Green, *Moira. Fate, Good and Evil in Greek Thought.* Gloucester, Mass.: Peter Smith, 1968. This book was originally published in 1944.

59. *Night Journey* libretto in Martha Graham's letter to William Schuman of October 28, 1946. William Schuman Papers and Records, Music Division, New York Public Library for the Performing Arts, box 18, folder 10.

60. Gay Morris, "Bourdieu, the Body, and Graham's Post-War Dance," in *Dance Research* 19/2 (Winter 2001), 70.

61. John Gould, "Tragedy and Collective Experience" in *Myth, Ritual Memory, and Exchange. Essays in Greek Literature and Culture* (Oxford: Oxford University Press, 2001), 384.

62. Morris, "Bourdieu, the Body, and Graham's Post-War Dance," 70–71.

63. Martha Graham letter to William Schuman, October 28, 1946, William Schuman Papers, New York Public Library for the Performing Arts at Lincoln Center, box 28, folder 10.

64. Program for performances at the Maxine Eliott's Theatre, 1948, Martha Graham Program file, Jerome Robbins Dance Collection, New York Public Library for the Performing Arts at Lincoln Center, *MGZB-Res. 01–8427 (box 1).

65. Typescript in Scrapbooks, Martha Graham Collection, Library of Congress, box 332.

66. Morris, "Bourdieu, the Body, and Graham's Post-War Dance," 71.

67. "Much of Jocasta's movement in her first solo is mimetic." Ibid., 71.

68. Bertram Ross Papers, Dance Collection, New York Public Library for the Performing Arts: box 10, folder 25.

69. Ted Hughes, *Shakespeare and the Goddess of Complete Being* (London: Faber & Faber, 1993), 36 & 54.

70. William Schuman interview with John Gruen, May 7, 1975, Jerome Robbins Dance Collection, New York Public Library for the Performing Arts: *MGTC 3–561.

71. Ben Belitt interview with David Sears, July 7, 1985, Jerome Robbins Dance Collection, New York Public Library for the Performing Arts: *MGZTL 4–1522.

72. David Vaughan, "Dissenting View on Graham" in *Dance Magazine* (July 1958), 26–27. See Gay Morris's discussion of this article in *A Game for Dancers*, 198–199.

73. Others followed Vaughan's lead. The backlash to this rereading of the theatricality of dance in modernism is doubtless Michael Fried's "Art and Objecthood" in which he brings the term theatrical to bear on minimalism. For a history of the discursive relationship of Graham's work to the idea of theater, see Diana Snyder, "'The Most Important Lesson for Our Theater'" in *Ballet Review* 7 (1982), 7–20.

74. Yvonne Rainer, "The Mind is a Muscle," in *Work: 1961–1973* (New York: New York University Press, 1974), 64.

75. Jill Johnston, "Martha Graham: An Irresponsible Study . . . The Head of her Father," in *Ballet Review* 2/4 (1968), 9. I thank Ramsay Burt for calling this article to my attention.

76. I purposely leave aside the work of the 1930s here because I have studied them elsewhere, and because insufficient attention has been given to the works of the 1940s and 1950s.

77. Gay Morris, *A Game for Dancers*, 199.

78. Yvonne Rainer, "Where's the Passion? Where's the Politics? Or, How I Became Interested in Impersonating, Approximating, and End Running around My Selves and Others', and Where Do I Look When You're Looking at Me?" in *Theater* 40:1 (2010), 53.

79. See, Mark Franko, "Some Notes on Yvonne Rainer, Modernism, Politics, Emotion, Performance, and its Aftermath," in *Meaning in Motion. New Cultural Studies in Dance*, edited by Jane Desmond (Durham: Duke University Press, 1997), 289–303.

80. Yuriko interview with the author, September 26, 2010, New York City.

81. "It was Erick's joy and privilege to teach Martha." De Mille, *Martha*, 279.

82. Both Eugenie Sellers (Mrs. Arthur Strong). and Harrison, according to Mary Beard, were "linking the visual arts and archaeology to a cultural anthropology of the ancient world." *The Invention of Jane Harrison* (Cambridge, Mass.: Harvard University Press, 2000), 28.

83. "It is clear that Jane Harrison played a much larger role in the modernist understanding of myth and ritual and their relation to classical literature than has hitherto been recognized."

Martha C. Carpentier, *Ritual, Myth, and the Modernist Text. The Influence of Jane Ellen Harrison on Joyce, Eliot, and Woolf* (Amsterdam: Gordon & Breach Publishers, 1998), 37.

84. Beard, *The Invention of Jane Harrison*, 7.
85. Jean Erdman interview with Don McDonagh, October 4, 1993. Jerome Robbins Dance Collection, New York Public Library for the Performing Arts: NYPL: *MGZTL 4–2567.
86. Erick Hawkins interview with David Sears, June 9, 1985, Typescript: "Erick Hawkins 6/9/85 on the Maze—in his studio on 5th Avenue," David Sears Papers, Jerome Robbins Dance Collection, New York Public Library for the Performing Arts, box 22, folder 9, p. 8.
87. I am grateful to Don McDonagh for this formulation.
88. Hawkins put it on a list of books to read in 1932 along with Otto Rank's *Art and Artist* (Erick Hawkins Collection, Music Division, Library of Congress, box 77, folder 4).
89. Carr, *The Verse Revolutionaries*, 263.
90. Lefevbre, *The Production of Space*, 235.
91. Merle Armitage interview with Don McDonagh, 1972, Jerome Robbins Dance Collection, New York Public Library for the Performing Arts: *MGZTL 4–2524.
92. Erick Hawkins interviewed by Don McDonagh, November 17, 1972, Dance Collection, New York Public Library for the Performing Arts at Lincoln Center, *MGZTL 4–2556.
93. Nadine Hubbs, *The Queer Composition of America's Sound. Gay Modernists, American Music, and National Identity* (Berkeley & Los Angeles: University of California Press, 2004), 181.
94. T. S. Eliot, "Ulysses, Order and Myth," in *the Selected Prose of T.S. Eliot*, edited by Frank Kermode (London: Faber & Faber, 1975), 177. This essay was originally published in 1923.
95. "Psychology (such as it is, and whether our reaction to it be comic or serious), ethnology, and *the Golden Bough* have concurred to make possible what was impossible even a few years ago." T.S. Eliot, "Ulysses," 178 [inc. pages = 175–178].
96. Erich Fromm, *Love, Sexuality, and Matriarchy. About Gender* edited by Rainer Funk (New York: Fromm International Publishing Corporation, 1994), 19–45.
97. Erich Fromm, *The Forgotten Language. An Introduction to the Understanding of Dreams, Fairy Tales, and Myths* (New York & Toronto: Rinehart & Company, 1951), 210. Fromm returned to this theme in his writings of the late 1960s and early 1970s. See, in particular, "The Significance of the Theory of Mother Right Today," in *The Erich Fromm Reader* edited by Rainer Funk (New Jersey: Humanities Press, 1985), 59–62. Robert Graves who in 1948 published *The White Goddess* may also have influenced Graham. ". . . [T]he book's argument is that in late prehistoric times, throughout Europe and the Middle East, matriarchal cultures, worshipping a supreme Goddess and recognizing male gods only as her son, consort or sacrificial victim, were subordinated by aggressive proponents of patriarchy who deposed women from their positions of authority, elevated the Goddess's male consorts into positions of divine supremacy and reconstructed myths and rituals to conceal what had taken place." Grevel Lindop, "Editorial Introduction," in Robert Graves, *The White Goddess. A Historical Grammar of Poetic Myth*, edited by Grevel Lindop (Manchester: Carcanet Press, 1997), ix–x. As Lindop points out, Graves forms a bridge between Frazer, Yeats, and Northrop Frye.
98. Bronislaw Malinowski, *Mutterrechtliche Familie und Oedipus-Komplex. Eine ethnologisch-psychoanalytische Studie* (Leipzig/Wien/Zürich: Internationaler Psychoanalytischer Verlage, 1924). This essay was also published in English as "Psycho-Analysis and Anthropology" in *Psyche* IV (1924).
99. Michael A. Young, *Malinowski. Odyssey of an Anthropologist, 1884–1920* (New Haven & London: Yale University Press, 2004), 178.
100. Fiona Macintosh cites *Night Journey* as a feminist rewriting of *Oedipus Tyrranus* "in which the Kleinian psychoanalytical theory provides the frame." See Fiona Macintosh, *Sophocles: Oedipus Tyrannus* (Cambridge: Cambridge University Press, 2009), 162.
101. J.J. Bachofen, *Myth, Religion, and Mother Right. Selected Writings of J.J. Bachofen*, translated by Ralph Manheim (Princeton: Princeton University Press, 1967). This partial translation of Bachofen first appeared in 1926. Graham could not have read the complete text.
102. Ibid., 93. That Graham adopted an East-West binary, trisecting it with theatrical irony into embodiments of Egypt, India and Greece, is indicated in her poem "Satirical Perspective." Martha Graham Collection, Music Division, Library of Congress, box 224, folder 6.
103. See Anthea Kraut, "White Womanhood, Property Rights, and the Campaign for Choreographic Copyright: Loïe Fuller's *Serpentine Dance*," in *Dance Research Journal* 43/1

(Summer 2011), 3–26; Priya Srinivasan, "The Bodies Beneath the Smoke or What's Behind the Cigarette Poster: Unearthing Kinesthetic Connections in American Dance History" in *Discourses in Dance* 4/1 (2007): 7–47; Amy Koritz, *Gendering Bodies/Performing Art: Dance and Literature in Early Twentieth-Century British Culture* (Ann Arbor: University of Michigan Press, 1995).

104. Hawkins commissioned the score from the Czech composer Bohuslav Martinu (1890–1959) whom he probably met at the Berkshire School of Music in Tanglewood, Massachusetts, in the summer of 1941 where they had both been invited to teach by Serge Kossuvitsky. *Time* (August 12, 1940) shows a picture of Erick Hawkins teaching podium gestures to conductors.

105. *Night Journey* script in Martha Graham letter to William Schuman, October 28, 1946, William Schuman Papers & Records, Music Collection, New York Public Library for the Performing Arts: JPB 87–33, box 18, folder 10. It shall be referred to hereafter as the *Night Journey* script.

106. Erick Hawkins letter to Aaron Copland, April 28, 1948. Erick Hawkins Collection, Music Division, Library of Congress, box 56, folder 5.

107. Ethel Winter interview with the author, July 27, 2010, New York City. Winter was an undergraduate at Bennington majoring in theater arts when she met Graham. She joined the Graham Company before she graduated in 1944 to replace Ethel Butler. She told me that because of the lack of gas during the war the summer program had been cancelled and the Company came to Bennington during the year. Graham first met Erich Fromm who was teaching there in 1943. Winter took a course with Fromm at Bennington on Freud. Graham mentioned the presence of psychoanalysis on campus in a letter to David Zellmer. Her major exposure to psychoanalysis was through the post-Freudians.

108. Martha Graham Center of Dance Records (1944–45), Jerome Robbins Dance Collection, New York Public Library for the Performing Arts: (S)*MGZMD 152 (folder 10). The performance was billed as "Erick Hawkins in Theatre Dance Pieces," and occasionally as Erick Hawkins Dance Company.

109. Erick Hawkins letter to William Schuman, March 29, 1948, William Schuman Papers, Music Collection, New York Public Library for the Performing Arts at Lincoln Center, box 20, folder 5. In the wake of the success of *Night Journey*, Hawkins was writing to Schuman about his idea for a ballet on Melville's *Moby Dick* to be entitled *The Fiery Hunt*. Hawkins reported he already had commissioned the text of poet Charles Olsen. Schuman demurred for lack of time in a letter of April 9, 1948.

110. Cited in Carr, *The Verse Revolutionaries*, 436.

111. Graham, *Notebooks*, 297.

112. *Night Journey* script, 2.

113. Ibidem.

114. Jane Harrison, *Prolegomena to the Study of Greek Religion* (1903; Princeton: Princeton University Press, 1991), 215. Graham would develop the theme of revenge in the context of incest with *Clytemnestra* in 1958.

115. Graham, *Notebooks*, 297.

116. Ethel Winter interview with the author. Winter was in the original rehearsals as she danced in the premiere.

117. *Night Journey* script, 2.

118. Erick Hawkins interview with David Sears, December 12, 1982, David Sears Papers, Jerome Robbins Dance Collection, New York Public Library for the Performing Arts: box 21, folder 4.

119. Margaret Lloyd, *The Borzoi Book of Modern Dance* (New York: Dance Horizons, 1969), 45.

120. William Schuman interview with John Gruen, May 7, 1975, Jerome Robbins Dance Collection, New York Public Library for the Performing Arts: *MGTC 3–561.

121. Joseph Frank, *The Idea of Spatial Form* (New Brunswick & London: Rutgers University Press, 1991), 10.

122. Ernst Cassirer, *The Philosophy of Symbolic Forms. Volume Two: Mythical Thought*, translated by Ralph Mannheim (New Haven & London: Yale University Press, 1955), 106.

123. Pound cited in Carr, *The Verse Revolutionaries*, 78.

124. Joseph Frank, *The Idea of Spatial Form*, 11.
125. Cassirer, *The Philosophy of Symbolic Forms*, 39.
126. William Schuman interview with John Gruen, May 7, 1975, Jerome Robbins Dance Collection, New York Public Library for the Performing Arts: *MGTC 3–561.
127. W. B. Yeats, *The Collected Plays of W. B. Yeats* (London: MacMillan & Company, 1952), 475.
128. *Night Journey* script, 5.
129. Doris Hering, "The Season in Review," *Dance Magazine* (April 1948), 12.
130. *Night Journey* script.
131. "Martha Graham Presents New Work "Night Journey," with Score by William Schuman, at Harvard University Festival" in *Dance Observer* 14/6 (June–July 1947), 64. Another critic similarly remarked that Graham overshadowed the cast at the premiere, citing a problem with "the formal reference of Jocasta, who now dominates the action too much, to the rest of the dancers." Cecil Smith, "Music and Dance Review: Gertrude S., Virgil T., and Susan B.," in *Theatre Arts Monthly* XXXI/7 (July 1947), 18.
132. Isamu Noguchi, "Collaborating With Graham," in *Isamu Noguchi. Essays and Conversations* edited by Diane Apostolos-Cappadona and Bruce Altshuler (New York: Harry N. Abrams, 1994), 85.
133. Homer, *The Odyssey*, translated by Robert Fitzgerald (New York: Farrar, Straus & Giroux, 1998), book XI, 193–194.
134. Martha Graham letter to Erick Hawkins, July 27, 1950. Erick Hawkins Collection, Music Division, Library of Congress, box 55, folder 13.
135. Ibidem.
136. Erick Hawkins, "The Rite in Theater," reprinted in Hawkins, *The Body is a Clear Place and Other Statements on Dance* (Princeton: Dance Horizons, 1992), 3. The article is the text of a talk Hawkins gave at the National Theater Conference Annual Meeting in New York City on November 27, 1947.
137. Ibidem, 6.
138. *Night Journey* script, 2. Graham did, however, use the names Jocasta and Oedipus at the Cambridge premiere and in program notes thereafter.
139. This could lead to a reading of Suzanne Langer's notion of dance as "virtual energy."
140. Fiona Macintosh, "Parricide versus Filicide: Oedipus and Medea on the Modern Stage" in *Tragedy in Transition*, edited by Sarah Anne Brown and Catherine Silverstone (Oxford: Blackwell, 2007), 92.
141. "The Dance: Miss Hush Returns" newspaper clipping, dated February 17, 1948. Martha Graham Collection, Library of Congress.
142. Sigmund Freud, *The Interpretation of Dreams*, translated by James Strachey (New York: Basic Books, 1956), 262.
143. Sally Banes, "Night Journey," in *Dancing Women. Female Bodies on Stage* (London: Routledge, 1998), 159.
144. C.G. Jung, *Modern Man in Search of a Soul* (New York: Harcourt, Brace, & World, 1933), 120.
145. Sally Banes, *Dancing Women: Female Bodies on Stage* (London: Routledge, 1998), 163.
146. See Carl Gustav Jung, *Two Essays on Analytical Psychology*, translated by R.F. C. Hull (New York: Pantheon Books, 1953), 97–98. The night sea journey is a hero myth in which the hero is swallowed by the monster. This intertext with its free-floating iconographic variants suggests that *Errand into the Maze* and *Night Journey* are sister works. The monster in *Night Journey*, the Sphinx, which is a lion with a human head and woman's torso, is only implied.
147. Esther M. Harding, *Psychic Energy. Its Source and Transformation.* (Washington, D.C.: Bollingen Foundation, 1947), 288. Graham could also have read of the night sea journey myth in Maud Bodkin, *Archetypal Patterns in Poetry. Psychological Studies of the Imagination* (1934; rpt. London: Oxford University Press, 1963), 52.
148. Martha Graham, "Synopsis." Martha Graham Collection, Music Division, Library of Congress, box 224, folder 5.
149. Martha Graham letter to William Schuman, June 14, 1949, William Schuman Papers, Music Collection, New York Public Library for the Performing Arts at Lincoln Center, box 18, folder 10.

150. Ramsay Burt points out that Graham's *Notebooks* quote Freud only once. See Burt, "Dance, Gender and Psychoanalysis: Martha Graham's *Night Journey*," in *Dance Research Journal* 30/1 (Spring 1998), 41. On Freud's influence on twentieth-century culture, see Michael S. Roth, "Introduction," *Freud. Conflict and Culture. Essays on his life, work, and legacy*, edited by Michael S. Roth (New York: Alfred A. Knopf, 1998), 3–14.

151. "During 1906 to 1912 the Oedipus complex emerged as the touchstone of psychoanalytic truth." Peter L. Rudnytsky, "Introductory Essay" in Otto Rank. *The Incest Theme in Literature and Legend. Fundamentals of a Psychology of Literary Creation*, translated by Gregory C. Richter (Baltimore & London: The Johns Hopkins University Press, 1992), xii.

152. Rank, *The Incest Theme*, 209.

153. "Recognition, as the name indicates, is a change from ignorance to knowledge . . . The best form of recognition is coincident with a Reversal of the Situation, as in the *Oedipus*." Aristotle, *Aristotle's Poetics*, translated by S.H. Butcher (New York: Hill & Wang, 1961), 11:72.

154. Reik agrees with Rank that the Sphinx is a split image of the mother (". . . die Einführung der Sphinx eine Abspaltung gewisser anstössiger Züge von der Mutter gestatten sollte," p. 126). Theodor Reik, "Oedipus und die Sphinx," in *Imago. Zeitschrift für Anwendung der Psychoanalyse auf die Geisteswissenshaften* vol. 6 (1920), 95–131.

155. Rank, *Art and Artist*, 424.

156. Rank, *The Incest Theme*, 95.

157. Eric Bentley, "Martha Graham's Journey," 198.

158. "The figures of the ritual dance were theatre's pre-history (the vase was telling her), its origins and *raison d'être*." Julie Stone Peters, "Jane Harrison and the Savage Dionysus: Archaeological Voyages, Ritual Origins, and the Modern Theatre," in *Modern Drama* 51/1 (Spring 2008), 1.

159. Rank, *The Incest Theme*, xxxi.

160. Sigmund Freud, *On the History of the Psychoanalytic Movement*, translated by Joan Rivière (New York: Norton, 1966), 65.

161. Jane Ellen Harrison, *Themis. The Study of the Social Origins of Greek Religion* (Cambridge: Cambridge University Press, 1912), 43.

162. T.S. Eliot cited in Robert Crawford, *The Savage and the City in the Work of T.S. Eliot* (Oxford: Clarendon Press, 1987), 86.

163. Martha Graham letter to Erick Hawkins, October 14, 1946, Erick Hawkins Collection, Music Division, Library of Congress, box 53, folder 3.

164. Erick Hawkins letter to Martha Graham, August 21, 1950, Erick Hawkins Collection, Music Division, Library of Congress, box 55, folder 16.

165. Martha Graham letter to Erick Hawkins, September 3, 1950, Erick Hawkins Collection, Music Division, Library of Congress, box 55, folder 8.

166. Judith Butler, *Antigone's Claim. Kinship Between Life and Death* (New York: Columbia University Press, 2000), 78.

167. *Night Journey* script, 3.

168. Bertram Ross Papers, Jerome Robbins Dance Collection, New York Public Library for the Performing Arts, box 24, folder 9.

169. Ben Belitt interviewed by Theresa Bowers, 1979, Bennington Summer School of Dance Project, Columbia University, Office of Oral Archives.

170. Also in 1947 Claude Lévi-Strauss published *The Elementary Structures of Kinship* in which incest is examined as a cultural phenomenon. "The prohibition of incest has the universality of bent and instinct, and the coercive character of law and institution. Where then does it come from, and what is its place and significance?" Claude Lévi-Strauss, *The Elementary Structures of Kinship*, translated by James Harle Bell, John Richard von Sturmer and Rodney Needham (Boston: Beacon Press, 1969).

171. Otto Rank, *The Trauma of Birth* (New York: Dover, 1993), 144. Rank adds: "Reik has explained very ingeniously how the Sphinx episode really represents a duplicate of the Oedipus saga itself" (ibidem).

172. Erick Hawkins interview with David Sears, May 27, 1983, David Sears Papers, Jerome Robbins Dance Collection, New York Public Library for the Performing Arts, box 21, folder 4.

173. *The Strangler* premiered on August 28, 1948, in New London with a text by Robert Fitzgerald spoken by Joseph Wiseman and Hawkins. Anne Meacham played the Sphinx and Hawkins commissioned original music of the Czech composer Bohuslav Martinu. It was also performed in the January 1950 Company season in New York with Sarah Cunningham as The Sphinx, Hawkins as "Oidipous" and Richard Malek as Chorus.

174. Erick Hawkins, "Diaries," Erick Hawkins Collection, Music Division, Library of Congress, box 77, folder 6.

175. Geza Roheim, *The Riddle of the Sphinx* (London: International Psychoanalytic Library, 1934), 15.

176. Program in Martha Graham Clippings File, Jerome Robbins Dance Collection, New York Public Library for the Performing Arts: *MGZR, box 15 (1950–59). The note goes on: "Oedipus overcomes the Sphinx by discerning in her child's phantasy of the primal scene and by deciphering her riddle to mean the four-legged being of the primal scene, the two-legged image a naked human being, and the three-legged image a physically creative man. His name in Greek is a euphemism, Swollen Foot."

177. Walter Terry, "The Dance" in *The New York Herald Tribune* (January 24, 1950).

178. Robert Sabin, "Review of American Dance Festival" in the *Dance Observer* 15/7 (August–September 1948), 86.

179. McDonagh, *Martha Graham*, 209.

180. Martha Graham Dance Company Souvenir Program, 1949. Dance Collection, New York Public Library for the Performing Arts at Lincoln Center: MGZB Martha Graham Dance Company Souvenir Program, 1949.179. *Night Journey* script, 3.

181. *Night Journey* script, 3.

182. Graham, *Notebooks*, 298.

183. Roheim, *Riddle of the Sphinx*, 17.

184. Roheim, *Riddle of the Sphinx*, 21.

185. Graham directed Yuriko not to notice Medea's hostility so that the Princess would not appear dangerously seductive. In this way, Graham neutralized her rival and made the jealousy of Medea more autonomous, more absolute. Yuriko interview with the author, September 26, 2010, New York City.

186. According to the composer Vincent Persichetti, *Eye of Anguish* premiered on January 31, 1949, in Montclair, New Jersey. Vincent Persichetti interview with Katy Matheson, November 29, 1978, Jerome Robbins Dance Collection, New York Public Library for the Performing Arts: *MGZMT 5–436, p. 15.

187. Martha Graham, letter to David Zellmer, January 30, 1944, Jerome Robbins Dance Collection, New York Public Library for the Performing Arts.

188. Vincent Persichetti interviewed by Katy Matheson, Jerome Robbins Dance Collection, New York Public Library for the Performing Arts: *MGZMT 5–436, p. 21.

189. Ibidem.

190. Graham writes "besutiful." The Helen McGehee and Umana Collection of Dance Materials, Music Division, Library of Congress, box 9, folder 16.

191. Walter Terry, "the Dance," *New York Herald Tribune* (January 20, 1950).

192. "Martha thought through a work using her psyche, her emotions, but I don't think she could do it for a leading male role." Erick Hawkins in *Martha Graham. The Evolution of her Dance Theory and Training 1926–1991*, compiled by Marian Horosko (New Jersey: a cappella books, 1991), 76.

193. "Martha Graham and Dance Company," *Dance Observer* 17/3 (March 1950), 40.

194. Ibidem.

195. Stuart Hodes interview with the author, April 26, 2010, New York City.

196. Vincent Persichetti interviewed by Katy Matheson, Jerome Robbins Dance Collection, New York Public Library for the Performing Arts: *MGZMT 5–436, p. 40.

197. Winthrop Palmer, *Dance News* XVI/3 (March 1950), 5.

198. Vincent Persichetti interviewed by Katy Matheson, Jerome Robbins Dance Collection, New York Public Library for the Performing Arts: *MGZMT 5–436, p. 33–34.

199. Phone conversation with the author, August 10, 2010.

200. John Rosenfield, "Ballet in Review," in *The Dallas Morning News* (Friday, March 11, 1949), p. 10. Section 1. Erick Hawkins Collection, Music Division, Library of Congress, box 69, folder 1.

201. Ibidem.

202. Erick Hawkins Collection, Music Division, Library of Congress, box 55, folder 14.

203. Diary entry, Erick Hawkins Collection, Music Division, Library of Congress, box 55, folder 14.

204. De Mille, *Martha*, 299.

205. Unprocessed MG tour file, "European tour," Jerome Robbins Dance Collection, New York Public Library for the Performing Arts. A *New York Times* article of April 26, 1950 puts the Paris opening as June 27, 1950 ("Graham Dancers Will Tour Europe"). Martha Graham Clippings File, Jerome Robbins Dance Collection, New York Public Library for the Performing Arts: *MGZR-Res. box 15 (195–59).

206. Bertram Ross Papers, Jerome Robbins Dance Collection, New York Public Library for the Performing Arts, box 24, folder 8. Agnes de Mille cites Ross as telling a very different story in her biography. She attributes to Ross the claim that Hawkins himself caused Graham's debilitating injury during a Paris performance. *Martha*, 296.

207. Robert Cohan interview with Don McDonagh, 1972, Jerome Robbins Dance Collection, New York Public Library for the Performing Arts: *MGZTL 4–2530.

208. De Mille, *Martha*, 290–300.

209. Erick Hawkins interviewed with Don McDonagh, November 17, 1973, Dance Collection, New York Public Library for the Performing Arts at Lincoln Center, *MGZTL 4–2556.

210. Howard Gardner, *Creating Minds*, 292.

211. Erick Hawkins Collection, Music Division, Library of Congress, box 53, folder 4.

212. *Judith* premiered on January 4, 1950, in Louisville, Kentucky. See Robert Sabin, "The Dance Concerto" in *Dance Observer* 17/2 (February 1950), 22.

213. Erick Hawkins interviewed with Don McDonagh, November 17, 1973, Dance Collection, New York Public Library for the Performing Arts at Lincoln Center, *MGZTL 4–2556.

214. Martha Graham letter to William Schuman, June 24, 1949, William Schuman Papers & Records, Music Collection, New York Public Library for the Performing Arts: JPB 87–33, box 18, folder 10.

215. The letter, dated 21 August, with no year, must have been sent in 1950 after the return from London. Erick Hawkins Collection, Music Division, Library of Congress, box 55, folder 16.

216. *Man for Himself. An Inquiry Into the Psychology of Ethics* (1947; rpt. New York: Holt Paperbacks, 1990), 98.

217. Erick Hawkins letter to Martha Graham, August 21, 1950, Erick Hawkins Collection, Music Division, Library of Congress, box 55, folder 16.

218. Hawkins sustained this critique of Graham's choreography and technique throughout his career, but was reticent in print about her personality and their relationship.

219. David Sears interview with Lesley Farlow, March 27, 1992, Jerome Robbins Dance Collection, New York Public Library for the Performing Arts: *MGZMT 3–1657.

220. Erick Hawkins, interview with David Sears, May 27, 1983, Dance Collection, New York Public Library for the Performing Arts, box 21, folder 4.

221. Martha Graham letter to Erick Hawkins, September 3, 1950. Erick Hawkins Collection, Music Division, Library of Congress, box 55, folder 13.

222. Martha Graham letter to Erick Hawkins, July 27, 1950. Erick Hawkins Collection, Music Division, Library of Congress, box 55, folder 13.

223. De Mille, *Martha*, 278.

224. Martha Graham cited by Mary Virginia Stieb-Hales in Helga Croner, "Jungiana," *Bulletin of the Analytical Psychology Club of New York* 53/7 (November 1991), 4.

225. De Mille, *Martha*, 301–302.

226. See David Anfam, *Abstract Expressionism* (London: Thames & Hudson, 2010). The frequent identification of Graham with Abstract Expressionism is usually articulated through a comparison between Pollock and Graham. Dance Writer Roger Copeland writes: "Graham's variety of modern dance has much in common with abstract expressionism: both

[Pollock and Graham] were Jungian, gravity-ridden, and emotionally overwrought." Roger Copeland, "Merce Cunningham and the Politics of Perception" in Roger Copeland and Marshall Cohen, editors, *What is Dance? Readings in Theory and Criticism* (Oxford and New York: Oxford University Press, 1983), 309.

227. Steven Polcari, "Martha Graham and Abstract Expressionism," in *Smithsonian Studies in American Art* (Winter 1990), 9.

228. There is no evidence that either Graham or Hawkins frequented the Analytical Psychology Club although there is some evidence of Graham's influence there. The *Bulletins* of January 1950 (12/1) and of April 1962 (24/4) contain reviews of Graham concerts by Jessie E. Fraser. In the November 1991 the "Jungiana" section of the *Bulletin* (53/7) there is an account of the memorial service held for Frances Wickes in 1964 at which Graham spoke. The text of that talk was partially reproduced. Graham was eulogized in the *Bulletin* of October 1991 (53/6).

Chapter 5

1. These words are from notes for a scenario on one handwritten page that includes, "Elements of a Dilemma Happening," "an improbably somewhere, possible inhabitants" "A Duet, a Trio, a soliloquy, an aside," "abstractions from the absolute," and so on. Martha Graham Collection, Library of Congress, box 224, folder 17.

2. Martha Graham letter to Frances Wickes, July 16, 1951, Manuscript Division, Library of Congress, box 2, folder 8.

3. Graham's letters to Wickes are housed in the Manuscript Division of the Library of Congress, in the Papers of Frances Gillespy Wickes (1875–1967). The file contains Graham's letters to Wickes between 1951 and 1964. The letters that concern us here were written between 1951 and 1954. Several other letters to Wickes are stored in the Papers of Muriel Rukeyser, (also in the Manuscript Division of the Library of Congress).

4. "Pollock's psychiatrist may have utilized art therapy. In any case, it was Pollock who suggested that he use drawings as an aid in discussing himself with Henderson in 1939." C.L. Wysuph, Jackson Pollock: Psychoanalytic Drawings (New York: Horizon Press, 1970), 12.

5. Harding Psychic Energy, 14

6. See my discussion of these works in *Excursion for Miracles: Paul Sanasardo, Donya Feuer and Studio for Dance (1955–1964)* (Middletown: Wesleyan University Press, 2005).

7. There was also ironic commentary on the feminine persona in Gospel of Eve.

8. E-mail from Robert Cohan to the author, February 21, 2010.

9. Martha Graham letter to Frances Wickes, July 16, 1951. Papers of Frances G. Wickes, Manuscripts, Library of Congress (Graham wrote this letter on Martha Graham Dance Company stationery).

10. Martha Graham letter to Frances Wickes, June 25, 1953. Papers of Frances G. Wickes, Manuscript Division, Library of Congress (Graham wrote this letter on Martha Graham Dance Company stationery).

11. William Schuman interview with John Gruen, May 7, 1975. Jerome Robbins Dance Collection, New York Public Library for the Performing Arts: *MGTC 3–561. After the premiere of *Voyage*, Schuman sent Graham a set of subtitles for his score that included "Anticipation," "Caprice" "Realization" and "Retrospection." He considered them "Martha Graham type subtitles" that would help *Voyage* overcome audience skepticism.

12. William Schuman interview with John Gruen (May 7, 1975), Dance Collection, New York Public Library for the Performing Arts: *MGTC 3–561 (sound recording).

13. See Steve Swayne, Orpheus in Manhattan. *William Schuman and the Shaping of American Musical Life* (New York: Oxford University Press, 2011), 268–270.

14. Graham sent Schuman notes and a scenario for *Judith* in a letter of June 14, 1949. The scenario of six typewritten pages contains many references to the writing of T.S. Eliot, and is footnoted by Graham. William Schuman Papers & Records, Music Collection, New York Public Library for the Performing Arts: JPB 87–33, box 18, folder 10.

15. Martha Graham letter to Frances Wickes, Frances Wickes Papers, Manuscript Division, Library of Congress.

16. Martha Graham cited by Virginia Stieb-Hales in Helga Crona, "Jungiana [Virginia Stieb-Hales recalls Martha Graham's remarks at Frances Wickes's memorial service]," *Bulletin of the Analytical Psychology Club of New York* 53/7 (November 1991), 4.

17. A letter to Hawkins from Bethsabee de Rothschild of July 1, 1952, set the terms of payment for his teaching. She concluded: "I am writing this letter so that there will be no necessity for you to communicate with Martha in the future. It is my personal opinion that you should not write; I am certain this is her desire . . . Martha plans a divorce when it is materially practical to arrange it." It does not seem that de Rothschild was faithfully representing all of Graham's views in this letter. Erick Hawkins Collection, Music Division Library of Congress, box 53, folder 4.

18. A Letter from Graham to Wickes of July 12, 1959, talks of finally getting a divorce from Hawkins: "I am not depressed or sad. I am just through." Papers of Muriel Rukeyser, Manuscript Division, Library of Congress.

19. In the posthumous legal battles that took place over the ownership of Graham's work, *Voyage* is not mentioned on the list of disputed choreographies.

20. I thank Stuart Hodes and Robert Cohan for consenting to be interviewed about *Voyage*, and David Prensky for permission to reprint the remarks of Bertram Ross in his interviews preserved at the Jerome Robbins Dance Collection, New York Public Library for the Performing Arts. I am also grateful to Stuart Hodes for allowing me to read and quote from his unpublished manuscript on Martha Graham.

21. Gaston Bachelard, *The Poetics of Space*, 91. See also, C. G. Jung, *Two Essays on Analytical Psychology* translated by R.F. C. Hull (London: Routledge & Kegan Paul, 1953), 172. Of particular interest to us will be Part Two of the second essay, "Individuation," which was originally published in 1945.

22. Graham, *Notebooks*, 137.

23. Graham, *Notebooks*, 141.

24. Martha Graham, "Choreographic Notebooks," Martha Graham Collection, Music Division, Library of Congress, box 274.

25. Papers of Frances Wickes, Manuscripts, Library of Congress, box 15, folder 12.

26. Jean Laplanche and J.B. Pontalis, *The Language of Psycho-analysis* translated by Donald Nicholson-Smith (New York: W.W. Norton and Company, 1973), 211.

27. Ibidem.

28. "Here the projection phenomenon plays a special role because the elements of the opposite sex in the speaker's own psyche, the anima in the man and the animus in the woman, are experienced as the reality of the opposite sex." Erich Neumann, *The Great Mother. An Analysis of the Archetype* (Princeton: Princeton University Press, 1955), 24.

29. The phrase is Eric Gould's in *Mythical Intentions in Modern Literature* (Princeton: Princeton University Press, 1981), 16.

30. Graham, *Notebooks*, 133.

31. Graham, *Notebooks*, 143.

32. Martha Graham letter to Frances Wickes, June 25, 1953, Papers of Frances Wickes, Manuscripts, Library of Congress. (Graham wrote this letter on Martha Graham Dance Company stationery).

33. Ibidem.

34. William Schuman letter to Martha Graham, May 18, 1953, William Schuman Records and Papers, Music Division, New York Public Library for the Performing Arts, JPB 87–33, box 18, folder 10.

35. Robert Sabin, "Martha Graham Opens One-Week Season with New York—Entitled Voyage, it differs from anything else she has done before," in *Musical America* (June 1953), 5.

36. Ibidem.

37. Ibidem.

38. Martha Graham Letter to Erick Hawkins, December 30, 1950, Martha Graham Collection, Music Division, Library of Congress, box 224, folder 17.

39. Martha Graham letter to Frances Wickes, July 16, 1951, Papers of Frances Wickes, Manuscript Division, Library of Congress.

40. These notes can be found in Martha Graham Collection, Music Division, Library of Congress, folder 17. Parts of the notes are a draft of a letter to Hawkins of December 3, 1950.

41. On August 4, 1953, Graham wrote to Wickes: "I remember those dark days, dark in more than one way, when I had a drink with you after the green curtains were drawn and a light seemed to come into the room and the world because of you."

42. Martha Graham letter to Frances Wickes, August 26, 1951, Frances Wickes Papers, Manuscript Division, Library of Congress.

43. Martha Graham letter to Frances Wickes, July 16, 1951, Frances Wickes Papers, Manuscript Division, Library of Congress, box 2, folder 8.

44. Graham, *Notebooks*, 148.

45. Martha Graham letter to Frances Wickes, July 16, 1951, Frances Wickes Papers, Manuscript Division, Library of Congress.

46. Martha Graham letter to Frances Wickes, July 16, 1951, Papers of Frances Wickes, Manuscript Division, Library of Congress, box 2, folder 8.

47. Saint-John Perse, "Winds" (Vents) in Collected Poems (Princeton: Princeton University Press, 1971), 229.

48. Martha Graham letter to Frances Wickes, July 16, 1951, Frances Wickes Papers. Manuscript Division, Library of Congress, box 2, folder 8.

49. Graham, *Notebooks*, 93.

50. T.S. Eliot, *The Cocktail Party* (New York: Harcourt Brace & Co., 1950), 28.

51. Robert Sabin, "Martha Graham Opens One-Week Season with New York—Entitled Voyage, it differs from anything else she has done before," in *Musical America* (June 1953), 5.

52. Graham, *Notebooks*, 111.

53. Bertram Ross interview with Jean Nuchtern, June 30, October 18 & 22, 1976, Jerome Robbins Dance Collection, New York Public Library for the Performing Arts: *MGZMT 5–416, Typescript, 96.

54. Graham, *Notebooks*, 112.

55. Carlos Surinach interview with Katy Matheson, February 27, 1979, Jerome Robbins Dance Collection, New York Public Library for the Performing Arts: *MGZTC 3–434.

56. Lincoln Center Special Collections, Katharine Cornell Papers, Theater Collection, New York Public Library for the Performing Arts: T—Mss 1965–02, box 20, folder 12.

57. Martha Graham letter to Erick Hawkins, September 3, 1950, Erick Hawkins Collection, Music Division, Library of Congress, page 3.

58. Bertram Ross interview with David Sears, July 21, 1985, Jerome Robbins Dance Collection, New York Public Library for the Performing Arts: *MGZTL 4–1586.

59. Bertram Ross interview with Jean Nuchtern, June 30, October 18 & 22, 1976, Jerome Robbins Dance Collection, New York Public Library for the Performing Arts: *MGZMT 5–416, Typescript, 104.

60. Graham, *Notebooks*, 111 & 114.

61. Campbell, *The Hero with a Thousand Faces*, 258.

62. Martha Graham, "I Salute My Love," typescript, Martha Graham Archive, Library of Congress, box 224, folder 9.

63. Phone interview with the author, August 10, 2010.

64. Graham, *Notebooks*, 147.

65. Martha Graham Collection, Library of Congress, box 224, folder 4.

66. Ibidem.

67. Robert Payne, *The Wanton Nymph. A Study of Pride* (Melbourne, London & Toronto: William Heinemann Ltd., 1951), 70.

68. Bertram Ross interview with Jean Nuchtern, June 30, October 18 & 22, 1976, Jerome Robbins Dance Collection, New York Public Library for the Performing Arts: *MGZMT 5–416, Typescript, 98.

69. Pearl Lang tried a similarly de-theatricalized approach to her gesture and facial expression in a revival of *Letter to the World* in the 1970s. I recall how striking was her shift to the non-theatrical register, and also how daring. I say this to suggest Graham might have performed

Voyage this way based on my memory of Lang's uncharacteristic style, and on the fact that Lang likely made that choice based on something she had once seen Graham do.

70. Bertram Ross interview with Jean Nuchtern, June 30, October 18 & 22, 1976, Jerome Robbins Dance Collection, New York Public Library for the Performing Arts: *MGZMT 5–416, Typescript, 99.

71. Bertram Ross interview with David Sears, July 21, 1985, Jerome Robbins Dance Collection, New York Public Library for the Performing Arts: *MGZTL 4–1586.

72. Phone interview with the author, August 10, 2010, New York City.

73. Graham, *Notebooks*, 133.

74. Jacob L. Moreno, *Psychodrama* (New York: Beacon House, 1946), 11.

75. Bertram Ross interview with David Sears, 1985, Jerome Robbins Dance Collection, New York Public Library for the Performing Arts: *MGZTL 4–1586.

76. Stuart Hodes interview with John Gruen, April 27 and May 4, 1976, Oral History Project, Jerome Robbins Dance Collection, New York Public Library for the Performing Arts: *MGZT 5–966, Typescript, 180.

77. Interview with the author, August 10, 2010, New York City.

78. Bertram Ross interview with Jean Nuchtern, June 30, October 18 & 22, 1976, Jerome Robbins Dance Collection, New York Public Library for the Performing Arts: *MGZMT 5–416, Typescript, 92.

79. Bertram Ross interview with David Sears, 1985, Jerome Robbins Dance Collection, New York Public Library for the Performing Arts: *MGZTL 4–1586.

80. Moreno, *Psychodrama*, 11.

81. Bertram Ross interview with David Sears, July 21, 1985, Jerome Robbins Dance Collection, New York Public Library for the Performing Arts: *MGZTL 4–1586.

82. Bertram Ross interview with Jean Nuchtern, June 30, October 18 & 22, 1976. Jerome Robbins Dance Collection, New York Public Library for the Performing Arts: *MGZMT 5–416, p. 108.

83. Bertram Ross interview with Jean Nuchtern, June 30, October 18 & 22, 1976. Jerome Robbins Dance Collection, New York Public Library for the Performing Arts: *MGZMT 5–416, p. 100.

84. Interview with the author, April 26, 2010.

85. Walter Terry, "Dance," *New York Herald Tribune* (May 22, 1953).

86. Robert Sabin, "American Dance" in *The Dance Observer* 22/6 (June–July 1955), 83. The review is signed R.S.

87. Bertram Ross interview with Jean Nuchtern, June 30, October 18 & 22, 1976. Jerome Robbins Dance Collection, New York Public Library for the Performing Arts: *MGZMT 5–416.

88. Douglas Watt, "Musical Event: Tell it to Eliot," *The New Yorker* (May 30, 1953), 95.

89. Hodes remembers there was a formal party "not on stage." Graham explained to her cast that the Japanese do not distinguish between the ocean and the desert; she wished to maintain the ambiguity between these two suggested expanses that set the scene.

90. Email from Robert Cohan to the author, March 9, 2010.

91. Bertram Ross Interview with David Sears, July 21, 1985, Jerome Robbins Dance Collection, New York Public Library for the Performing Arts: *MGZTL 4–1586.

92. Bertram Ross Interview with David Sears, July 21, 1985, Jerome Robbins Dance Collection, New York Public Library for the Performing Arts: *MGZTL 4-1586.

93. Bertram Ross Interview with David Sears, July 21, 1985, Jerome Robbins Dance Collection, New York Public Library for the Performing Arts: *MGZTL 4–1586.

94. Interview with the author, April 26, 2010, New York City.

95. Bertram Ross interview with Jean Nuchtern, June 30, October 18 & 22, 1976, Jerome Robbins Dance Collection, New York Public Library for the Performing Arts: *MGZMT 5–416, Typescript: 98.

96. John Martin, "Martha Graham Begins Dance Engagement at Alvin Theatre With Premiere of 'Voyage'," *New York Times* (May 17, 1953).

97. Bertram Ross cited in Robert Tracy, *Goddess: Martha Graham's Dancers Remember* (New York: Limelight Editions, 1997): 159.

98. Robert Sabin, "Martha Graham Opens One-Week Season with New York—Entitled Voyage, it differs from anything else she has done before," in *Musical America* (June 1953), 5.
99. Interview with the author, April 26, 2010, New York City.
100. She refers to them in her notes as Matadors, which suggests the male costumes in *Embattled Garden.*
101. Walter Terry, "Dance: Martha Graham," in *New York Herald Tribune* (Monday, May 18, 1953).
102. Bertram Ross interview with David Sears, July 21, 1985, Jerome Robbins Dance Collection, New York Public Library for the Performing Arts: *MGZTL 4–1586.
103. Graham, *Notebooks,* 141.
104. Robert Cohan email to the author, March 16, 2010.
105. Bertram Ross interview with Jean Nuchtern, June 30, October 18 & 22, 1976, Jerome Robbins Dance Collection, New York Public Library for the Performing Arts: *MGZMT 5–416, Typescript, 104–105.
106. Robert Cohan email to the author, March 6, 2010.
107. Bertram Ross interview with Jean Nuchtern, June 30, October 18 & 22, 1976, Jerome Robbins Dance Collection, New York Public Library for the Performing Arts: *MGZMT 5–416, Typescript, 105.
108. Ibidem.
109. Douglas Watt, "Musical Event: Tell it to Eliot," *The New Yorker* (May 30, 1953), 95.
110. Bertram Ross interview with David Sears, July 21, 1985, Jerome Robbins Dance Collection, New York Public Library for the Performing Arts: *MGZTL 4–1586.
111. Bertram Ross interview with Jean Nuchtern, June 30, October 18 & 22, 1976, Jerome Robbins Dance Collection, New York Public Library for the Performing Arts: *MGZMT 5–416, Typescript, 101.
112. Bertram Ross interview with David Sears, July 21, 1985, Jerome Robbins Dance Collection, New York Public Library for the Performing Arts: *MGZTL 4–1586.
113. Douglas Watt, "Musical Event," *The New Yorker* (May 30, 1953), 95.
114. This cynicism was mordantly summed up and caricatured in *Embattled Garden* (1958).
115. Bertram Ross interview with David Sears, July 21, 1985, Jerome Robbins Dance Collection, New York Public Library for the Performing Arts: *MGZTL 4–1586.
116. Graham, *Notebooks,* 171.
117. In making *Deaths and Entrances* Graham characterized that work as more "wild," "elemental" and "abstract" than *Letter to the World.* Martha Graham letter to David Zellmer, December 14, 1942, Jerome Robbins Dance Collection, New York Public Library for the Performing Arts: (S) *MGZMD 117.
118. "Martha Graham and Dance Company" in *The Dance Observer* 20/7 (August–September 1953), 103.
119. Richard Hayes, "Martha Graham's Theater," *The Commonweal* LVIII/16 (July 24, 1953), 394.
120. Martha Graham letter to Frances Wickes, June 25, 1953, Manuscript Division, Library of Congress (Graham wrote this letter on Martha Graham Dance Company stationery).
121. Martha Graham archive, Music Division, Library of Congress, box 218, folder 2.
122. Of *Gospel of Eve* Walter Terry wrote:

> It is in the area of gesture, rather than in large scale movement, where the choreographer has worked major miracles of hilarity and dramatic point. These gestures—the useless flutter of a hand, a shrug, a grimace of exasperation, a prissy manipulation of stage props—all contribute to a characterization of a woman whose whole life appears to be dedicated to self-embellishment, self-admiration and the arrangement of surrounds to enhance that self. "Gospel of Eve" is, of course, cruel while it is being immensely funny. It is also, in the tradition of fine comedy, sad and Miss Graham in one particularly eloquent passage discards the empty mannerisms of a foolish female and permits us to see the real anguish, the poignant loneliness of a woman whose attempts to build beauty end with the veneer.

> Walter Terry, "The Dance," *New York Herald Tribune* (Tuesday, January 24, 1950). Doris Hering's review related *Gospel of Eve* to the earlier *Every Soul is a Circus*: "Like the heroine of Every

Soul Eve has an acute case of ennui which she tries to eradicate by changing her surroundings, instead of herself. The lady in Every Soul trifles with me. Eve trifles with hats and chairs. Both end in a void." Doris Hering, "The Season in Review," *Dance Magazine* XXIV/3 (March 1950), 13–14. Hering also panned *Eye of Anguish* and *The Strangler* on the same program.

123. Bertram Ross Papers, Jerome Robbins Dance Collection, New York Public Library for the Performing Arts: box 10, folder 19.

124. Bertram Ross interview with David Sears, July 21, 1985, Jerome Robbins Dance Collection, New York Public Library for the Performing Arts: *MGZTL 4–1586.

125. "The time has come to discipline myself to see Truth and to find the best possible way of arriving at a state of peace from which creative living can proceed." Martha Graham Letter to Erick Hawkins, March 10, 1951. Erick Hawkins Collection, Music Division, Library of Congress.

126. Esther M. Harding, *Psychic Energy. Its Source and its Transformation* (1947; rpt. Washington, D.C.: Bollingen Foundation, 1963), 13.

127. Martha Graham letter to Frances Wickes, August 26, 1951, Papers of Frances Wickes, Manuscript Division, Library of Congress.

128. C. G. Jung, *Two Essays on Analytical Psychology* translated by R.F. C. Hull (London: Routledge & Kegan Paul, 1953), 171–172.

129. Ibid., 155–156.

130. Ibid., 284.

131. Ibid., 172.

132. The mythic genre drifted by the 1960s toward self-caricature, the quality of which has inspired the phenomenon of cross-dressed Graham impersonation in recent years.

133. C.G. Jung, "Concerning Rebirth," in *The Archetypes and the Collective Unconscious* translated by R.F.C. Hull (Princeton: Princeton University Press, 1969), 114.

134. Ibidem.

135. Martha Graham letter to William Schuman, June 14, 1949, William Schumann Papers & Records, Music Division, New York Public Library for the Performing Arts: JPB 87–33, box 18, folder 10.

136. Graham did not appear in any of these works with the exception of *Voyage*.

137. Ben Belitt interview with David Sears, July 7, 1985, Dance Collection, New York Public Library for the Performing Arts at Lincoln Center, *MGZTL 4–1522.

138. Martha Graham Collection, Library of Congress, box 224, folder 4.

139. Ben Belitt interview with David Sears, July 2, 1985, Dance Collection, New York Public Library for the Performing Arts at Lincoln Center, *MGZTL 4–1522.

140. Isamu Noguchi, *A Sculptor's World* (New York & Evanston: Harper & Row, 1968), 127.

141. Carlos Surinach interview with Katy Matheson, February 27, 1979, New York. Jerome Robbins Dance Collection, New York Public Library for the Performing Arts: *MGZTC 3–434.

142. Henri Lefebvre, *The Production of Space* translated by Donald Nicholson-Smith (Oxford: Blackwell, 1991), 363.

Conclusion

1. Adrienne Rich, *Of Woman Born: Motherhood as Experience and Institution* (New York & London: W.W. Norton & Co., 1995), 160.

2. Graham wrote Wickes on August 4, 1953, that she was reading *Essays on a Science of Mythology* by Jung and Kerenyi.

3. Jung, "The Psychological Aspects of the Kore" in Jung & Kerenyi, *Essays on a Science of Mythology. The Myth of the Divine Child and the Mysteries of Eleusis* translated by R.F.C. Hull (Princeton: Bollingen Series, 1949), 158.

4. Jane Ellen Harrison, *Prolegomena to the Study of Greek Religion* (Princeton: Princeton University Press, 1991), 274.

5. Esther Harding, *Psychic Energy* (Washington, D.C.: Bollingen Foundation, 1963), 165.

6. Jung quoted by Kerényi in *Eleusis. Archetypal Image of Mother and Daughter*, translated by Ralph Mannheim (New York: Bollingen Foundation, 1967), xxxi–xxxii.

7. Bertram Ross Papers, Dance Collection, New York Public Library for the Performing Arts at Lincoln Center, box 10, folder 19, page. 29.

8. Jill Johnston, "Martha Graham: An Irresponsible Study . . . The Head of Her Father" in *Ballet Review* 2/4 (1968), 11. I thank Ramsay Burt for calling my attention to this article.

9. Leroy Leatherman letter to Jeannette Roosevelt, November 9, 1969, Bertram Ross Papers, Dance Collection, New York Public Library for the Performing Arts at Lincoln Center, box 10, folder 1. Leatherman handed in his resignation on September 20, 1972, and urged that Graham be confronted.

10. Karl Stern, *The Flight From Woman* (New York: Noonday Press, 1965); Philip Slater's *The Glory of Hera* (Boston: Beacon Press, 1968), Elizabeth Gould Davis, *The First Sex* (Baltimore: Penguin, 1971).According to Adrienne Rich, "the first extensive analysis of patriarchy in contemporary American feminist literature is that of Kate Millett in *Sexual Politics*." *Of Woman Born*, 56.

11. Warren I. Susman, *Culture as History. The Transformation of American Society in the Twentieth Century* (New York: Pantheon Books, 1973), 284.

12. Ibid., 207.

BIBLIOGRAPHY

"A Dancer and an Educator on Fascism," *Dance Observer* (March 1937): 39.

Anderson, Benedict. *Imagined Communities: reflections on the origin and spread of nationalism.* London & New York: Verso, 1991.

Andrews, Edward D. *The Gift to be Simple. Songs, Dances and Rituals of the American Shakers.* New York: Dover Publications, Inc., 1940.

Anfam, David. *Abstract Expressionism.* London: Thames & Hudson, 2010.

Ankersmit, F.R. *Aesthetic Politics: Political Philosophy Beyond Fact and Value.* Stanford: Stanford University Press, 1996.

Anthony, Maggy. *The Valkyries. The Women Around Jung.* Longmead, Shaftesbury and Dorset: Element Books, 1990.

Apostolos-Cappadona, Diane & Bruce Altshuler. Editors. *Isamu Noguchi. Essays and Conversations.* New York: Harry N. Abrams, Inc., 1994.

Aristotle. *Aristotle's Poetics,* translated by S.H. Butcher. New York: Hill & Wang, 1961.

Armitage, Merle. *Martha Graham.* 1937; New York: Dance Horizons, 1966.

"Auditorium for Chamber Music in the Library of Congress." December 1, 1924–March 4, 1925. *Miscellaneous.* Washington: Government Printing Office. 1925.

Bachelard, Gaston. *The Poetics of Space.* Translated by Maria Jolas. Boston: Beacon Press, 1969.

Bachofen, Johann Jakob. *Das Mutterrecht: eine Untersuchung über die Gynaikokratie der alten Welt nach ihrer religiösen und rechtlichen Natur.* Frankfurt am Main: Suhrkamp, 1975.

Bachofen, Johann Jakob. *Myth, Religion, and Mother Right. Selected Writings of J.J. Bachofen,* translated by Ralph Manheim. Princeton: Princeton University Press, 1967.

Bandel, Betty. "Graham's Art Pleases Here." In *Arizona Daily Star* (March 7, 1939).

Banes, Sally. *Dancing Women: Female Bodies on Stage.* London: Routledge, 1998.

Bannerman, Henrietta. "An Overview of the Development of Martha Graham's Movement System (1926–1992)." In *Dance Research* 17, no.2 (Winter 1999): 9–46.

Bannerman, Henrietta. "Martha Graham's House of the Pelvic Truth: The Figuration of Sexual Identities and Female Empowerment." *Dance Research Journal* 42, Number 1 (Summer 2010): 30–45.

Baigell, Matthew, and Julia Williams, editors. *Artists against War and Fascism: Papers of the First American Artists' Congress.* Rutgers: Rutgers University Press, 1986.

Barthes, Roland. *Mythologies.* Translated by Annette Lavers. New York: Hill & Wang, 1982.

Baxmann, Inge. *Mythos Gemeinschaft: Körper und Tanzkulturen in der Moderne* Munich: Wilhelm Fink, 2000.

Beard, Charles A., and Mary R. *America in Midpassage,* 2 volumes. New York: Macmillan Company, 1939.

Beard, Mary. *The Invention of Jane Harrison.* Cambridge, Mass.: Harvard University Press, 2000.

Bedford, William Charles. *Elizabeth Sprague Coolidge: the education of a patron of chamber music: the early years*. Ph.D. Dissertation: University of Missouri, 1964.

Beiswanger, George W. "The New Theatre Dance." *Theatre Arts Monthly* 23, no.1 (January 1939): 51–54.

Belitt, Ben. *Wilderness Stair*. New York: Grove Press, 1955.

Benjamin, Walter. *Illuminations*. Edited by Hannah Arendt. New York: Schocken Books, 1969.

Bock, Gisela. "Racism and Sexism in Nazi Germany: Motherhood, Compulsory Sterilization, and the State." In *When Biology Became Destiny. Women in Weimar and Nazi Germany*, edited by Renate Bridenthal, Anita Grossman, and Marion Kaplan. New York: Monthly Review Press, 1984: 271–296.

Bodkin, Maud. *Archetypal Patterns in Poetry. Psychological Studies of the Imagination*. 1934. London: Oxford University Press, 1963.

Briffault, Robert. *The Mothers. The Matriarchal Theory of Social Origins*. 1927; rpt. New York: Howard Fertig, 1993.

Burke, Owen. "An American Document." *New Masses* 24, no.4 (October 18, 1938).

Burt, Ramsay. "Dance, Gender and Psychoanalysis: Martha Graham's Night Journey." In *Dance Research Journal* 30, no.1 (1998): 34–53.

Burt, Ramsay. "Memory, Repetition and Critical Intervention. The Politics of Historical Reference in Recent European Dance Performance." In *Performance Research* 8, no.2 (2003): 34–41.

Butler, Judith. *Antigone's Claim. Kinship Between Life and Death*. New York: Columbia University Press, 2000.

Caldwell, Helen. *Michio Ito. The Dancer and his Dances*. Berkeley & Los Angeles: University of California Press, 1977.

Campbell, Joseph. *The Hero With a Thousand Faces*. Princeton: Princeton University Press, 1949.

Carpentier, Martha C. *Ritual, Myth, and the Modernist Text. The Influence of Jane Ellen Harrison on Joyce, Eliot, and Woolf*. Amsterdam: Gordon & Breach Publishers, 1998.

Carr, Helen. *The Verse Revolutionaries. Ezra Pound, H.D. and the Imagists*. London: Jonathan Cape, 2009.

Carruthers, Mary. "Rhetorical Ductus, or, Moving through a Composition." In *Acting on the Past: Historical Performance Across the Disciplines*, edited by Mark Franko and Annette Richards, 99–117. Middletown: Wesleyan University Press, 2000.

Cassirer, Ernst. *The Philosophy of Symbolic Forms. Volume Two: Mythical Thought. Translated by Ralph Mannheim*. New Haven & London: Yale University Press, 1955.

Chafe, William H. *The Paradox of Change. American Women in the Twentieth Century*. New York & Oxford: Oxford University Press, 1991.

Copeland, Roger. "Merce Cunningham and the Politics of Perception." In Roger Copeland and Marshall Cohen, editors, *What is Dance? Readings in Theory and Criticism*. Oxford and New York: Oxford University Press, 1983: 307–324.

Copland, Aaron, and Vivian Perlis. *Copland since 1943*. New York: Saint Martin's Press, 1989.

Crawford, Robert. *The Savage and the City in the Work of T.S. Eliot*. Oxford: Clarendon Press, 1987.

Crist, Elizabeth B. *Music for the Common Man. Aaron Copland During the Depression and the War*. Oxford & New York: Oxford University Press, 2005.

Croner, Helga. "Jungiana. Virginia Stieb-Hales recalls Martha Graham's Remarks at Frances Wickes's memorial service." *Bulletin of the Analytical Psychology Club of New York* 53, no. 7 (November 1991): 4.

Davis, Elizabeth Gould. *The First Sex*. Baltimore: Penguin Books, 1971.

de Lauretis, Teresa. *Alice Doesn't. Feminism, Semiotics, Cinema*. Bloomington: Indiana University Press, 1984.

de Mille, Agnes. *Martha: The Life and Works of Martha Graham*. New York: Random House, 1991.

Denby, Edwin. *Dance Writings*. Edited by Robert Cornfield and William Mackay. New York: Knopf, 1986.

Denning, Michael. *The Cultural Front. The Laboring of American Culture in the Twentieth Century*. London & New York: Verso, 1996.

Diamond, David. "With the Dancers." *Modern Music* 17, no.2 (January–February 1940).

Doob, Penelope Reed. *The Idea of the Labyrinth from Classical Antiquity through the Middle Ages.* Ithaca & London: Cornell University Press, 1990.

Doss, Erika Lee. *Benton, Pollock and the Politics of Modernism: from Regionalism to Abstract Expressionism.* Chicago: University of Chicago Press, 1991.

Duberman, Martin. *The Worlds of Lincoln Kirstein.* New York: Knopf, 2007.

Du Bois, W.E.B. *A Reader.* Edited by David Levering Lewis. New York: Henry Holt & Co., 1995.

Du Bois, W.E.B. *John Brown.* New York: the Modern Library, 2001.

Eliot, T.S. *The Cocktail Party.* New York: Harcourt Brace & Co., 1950.

Eliot, T.S. "Ulysses, Order and Myth." *The Selected Prose of T.S. Eliot.* Edited by Frank Kermode. London: Faber & Faber, 1975: 175–178.

Ellwood, Robert. *The Politics of Myth. A Study of C.G. Jung, Mircea Eliade, and Joseph Campbell.* Albany: State University of New York Press, 1999.

Foulkes, Julia. *Modern Bodies. Dance and American Modernism from Martha Graham to Alvin Ailey.* Chapel Hill & London: University of North Carolina Press, 2002.

Franco, Susanne. *Martha Graham.* Palermo: L'Epos, 2003.

Frank, Joseph. *The Idea of Spatial Form.* New Brunswick & London: Rutgers University Press, 1991.

Franko, Mark. *Dancing Modernism/Performing Politics.* Bloomington: Indiana University Press, 1995.

Franko, Mark. "History/Theory—Criticism/Practice" in *Corporealities. Body, Knowledge, Culture, and Power.* Edited by Susan Leigh Foster. London: Routledge, 1995, 25–52.

Franko, Mark. "Some Notes on Yvonne Rainer, Modernism, Politics, Emotion, Performance, and its Aftermath." In *Meaning in Motion. New Cultural Studies in Dance*, edited by Jane Desmond. Durham: Duke University Press, 1997, 289–303.

Franko, Mark. *The Work of Dance: Labor, Movement, and Identity in the 1930s.* Middletown: Wesleyan University Press, 2002.

Franko, Mark. "L'utopie antifasciste: American Document de Martha Graham." In *Etre ensemble.* Pantin: Centre National de la Danse, 2003: 283–306.

Franko, Mark. *Excursion for Miracles: Paul Sanasardo, Donya Feuer and Studio for Dance (1955–1964).* Middletown: Wesleyan University Press, 2005.

Franko, Mark. "Die Ausradierung des Politischen: Regionalismus im Tanz als Verschlusselungstaktik." In *Tanz—Metropole—Provinz.* Edited by Yvonne Hardt and Kirsten Maar. Berlin: Jahrbuch der Gesellschaft für Tanzforschung 17, 2007: 101–119.

Frascina, Frances. *Pollock and After. The Critical Debate.* New York: Harper & Row, 1985.

Fraser, Jessie E. "Martha Graham, modern artist." *Bulletin of the Analytical Psychology Club of New York* 12 (1950): 10–14.

Fraser, Jessie E. "Martha Graham." *Bulletin of the Analytical Psychology Club of New York* 24, no. 4 (April 1962): 15–17.

Freud, Sigmund. *The Interpretation of Dreams,* translated by James Strachey. New York: Basic Books, 1956.

Freud, Sigmund. *On the History of the Psychoanalytic Movement.* Translated by Joan Rivière. New York: Norton, 1966.

Fromm, Erich. *Escape from Freedom.* New York: Rinehart & Company, 1941.

Fromm, Erich. "Faith as a Character Trait." Reprint from *Psychiatry: Journal of Biology and Pathology of Interpersonal Relations* 5, no.3 (August 1942).

Fromm, Erich. *The Forgotten Language. An Introduction to the Understanding of Dreams, Fairy Tales, and Myths.* New York & Toronto: Rinehart & Company, 1951.

Fromm, Erich. "The Significance of the Theory of Mother Right Today." In *The Erich Fromm Reader,* edited by Rainer Funk, 59–62. New Jersey: Humanities Press, 1985: 59–62.

Fromm, Erich. *Man for Himself. An Inquiry Into the Psychology of Ethics,* 1947; New York: Holt Paperbacks, 1990.

Fromm, Erich. *Love, Sexuality, and Matriarchy. About Gender.* Edited by Rainer Funk. New York: Fromm International Publishing Corporation, 1994.

Gardner, Howard. *Creating Minds. An Anatomy of Creativity Seen Through the Lives of Freud, Einstein, Picasso, Stravinsky, Eliot, Graham, and Gandhi.* New York: Basic Books, 1993.

Geduld, Victoria. "Dancing Diplomacy: Martha Graham and the Strange Commodity of Cold-War Cultural Exchange in Asia, 1955 and 1974." In *Dance Chronicle* 33 (2010): 44–81.

Geduld, Victoria. "Martha Graham's Gilded Cage: *Blood Memory: An Autobiography* (1991)." *Dance Research Journal* (forthcoming).

Gianinazzi, Willy. *Naissance du mythe moderne. Georges Sorel et la crise de la pensée savante (1889–1914)*. Paris: Editions de la Maison des Sciences de l'Homme, 2006.

"Gift by Elizabeth Sprague Coolidge to the Library of Congress." *House Reports 1063, 68th Congress, 2nd Session. December 1, 1924–March 4, 1925.* Volume 1(8390). Washington: Government Printing Office, 1925.

Golder, Herbert. "Making a Scene: Gesture, Tableau, and the Tragic Chorus." *Arion* 2 (Spring 1996): 1–19.

Gould, Eric. *Mythical Intentions in Modern Literature.* Princeton: Princeton University Press, 1981.

Gould, John. "Tragedy and Collective Experience" in *Myth, Ritual Memory, and Exchange. Essays in Greek Literature and Culture.* Oxford: Oxford University Press, 2001: 378–404.

Graff, Ellen. *Stepping Left. Dance and Politics in New York City, 1928–1942.* Durham & London: Duke University Press, 1997.

Graham, Martha. "Dance Libretto: American Document." *Theatre Arts* 26, no. 9 (September 1942): 565–574.

Graham, Martha. *The Notebooks of Martha Graham.* New York: Harcourt, Brace, Jovanovich, 1973.

Graebner, Martin. *The Age of Doubt. American Thought and Culture in the 1940s.* Boston: Twayne Publishers, 1991.

Graves, Robert. *The White Goddess. A Historical Grammar of Poetic Myth.* Edited by Grevel Lindop. 1948; Manchester: Carcanet Press, 1997.

Greene, William Chase. *Moira. Fate, Good and Evil in Greek Thought.* Gloucester, Mass.: Peter Smith, 1968.

Gross, David. "Myth and Symbol in Georges Sorel." In *Political Symbolism in Modern Europe. Essays in Honor of George L. Mosse,* edited by Seymour Drescher, David Sabean, and Allan Sharlin. New Brunswick & London: Transaction Books, 1982.

Guilbert, Laure. *Danser avec le IIIe Reich. Les danseurs modernes sous le nazisme.* Brussels: Editions Complexe, 2000.

H.D. *Collected Poems (1912–1944).* Edited by Louis L. Martz. New York: New Directions, 198?.

Harding, Esther M. *Woman's Mysteries. Ancient and Modern.* London, New York, Toronto: Longman's, Green & Co., 1935.

Harding, Esther M. *Psychic Energy. Its Source and its Transformation.* 1947; rpt. Washington D.C.: Bollingen Foundation, 1963.

Harrison, Jane Ellen. *Themis. The Study of the Social Origins of Greek Religion.* Cambridge: Cambridge University Press, 1912.

Harrison, Jane Ellen. *Prolegomena to the Study of Greek Religion,* 1903. rpt. Princeton: Princeton University Press, 1991.

Harrison, Jane Ellen. *Mythology.* Boston: Marshall Jones Company, 1924.

Hayes, Richard. "Martha Graham's Theater," *The Commonweal* 58, no. 16 (July 24, 1953): 394.

Hawkins, Erick. "The Rite in Theater." Reprinted in Hawkins, *The Body is a Clear Place and Other Statements on Dance.* Princeton: Dance Horizons, 1992: 1–7.

Hering, Doris. "The Season in Review." In *Dance Magazine* (April 1948): 12–13.

Herzog, Dagmar. *Sex after Fascism. Memory and Morality in Twentieth-Century Germany.* Princeton: Princeton University Press, 2005.

Hobsbawm, E.J. *Nations and Nationalism since 1780: Programme, Myth, Reality.* Cambridge: Cambridge University Press, 1990.

Homer. *The Odyssey.* Translated by Robert Fitzgerald. New York: Farrar, Straus & Giroux, 1998.

Horkheimer, Max. *Authority and the Family.* Translated by A. Lissance. New York: Works Progress Administration, 1937.

Horosko, Marian, Compiler. *Martha Graham: the Evolution of her Dance Theory and Training. 1926–1991.* Pennington, NJ: A Cappella Books, 1992.

Hubbs, Nadine. *The Queer Composition of America's Sound. Gay Modernists, American Music, and National Identity.* Berkeley & Los Angeles: University of California Press, 2004.

Hughes, Langston. *The Langston Hughes Reader.* New York: George Brazillier, Inc., 1958.

Hughes, Langston. *The Collected Poems of Langston Hughes*. Edited by Arnold Rampersad. New York: Alfred A. Knopf, 2001.

Hughes, Langston. *The Collected Works of Langston Hughes*. Edited by Arnold Rampersad. Columbia & London: University of Missouri Press, 2001.

Hughes, Ted. *Shakespeare and the Goddess of Complete Being*. London: Faber & Faber, 1993.

Hunt, Jacqueline. "Dance for Poise, Grace, Martha Graham Urges." *Tulane California Advance Register* (August 1, 1942).

"Hush Hubbub." *Life 23, no.* 25 (December 22, 1947): 69–70.

Jameson, Frederic. *The Political Unconscious: Narrative as a Socially Symbolic Act*. Ithaca: Cornell University Press, 1981.

Janson, H.W. "Benton and Wood, Champions of Regionalism." In *Magazine of Art* 39, no.5 (May 1946): 184–186; 198–200.

Johnston, Jill. "Martha Graham: An Irresponsible Study . . . The Head of her Father." *Ballet Review* 2, no.4 (1968): 6–13.

Jolles, André. *Einfache Formen*. Tübingen: Max Niemeyer Verlag, 1958.

Jones, Isabel Morse. "American Dance Play Impressive." In *Los Angeles Times*. March 11, 1939.

Jones, Susan. "'At the Still Point.' T.S. Eliot, Dance, and Modernism." *Dance Research Journal* 41, no.2 (Winter 2009): 31–51.

Jung, Carl Gustav. *Modern Man in Search of a Soul*. New York: Harcourt, Brace, & World, 1933.

Jung, Carl Gustav. "Wotan. A Psychologist Explores the Forces Behind German Fascism." *The Saturday Review of Literature* (October 16, 1937): 3–4, 19.

Jung, Carl Gustav. *Two Essays on Analytical Psychology*. Translated by R.F.C. Hull. New York: Pantheon Books, 1953.

Jung, Carl Gustav. *The Archetypes and the Collective Unconscious*, translated by R.F.C. Hull. Princeton: Princeton University Press, 1959.

Jung, Carl Gustav. *Man and His Symbols*. London: Aldus Books, 1964.

Jung, Carl Gustav & Carl Kerenyi. *Essays on a Science of Mythology. The Myth of the Divine Child and the Mysteries of Eleusis*. Translated by R.F.C. Hull. Princeton: Bollingen Series, 1949.

Kain, Ida. "Martha Graham, Dancer, Coaches Women Workers." *Courier-Journal*. April 9, 1943.

Kandinsky, Wassily. *Concerning the Spiritual in Art*. Translated by M.T.H Sadler. New York: Dover Books, 1977.

Kaplan, Alice Yaeger. *Reproductions of Banality: Fascism, Literature, and French Intellectual Life*. Minneapolis: University of Minnesota Press, 1986.

Karina, Lilian, and Marion Kant. *Hitler's Dancers. German Modern Dance and the Third Reich*. Translated by Jonathan Steinberg. New York and Oxford: Berghahn Books, 2003.

Kerényi, Carl. *Eleusis. Archetypal Image of Mother and Daughter*, translated by Ralph Mannheim. New York: Bollingen Foundation, 1967.

Kirstein, Lincoln. "Dance: Martha Graham at Bennington." *The Nation*. September 3, 1938.

Kirstein, Lincoln. "Our Ballet and Our Audience" and "Transcontinental Caravan." In *Ballet: Bias and Belief. Three Pamphlets Collected and Other Dance Writings of Lincoln Kirstein*. New York: Dance Horizons, 1983: 53–67.

Kirstein, Lincoln. "Art in the Third Reich—Survey, 1945." *Magazine of Art* 35, no.6 (October 1945): 223–238, 240–242.

Kirstein, Lincoln. *Program Notes 1934–1991*. Edited by Randall Bourscheidt. New York: Eakins Press Foundation Alliance for the Arts, 2009.

Koritz, Amy. *Gendering Bodies/Performing Art: Dance and Literature in Early Twentieth-Century British Culture*. Ann Arbor: University of Michigan Press, 1995.

Koritz, Amy. *Culture Makers. Urban Performance and Literature in the 1920s*. Urbana & Chicago: University of Illinois Press, 2009.

Kowal, Rebekah J. *How to Do Things With Dance. Performing Change in Postwar America*. Middletown: Wesleyan University Press, 2010.

Kraut, Anthea. "White Womanhood, Property Rights, and the Campaign for Choreographic Copyright: Loïe Fuller's Serpentine Dance." In *Dance Research Journal* 43, no.1 (Summer 2011): 3–26.

Kriegsman, Ann. *Modern Dance in America—the Bennington Years*. Boston, Mass.: G.K. Hall, 1981.

La Place, Maria. "Bette Davis and the Ideal of Consumption." *Wide Angle* 6, no. 4 (1985): 34–43.

Lacoue-Labarthe, Philippe and Jean-Luc Nancy. "The Nazi Myth," translated by Brian Holmes. In *Critical Inquiry* 16/2 (Winter 1990): 291–312.

LaMothe, Kimerer L. *Nietzsche's Dancers. Isadora Duncan, Martha Graham, and the Revaluation of Christian Values*. London: Palgrave Macmillan, 2006.

Laplanche, Jean, and J.B. Pontalis. *The Language of Psycho-analysis*, translated by Donald Nicholson-Smith. New York: W.W. Norton and Company, 1973.

Lawson, R. Alan. *The Failure of Independent Liberalism (1930–1941)*. New York: G.P. Putnam's Sons, 1971.

Lears, T. J. Jackson. "From Salvation to Self-Realization. Advertising and the Therapeutic Roots of Consumer Culture, 1880–1930." *The Culture of Consumption: Critical Essays in American History, 1880–1930*. Edited by Richard Wightman Fox and T.J. Jackson Lears. New York: Pantheon Books, 1983.

Lefebvre, Henri. *The Production of Space*, translated by Donald Nicholson-Smith. Oxford: Blackwell, 1991.

Leja, Michael. *Reframing Abstract Expressionism. Subjectivity and Painting in the 1940s*. New Haven & London: Yale University Press, 1993.

Levin, Gail, and Judith Tick. *Aaron Copland's America. A Cultural Perspective*. New York: Watson-Guptill Publications, 2000.

Lévi-Strauss, Claude. *The Elementary Structures of Kinship*. Translated by James Harle Bell, John Richard von Sturmer, and Rodney Needham. Boston: Beacon Press, 1969.

Lieberman, E. James. *Acts of Will. The Life and Work of Otto Rank*. New York: The Free Press, 1985.

Limón, José. *An Unfinished Memoir*. Edited by Lynn Garafola. Hanover & London: University Press of New England, 1999.

Lloyd, Margaret. *The Borzoi Book of Modern Dance*. New York: Dance Horizons, 1969.

Macintosh, Fiona. "Parricide versus Filicide: Oedipus and Medea on the Modern Stage." In *Tragedy in Transition*, edited by Sarah Anne Brown and Catherine Silverstone, 193–211. Oxford: Blackwell, 2007.

Macintosh, Fiona. *Sophocles: Oedipus Tyrannus*. Cambridge: Cambridge University Press, 2009.

MacLeish, Archibald. *Panic. A Play in Verse*. Boston & New York: Houghton Mifflin Company, 1935.

Malinowski, Bronislaw. *Mutterrechtliche Familie und Oedipus-Komplex. Eine ethnologisch-psychoanalytische Studie*. Leipzig/Wien/Zürich: Internationaler Psychoanalytischer Verlage, 1924.

Manganaro, Marc. *Myth, Rhetoric, and the Voice of Authority. A Critique of Frazer, Eliot, Frye, and Campbell*. New Haven & London: Yale University Press, 1992.

Manning, Erin. *Relationscapes: movement, art, philosophy*. Cambridge, Mass.: MIT, 2009.

Manning, Susan. *Ecstasy and the Demon: Feminism and Nationalism in the Dances of Mary Wigman*. Berkeley: University of California Press, 1993.

Manning, Susan. "American Document and American Minstrelsy." In *Moving Words, re-writing dance*, edited by Gay Morris, 183–202. London: Routledge, 1996.

Manning, Susan. *Modern Dance/Negro Dance. Race in Motion*. Minneapolis: University of Minnesota Press, 2004.

Marcus, Phillip L. "'A Healed Whole Man': Frazer, Lawrence and Blood Consciousness." In *Sir James Frazer and the Literary Imagination. Essays in Affinity and Influence*. Edited by Robert Fraser. London: The Macmillan Press, 1990: 232–252.

Marcuse, Herbert. *Negations. Essays in Critical Theory*. London: Free Association Books, 1988.

Martin, John. "The Dance: Annual Award." In *The New York Times* (August 1945).

Martin, John. "Martha Graham Begins Dance Engagement at Alvin Theatre With Premiere of 'Voyage.'" *New York Times* (May 17, 1953).

McCully, Robert S. "A Bit of History and Martha Graham." *Bulletin of the Analytical Psychology Club of New York* 53, no. 6 (October 1991): 4.

McDonagh, Don. *Martha Graham. A Biography*. New York: Praeger, 1973.

McGehee, Helen. *To Be a Dancer*. Lynchburg, Virginia: Editions Heraclita, 1989.

Meglin, Joellen. "Blurring the Boundaries of Genre, Gender, and Geopolitics: Ruth Page and Harald Kreutzberg's Transatlantic Collaboration in the 1930s." *Dance Research Journal* 41, no.2 (Winter 2009): 52–75.

Meglin, Joellen A., and Lynn Matluck Brooks. "Why a Special Issue on Martha Graham?" in *Dance Chronicle* 33, no.1 (2010): 1–4.

Melosh, Barbara. *Engendering Culture: Manhood and Womanhood in New Deal Public Art and Theater*. Washington, D.C.: Smithsonian Institution Press, 1991.

Michaels, Walter Benn. *Our America. Nativism, Modernism, and Pluralism*. Durham & London: Duke University Press, 1995.

Minor, Marcia. "Graham Interprets Democracy. Uses Militant Theme as Climax of Dance Presented in the Form of a Documentary Play." *The Daily Worker* (October 4, 1938).

Moi, Toril. *Feminist Theory and Simone de Beauvoir*. Oxford: Blackwell, 1990.

Moreno, Jacob L. *Psychodrama*. New York: Beacon House, 1946.

Morgan, Barbara. "Dance Into Photography." In *Martha Graham: Sixteen Dances in Photographs*. Hastings-on-Hudson: Morgan & Morgan, 1941: 149–152.

Morgan, Barbara. "Dance Photography." *The Complete Photographer* 18, no.3. New York: National Educational Alliance, 1942: 1132–1146.

Morgan, Barbara. "Modern Dance." *Popular Photography* 16, no.16 (June 1945): 44–47 & 68.

Morris, Gay. "Bourdieu, the Body, and Graham's Post-War Dance." In *Dance Research* 19, no.2 (Winter 2001): 52–82.

Morris, Gay. *A Game for Dancers: Performing Modernism in the Postwar Years, 1945–1960*. Middletown: Wesleyan University Press, 2006.

Mumford, Lewis. *Men Must Act*. New York: Harcourt, Brace and Company, 1939.

Mumford, Lewis. "A Call to Arms." *New Republic* 95, no.1124 (May 18, 1938): 39–42.

Mumford, Lewis. *Faith for Living*. New York: Harcourt, Brace & Co., 1940.

Needham Costonis, Maureen. "*American Document*: A Neglected Graham Work." *Proceedings Society of Dance History Scholars, Twelfth Annual Conference*. Arizona State University, February 17–19, 1989: 72–81.

Neumann, Erich. *The Great Mother. An Analysis of the Archetype*. Princeton: Princeton University Press, 1955.

Neumann, Erich. *The Origins and History of Consciousness*. London: Maresfield Library, 1989.

Noguchi, Isamu. *A Sculptor's World*. New York & Evanston: Harper & Row Publishers, 1968.

Payne, Robert. *The Wanton Nymph. A Study of Pride*. Melbourne, London & Toronto: William Heinemann Ltd., 1951.

Perse, Saint-John. *Collected Poems*. Princeton: Princeton University Press, 1971.

Peters, Julie Stone. "Jane Harrison and the Savage Dionysus: Archaeological Voyages, Ritual Origins, and the Modern Theatre." *Modern Drama* 51, no.1 (Spring 2008): 1–41.

Polcari, Stephen. "Martha Graham and Abstract Expressionism." *Smithsonian Studies in American Art* 1 (Winter 1990): 3–26.

Pollack, Howard. *Aaron Copland. The Life and Work of an Uncommon Man*. New York: Henry Holt & Co., 1999.

Porterfield, Amanda. *Feminine Spirituality in America. From Sarah Edwards to Martha Graham*. Philadelphia: Temple University Press, 1980.

Posert, Natlee. "Martha Graham Dances Ideas and Interprets Our America." *The Memphis Commercial Appeal* (March 2, 1939).

Posner, Richard. A. Editor. *The Essential Holmes. Selections from the Letters, Speeches, Juridical Opinions, and other writings of Oliver Wendell Holmes, Jr.* Chicago & London: University of Chicago Press, 1992.

Pound, Ezra, and Ernst Fenollosa, *The Classic Noh Theatre of Japan*. Westport, Connecticut: Greenwood Press, 1977.

Pound, Ezra, and Ernst Fenollosa. *The Translations of Ezra Pound*. London: Faber & Faber, 1970.

"Purely Symbolic." *Time* (May 28, 1945).

Rabinbach, Anson. "The Body Without Fatigue: A Ninetheenth-Century Utopia." *Political Symbolism in Modern Europe. Essays in Honor of George L. Mosse*, edited by Seymour Drescher, David Sabean, and Allan Sharlin, 42–62. New Brunswick & London: Transaction Books, 1982.

Rainer, Yvonne. *Work: 1961–1973*. New York: New York University Press, 1974.

Rainer, Yvonne. "Where's the Passion? Where's the Politics? Or, How I Became Interested in Impersonating, Approximating, and End Running around My Selves and Others', and Where Do I Look When You're Looking at Me?" In *Theater* 40, no.1 (2010): 47–55.

Rank, Otto. *The Incest Theme in Literature and Legend*. 1912; Baltimore: Johns Hopkins University Press, 1991.

Rank, Otto. *The Trauma of Birth*. 1924; New York: Dover, 1993.

Rank, Otto. *Art and Artist. Creative Urge and Personality Development*. Translated by Charles Frances Atkinson. New York & London: W.W. Norton & Company, 1932.

Reik, Theodor. "Oedipus und die Sphinx." In *Imago. Zeitschrift für Anwendung der Psychoanalyse auf die Geisteswissenshaften* vol. 6 (1920): 95–131.

Reynolds, Dee. *Rhythmic Subjects: Uses of Energy in the Dances of Mary Wigman, Martha Graham and Merce Cunningham*. Hampshire: Dance Books, 2007.

Rich, Adrienne. *Of Woman Born: Motherhood as Experience and Institution*. New York & London: W.W. Norton & Co., 1995.

Ricoeur, Paul. *Time and Narrative*. Translated by Kathleen McLaughlin and David Pellauer. Chicago & London: University of Chicago Press, 1983.

Robertson, Marta Elaine. "'A Gift to be Simple': The Collaboration of Aaron Copland and Martha Graham in the Genesis of Appalachian Spring." (Ph.D. Dissertation: University of Michigan, 1992).

Robertson, Marta Elaine. "Musical and Choreographic Integration in Copland's and Graham's 'Appalachian Spring.'" In *The Musical Quarterly* 83, no. 1 (Spring, 1999): 6–26.

Robinson, Harlow. *The Last Impressario. The Life, Times, and Legacy of Sol Hurok*. New York: Viking, 1944.

Roheim, Geza. *The Riddle of the Sphinx*. London: International Psychoanalytic Library, 1934.

Rosenfield, John. "Ballet in Review." *The Dallas Morning News*. (Friday, March 11, 1949), p. 10. Section 1.

Rosenman, Samuel, editor. *The Public Papers of Franklin D. Roosevelt, Volume Two: The Year of Crisis, 1933*. New York: Random House, 1938.

Roth, Michael S. *Freud. Conflict and Culture. Essays on his life, work, and legacy*. Edited by Michael S. Roth. New York: Alfred A. Knopf, 1998.

Sabin, Robert. "Dance at the Coolidge Festival." *Dance Observer* 11, no.10 (December 1944): 120–121.

Sabin, Robert. "Martha Graham and Her Company Give Repertory Season." *Dance Observer* 14, no.4 (April 1947): 43–44.

Sabin, Robert. "The Dance Concerto: Martha Graham and William Schuman Create a New Form for the Theatre." *Dance Observer* 17, no.2 (February 1950): 22–23.

Sabin, Robert. "Martha Graham Opens One-Week Season with New York – Entitled Voyage, it differs from anything else she has done before," in *Musical America* (June 1953): 5.

Sabin, Robert. "American Dance." *The Dance Observer* 22, no. 6 (June–July 1955): 83–84.

Samuels, Andrew. *The Political Psyche*. London & New York: Routledge, 1993.

Schnapp, Jeffrey. *Staging Fascism: 18BL and the Theater of Masses for Masses*. Stanford: Stanford University Press, 1996.

Schwartz, Selby Wynn. "Martha@Martha: a Seance with Richard Move." In *Women & Performance* 20, no.1 (March 2010): 61–87.

Scobie, Alex. *Hitler's State Architecture. The Impact of Classical Antiquity*. University Park & London: The Pennsylvania State University Press, 1990.

Scott, Jonathan. *Socialist Joy in the Writing of Langston Hughes*. Columbia & London: University of Missouri Press, 2006.

Sears, David. "Martha Graham: The Golden Thread." *Ballet Review* 14, no. 3 (Fall 1986): 44–64.

Sears, David. "Graham Masterworks in Revival." *Ballet Review* 11, no. 12 (1982): 25–34.

Shea-Murphy, Jacqueline. *The People Have Never Stopped Dancing: Native American Modern Dance Histories*. Minneapolis: University of Minnesota Press, 2007.

Shelton, Suzanne. "Jungian Roots of Martha Graham's Dance Imagery." In *Dance History Scholars Proceedings*. Riverside: Dance History Scholars, 1983: 119–132.

Shirley, Wayne D. *Ballet for Martha and Ballets for Martha*. Washington: Library of Congress, 1997.

Siegel, Marcia B. *The Shapes of Change. Images of American Dance*. Boston: Houghton Mifflin, 1979.

Siegmund, Gerald. *Abwesenheit: eine performative Ästhetik des Tanzes; William Forsythe, Jérôme Bel, Xavier Le Roy, Meg Stuart*. Bielefeld: Transcript Verlag, 2006.

Slater, Philip E. *The Glory of Hera. Greek Mythology and the Greek Family*. Boston: Beacon Press, 1968.

Smith, Cecil. "Music and Dance Review: Gertrude S., Virgil T., and Susan B." *Theatre Arts* XXXI/7 (July 1947): 17–20.

Smith, David. *Medals for Dishonor*. New York: Independent Curators Incorporated, 1996.

Snyder, Diana. "'The Most Important Lesson for Our Theater.'" *Ballet Review* 7 (1982): 7–20.

Soares, Janet Mansfield. *Louis Horst. Musician in a Dancer's World*. Durham & London: Duke University Press, 1992.

Sorel, Georges. *Reflections on Violence*. Translated by T.E. Hulme and J. Roth. Glencoe. Illinois: the Free Press, 1950.

Srinivasan, Priya. "The Bodies Beneath the Smoke or What's Behind the Cigarette Poster: Unearthing Kinesthetic Connections in American Dance History." *Discourses in Dance* 4, no.1 (2007): 7–47.

Stern, Karl. *The Flight From Woman*. New York: Noonday Press, 1965.

Steuben, Frances. "Symbolism and Surrealism in Dance." *New Masses* (April 2, 1946).

Susman, Warren I., *Culture as History. The Transformation of American Society in the Twentieth Century*. New York: Pantheon Books, 1973.

Stich, Sidra. "Picasso's Art and Politics in 1936." *Arts Magazine* 58 (October 1983): 113–118.

Stodelle, Ernestine. *Deep Song: the Dance Story of Martha Graham*. New York: Schirmer Books, 1984.

Stout, Harry S. "Edwards as Revivalist." In *The Cambridge Companion to Jonathan Edwards*. Edited by Stephen J. Stein, 125–143. Cambridge: Cambridge University Press, 2007.

Swayne, Steve. *Orpheus in Manhattan. William Schuman and the Shaping of American Musical Life*. New York: Oxford University Press, 2011.

Taylor, Gladys and Warren, Josephine Jenks. "The Artist and the Life About Him." *Bulletin of the Analytical Psychology Club of New York* 1/2 (March 1939): 1–2.

Terry, Walter. "Dance: Martha Graham." *New York Herald Tribune* (May 18, 1953).

Terry, Walter. "The Dance." *The New York Herald Tribune* (January 24, 1950).

Thomas, Helen, *Dance Modernity and Culture: explorations in the sociology of dance*. London: Routledge, 1995.

Thompson, Virgil. "Two Ballets." *New York Herald Tribune* (May 20, 1945).

Tokunaga, Emiko. *Yuriko. An American Japanese Dancer: To Wash in the Rain and Polish With the Wind*. N.p.: Tokunaga Dance Ko, 2008.

Tracy, Robert. *Goddess. Martha Graham's Dancers Remember*. New York: Limelight Editions, 1997.

Utley, Gertje R. *Picasso: the Communist Years*. New Haven & London: Yale University Press, 2000.

Vaughan, David. "Dissenting View on Graham." *Dance Magazine* (July 1958): 26–27.

Vickery, Catherine. "'American Document' Tours America." *Dance Observer* 6/4 (April 1939): 205–206.

Viereck, Peter. *Metapolitics. From the Romantics to Hitler*. New York: Alfred A. Knopf, 1941.

Watt, Douglas. "Musical Event: Tell it to Eliot." *The New Yorker* (May 30, 1953).

Wegner, Phillip E. *Imaginary Communities: Utopia, the Nation, and the Spatial Histories of Modernity*. Berkeley & Los Angeles: University of California Press, 2002.

Weston, Jessie. *From Ritual to Romance*. 1920. New York: Anchor Books, 1957.

Whiting, Cecile. *Antifascism in American Art*. New Haven & London: Yale University Press, 1989.

Williams, William Carlos. *In the American Grain*. New York: New Directions, 1956.

Williams, William Carlos. *The Autobiography of William Carlos Williams*. New York: Random House, 1948.

White, Hayden. "Bodies and Their Plots." In *Choreographing History*, edited by Susan Leigh Foster. Bloomington: Indiana University Press, 1995: 229–234.

White, Hayden. "The Value of Narrativity in the Representation of Reality." *The Content of the Form. Narrative Discourse and Historical Representation*. Baltimore and London: The Johns Hopkins University Press, 1987: 1–25.

Wickes, Frances. *The Inner World of Man*. London: Methuen, 1950.

Wong, Yutian. "Artistic Utopias: Michio Ito and the Trope of the International." In *Worlding Dance*, edited by Susan Leigh Foster, 144–162. London: Palgrave Macmillan, 2009.

Wood, Paul, Frascina, Frances, Harris, Jonathan, Harrison, Charles. *Modernism in Dispute: Art since the forties*. New Haven & London: Yale University Press, 1993.

Wysuph, C.L. *Jackson Pollock: Psychoanalytic Drawings*. New York: Horizon Press, 1970.

Yeats, William Butler. *The Collected Plays of W.B. Yeats*. London: MacMillan & Company, 1952.

Young, Michael A. *Malinowski. Odyssey of an Anthropologist, 1884–1920*. New Haven & London: Yale University Press, 2004.

Young, Stark. "Martha Graham." *New Republic* 112/23 (June 4, 1945): 790–791.

Zytaruk, George J. & James T. Boulton. Editors. *The Letters of D.H. Lawrence*. Cambridge: Cambridge University Press, 1981.

INDEX